Author Stephen Walker br. memorable season to life ~~~ *1969 Washington Senators.* He ~~~ portraits of players such as Jim French, Dave Baldwin, Ed Stroud, Hank Allen, Bernie Allen, Darold Knowles, Dick Bosman, Ed Brinkman, Frank Howard and others. The portraits of some of the Washington "irregulars" such as Stroud, Allen and Bob Humphreys prove to be most interesting. This book is rich with personalities and anecdotes. For those who remember the 1969 Senators, it's a delightful trip down memory lane, featuring many aspects of the players and the season that you didn't know or have forgotten. For those too young to remember, it will make you sorry you missed that memorable season.

-Barry Sparks, Member, Amazon Vine Voice

In his book *A Whole New Ballgame*, Stephen J. Walker captures the essence of a team that exceeded everyone's expectations. Walker weaves his tale as seen through the eyes of players, coaches, play-by-play announcer Ron Menchine, bat boy Paul Oppermann and Senators fans. The funny and often poignant moments in the lives of the players themselves keep the reader entertained from start to finish. Much like the 1969 season itself, readers will not want the book to end.

-Jim Hartley, President, Washington Baseball Historical Society

As I read your book, I could feel the passion that you have for the '69 Senators and Washington baseball.

-Mark Hornbaker, President, D.C. Baseball History: D.C. Baseball Yesterday and Today

I love this book because it brought back so many memories of that 1969 Washington Senators team and the entire memorable season. If you, like me, remember that wonderful season, or are just a sports fan, I think you will enjoy reading this book.

-William G. Straub on Amazon.com

i

Author Stephen J. Walker has done a nice job of recreating the 1969 Washington Senators environment for the reader. There are stories from just about everyone on the Senators roster talking about the 1969 season and the effect that Ted Williams had on them. *A Whole New Ballgame* really captures the essence of who Ted Williams was as a manager and how most of the players really respected him. Walker (writes) about the personalities on the team like Frank Howard, Casey Cox, Ed Brinkman, and Mike Epstein and how they intermingled with each other.

-M.A. Filippelli on Amazon.com

Enjoy this book as a poignant essay of one man's favorite team and its best season. Recommended for any true baseball fan.

-Ed Cuneo on Amazon.com

An enjoyable read that has brought back many warm memories of a simpler time!

-J.W. Deibert on Amazon.com

A fantastic book. The story of the 1969 Washington Senators and a larger story of Life, as told through the lives of the players who came together to form this ball club in that moment in time and U.S. history. I was especially interested to read and learn about a side of Ted Williams that we don't often see revealed. A great book for anyone interested in Washington Baseball and the larger stories where sports intersect with Life.

-Paul Golder on Amazon.com

Anybody who spent time watching or even listening to the old Senator games on the radio would really enjoy this.

-Allen Derwent on Amazon.com

A Whole New Ballgame: The 1969 Washington Senators 50th Anniversary Edition

Stephen J. Walker

Pocol Press
Punxsutawney, PA

POCOL PRESS

Published in the United States of America
by Pocol Press
320 Sutton Street
Punxsutawney, PA 15767
www.pocolpress.com

Publisher's Cataloging-in-Publication Data

Names: Walker, Stephen J., author.
Title: A Whole new ballgame : the 1969 Washington Senators 50th anniversary edition / Stephen J. Walker
Description: Includes bibliographical references and index. | Punxsutawney, PA: Pocol Press, 2019.
Identifiers: LCCN 2019936222 | ISBN 978-1-929763-88-7
Subjects: LCSH Washington Senators (Baseball team : 1961- 1971)--History--1969. | Baseball--Washington (D.C.)--History. | Baseball players--United States--Biography. | Williams, Ted, 1918-2002. BISAC SPORTS & RECREATION / Baseball / History
Classification: LCC GV875.W3 W35 2019 | DDC 796.357/6409753--dc23

Library of Congress Control Number: 2019936222

Dedication

*To Charles and Tommy, Brent and Craig, Jimmy and Vince, Ben, Rusty
and Mike, the boys of Greymont Drive, who taught me to love sports,
especially baseball; to my deceased Uncle and godfather, John "Kirk"
Kirkpatrick, who taught me to win with grace and lose with dignity.*

And to all who remember and love the 1969 Washington Senators.

*And to the incomparable men who managed, coached, played for, or
broadcast the triumphs and trials of this team who have passed to the
other side:*

> *Frank Bertaina*
> *Sam Bowens*
> *Ed Brinkman*
> *Joe Camacho*
> *Paul Casanova*
> *Nellie Fox*
> *Sid Hudson*
> *Arthur Lee Maye*
> *Ron Menchine*
> *Ed Stroud*
> *George Susce*
> *Zoilo Versalles*
> *Ted Williams*

May they rest in peace.

Acknowledgements

My love for baseball began the day my father took me to my first Washington Senators' game at RFK Stadium in 1969. The details are lost in a jumble of childhood memories, but I remember Tim Cullen, the quintessential good glove, no-hit utility infielder, blasted a home run. Through the wonders of Retrosheet, the gold standard of baseball web sites, I learned that Cullen hit one homer that season, on July 15, 1969 against the Detroit Tigers. Cullen performed his feat before President Nixon, Julie and David Eisenhower, astronaut Frank Borman and 16,118 other fans including me and my dad.

Nearly 26 years later, my father, James Henry Walker, the man who imbued me with love for baseball with his stories of riding the steam train from Altoona, Pennsylvania to Pittsburgh's Forbes Field with his brothers to see Ralph Kiner, Willie Mays, Stan Musial, and Jackie Robinson, died in a hospital room in Chantilly, Virginia. In the midst of my grief, the idea for this book was born. The 1969 Senators' story connects us again.

So many people helped bring *A Whole New Ballgame* to life. Jim Hartley, David Gough, Tom Holster, and Jim Bard, all devoted members of the Washington Baseball Historical Society (WBHS) gave me research leads and contact information for nearly every player and coach I interviewed. Jim Hartley's stories of watching the 1969 Senators' storybook season with his little brother from their choice seats in Section 422 put flesh on my research skeleton. Mark Hornbaker, of the D.C. Baseball History (DCBH) group was instrumental in leading me to updated information about the 1969 Senators. Mark introduced me to Bernie Allen, Dick Bosman, Jim French, and Darold Knowles at the group's 2019 meeting. The dedicated souls of the WBHS and DCBH retained a fervent hope for baseball's return to the nation's capital that sustained them through 33 seasons of rainouts and off days. April 14, 2005 stands as just reward for their faithfulness.

The first person I interviewed, Sid Hudson, who died on October 10, 2008, treated me with kindness beyond measure. Ron Menchine prefaced our interview with the gift of a savory dinner at the stately Country Club of Maryland. Ron, who died on September 10, 2010, always gave me far more than I asked. Old Senators' fans like me wish the Nationals would have invited him into the booth for a game or ten. Dave Baldwin and Bob Humphreys went above and beyond to help me find their teammates.

I am deeply indebted to: Rob Johnson, who shared his programs, 1969 Senators Press-TV Guide, the 1969 All-Star Game program, scorecards, and ticket stubs; Jack Summers, Richard Schlessinger, Keith Gallagher, Charles "Tripp" Morgan, Dan McGarvey, Steve Goode, Rob Cassell, Chuck Eisenhauer, Mark Byrd, Kevin Hamlin, Charlie Descalzi, and Carol Allen, who shared their memories; Paul Oppermann, who recounted his years as a Senators' bat boy; Penney Gentile, of Nelson Avenue Pines Bed and Breakfast in Cooperstown, who made my stay there both pleasant and productive; Freddy Berowski, Gabe Schechter, Bill Francis and Andrew Newman of the National Baseball Hall of Fame Library unearthed a cornucopia of photographs and information; the staff at Wheaton Regional Library and the Washingtoniana section of the Martin Luther King, Jr. Library endured my misadventures with microfilm; Allen Rice, of the National Archives and Records Administration, Nixon Presidential Materials Staff helped me locate images of 1969 Opening Day; Big Bruno and Ronnie Joyner shared their pictures and art from the 1969 Senators' Reunion; and Diane and Rob Floyd of Skyview Gymnastics let me use a quiet, makeshift office within their facility to write much of the manuscript.

Sean Dooley offered graphic design samples. Tom Rowe and Marty Niland edited portions of the manuscript. Msgr. Richard Tillman's insights into Scripture dared me to dream. Tim Michael shot down all excuses to quit.

Heartfelt thanks to: Dave Smith and his Retrosheet goldmine; the late David Vincent and Dr. Bruce Brown of the Society for American Baseball Research (SABR) and my fellow aficionados in SABR's Bob Davids Chapter; Richard McCloud, Dave Murphy, Yvette Ridenour, and Beth Mende Conny, for writing advice and mentoring; Jeanne Ford for showing me how a true professional writes; Sr. Janis McQuade, S.S.J., for moments of grace over chili at the Walker family dinner table; my Psalm 133 brothers, who renew my spirit every Saturday morning.

Chris Youstra and St. John the Evangelist's choir – thanks for the courage to sing loud, sing wrong and laugh at rejection.

J. Thomas Hetrick, of Pocol Press has my eternal gratitude for deciding to publish this 50th anniversary edition of the 1969 Senators' story.

My sister, Kathleen Walker, read every word of this manuscript and many others that failed to pass her uncompromising standards. Whatever is good and right herein exists because of her editorial talents. Whatever is wrong is my responsibility alone.

To my sons, Timothy, Matthew and Christian, superstars all, you inspire me to strive for excellence. I love you and am bursting with pride to be your dad.

Finally, every writer needs a muse. Debbie, my bride, my love, the woman of God's dreams for me, you make everything wonderful.

Foreword by Dick Bosman

People often say only championship seasons get remembered. Sometimes, though, other years stand out. Playing for the Washington Senators in 1969 was like that for me and my teammates.

It began at Spring Training Camp, after Marvin Miller led us in a brief strike for better pensions. Ted Williams put us to work. We certainly were eager to learn from him. Ted immediately changed the way we went about things and how we thought about the game. He did an outstanding job, despite the fact that us pitchers were banished to the back fields to bunt and field balls while he spent endless hours with the hitters.

Once we got into the season, it became clear to Ted and all of us that we had a darn good ball club. No one in the AL East was going to catch the Orioles, but we all wanted that winning season. A lot of us had to work hard to overcome several obstacles to get to and stay in the Major Leagues, so we chased that hard. It meant a lot to us to finally be called winners.

The years to come validated that we deserved that honor. Seven of my 1969 teammates earned World Series rings and six of us played in the League Championships. Looking back, most of my teammates agree with me that 1969 was one of the best seasons of our careers.

We were a close-knit bunch. We were always together. We played cards. We went to dinner. We played golf on off days. Myself, Barry Moore, Joe Coleman and Frank Howard shared an apartment that season. Even 50 years later, our club has an uncommon camaraderie. We still look forward to the times we can meet up for a drink or a round or two of golf.

That year was also memorable for people living in the Washington, D.C. metro area. I still hear from fans about how much they cherish that season. Obviously, losing the team two years later made 1969 even more memorable. Until baseball returned to D.C. in 2005, it was the only good season most fans remembered.

I remember the huge crowd that welcomed us back at National Airport on Sunday night, July 6, after our 6-3 road trip and the even bigger crowd the next night at RFK. The fans gave a standing ovation to Ted when he came out before the game to give the home plate umpire the line-up card and we rewarded them with a 7-3 win. And I remember thinking that evening, "This city is no different than any other city, if we win, they come see us."

Looking back, our 86-win season gave the town some good times and, for 33 years, more than a little hope that it could happen again. Fifty years later, it still surprises me how men and women's eyes light up when they see us. I appreciate that they'll never forget us. The standing ovation they gave me in 2007 when I threw out the first pitch for the last ballgame at RFK stadium shows that the fans will never forget.

Overall, from a professional and personal standpoint, 1969 was one of my best years. My dad's wisdom about how to pitch started to take on a new meaning. I got to work day after day with my mentor and pitching coach Sid Hudson. I learned more about the mental game of pitching from Ted Williams than any other coach in my career. I went from a young kid scuffling to make the club to pitching a 1-hitter on May 2 against Cleveland, overcoming my first arm injury, going 8-0 to close the season, and edging out Mike Cuellar and Jim Palmer, two fine pitchers, for the ERA title. I pitched well enough in 1969 to get the nod for the 1970 and 1971 Presidential Openers and the first home game for the Texas Rangers in 1972.

In 2018, I retired from professional baseball after nearly 60 years in the game. The 1969 Senators still remain very dear to my heart. When you think about it, the modern era of DC baseball began in 1969 and I'm proud I was part of it.

Dick Bosman played for the Washington Senators from 1966-1971. His record with the Senators was 49-49. No pitcher for a Washington ballclub won more games until Jordan Zimmerman's 7th win in 2014, giving him 50. He also pitched for the Texas Rangers (1972-73), Cleveland Indians (1974-75) and Oakland A's (1975-76). Dick served as pitching coach for the Chicago White Sox, Baltimore Orioles, and Texas Rangers. With Ted Leavengood, he is the co-author of Dick Bosman on Pitching: Lessons from the Life of a Major League Ballplayer and Pitching Coach, 2018, Rowman & Littlefield Publishers, ISBN 1538106612.

The mists of age may make these summer seasons dim –

-Thomas Caulfield Irwin

Table of Contents

Table of Illustrations

Introduction to the 50th Anniversary Edition

"The 1969 Senators are the finest group of athletes I have ever been associated with."

-Ron Menchine (1934-2010), Radio Broadcaster for the
Washington Senators, 1969-1971

Fifty years on, their relevance endures.

Baseball's return to the nation's capital in 2005 failed to dim longtime D.C. baseball fans' love for the 1969 Washington Senators. The gentlemen who wove their completely unexpected magic night after night at Robert F. Kennedy (RFK) Memorial Stadium still hold sway over fans' affections.

Why do they stir our hearts still? Why, in adulthood, is our admiration for them, our childhood heroes, even greater?

Did our respect for them mature once we learned their stories of redemption, the mountains of injury, derision, doubt, and prejudice that they had to overcome?

Is it our recollection of their plucky, hard-nosed play; how they knit together a divided community, inspired 1,700 people to greet them at National Airport after a winning road trip, drove the entire audience to stand and cheer when they were introduced at intermission of Burn Brae Dinner Theatre's performance of "Damn Yankees?"

Perhaps it's because they stand in everlasting contradiction to the false tales major league baseball and a certain owner in Baltimore told for years: that fans in the Washington Metro area never really cared about baseball, that D.C. "just isn't a baseball town" and would never support yet another club. The likely more than one million fans who clicked past RFK's turnstiles in 1969, the 6th highest attendance in the American League, refute that long-held bromide. (Owner Bob Short, for reasons that became obvious two years later, revised attendance figures downward by pro-rating them based on full gate receipts paid, thus the 918,106 "official" figure listed today).

Possibly, it's the witness of 500 people who, in one week, purchased all available tickets for the Washington Baseball Historical Society's 30-year reunion for the club, held November 8, 1998. The adulation the crowd showed at the Sunday morning breakfast for the team as Phil Hochberg introduced each player left even seasoned broadcaster and passionate D.C. baseball advocate Phil Wood

1

dumbfounded. In his closing remarks, Wood, his voice choked with emotion, said, "That 500 people would come out on a November Sunday morning 30 years later to see a 4th place baseball team...I thank you all for the memories of a lifetime."

It may be the testimony of relief pitcher Dave Baldwin who said, "I still get literally hundreds of requests from fans to autograph a baseball card or some piece of memorabilia from the 1969 season. It amazes me how much interest that year still generates."

The Senators' 1969 season wove an unbreakable thread that ties the late afternoon of October 1, 1969, the final game of that season, when the crowd saluted Ted Williams and his men with a standing ovation, to the twilight of April 14, 2005 when Livan Hernandez fired a first pitch fastball over the outside corner for strike one, bringing baseball back to Washington at last.

Like a Summer afternoon at the ballpark, the 1969 Washington Senators are the warm rays of happiness, the breath of fresh air that ever reminds us that baseball stands alone as the sport that grabs us by the heart -- and won't let go.

Bernie Allen. Hank Allen. Brant Alyea. Dave Baldwin. Frank Bertaina. Dick Billings. Dick Bosman. Sam Bowens. Ed Brinkman. Doug Camilli. Cisco Carlos. Paul Casanova. Joe Coleman. Casey Cox. Tim Cullen. Jan Dukes. Mike Epstein. Jim French. Jim Hannan. Toby Harrah. Dennis Higgins. Gary Holman. Frank Howard. Bob Humphreys. Darold Knowles. Frank Kreutzer. Lee Maye. Ken McMullen. Jim Miles. Barry Moore. Camilo Pascual. Jim Shellenback. Dick Smith. Ed Stroud. Del Unser. Zoilo Versalles.

Joe Camacho. Nellie Fox. Sid Hudson. George Susce. Wayne Terwilliger.

Ted Williams.

42 men.

Their hold on us remains.

Introduction: Together Again

"We all had our own stories."

-Bernie Allen, Second Baseman, Washington Senators

Sometimes, heroes hide in plain sight. On November 8, 1998, a bright morning with the chill of fall in the air, 25 middle-aged men mingled in the main ballroom of the Westfields Inn and Conference Center in Chantilly, Virginia, rubbing Sunday sleep from their eyes. With wrinkled faces, wide midsections, and gray or receding hairlines, they looked decidedly unremarkable.

Yet, to the eager throng who waited outside the locked ballroom doors to eat breakfast with them, spines tingling and goose bumps on their arms, heroes they were. The crowd, 500 strong, pressed toward the doors, boys and girls in adult bodies. They craved one final opportunity to claim an autograph, snap a picture, and converse over coffee with the men who gave them their happiest baseball moments.

Through the magic of memory, the ordinary old men these 500 yearned to see, the bulk of the 1969 Washington Senators baseball club, became young again. As the aroma of pancakes, sausage and coffee caressed their noses, the Senators and their fans prepared to celebrate the 30th anniversary of the astounding 1969 season. Dismissed as hopeless losers before a pitch was ever thrown, these men rode the enthusiasm and charm of rookie manager Ted Williams and their own resilience to play the best baseball anyone in Washington witnessed in more than 20 years. Williams transformed the same players who finished in last place in 1968 into his Battlin' Senators, gentlemen whose feats captured the heart of a weary, riot-torn nation's capital. Thirty years later in Chantilly, fans, players, coaches – even the club's radio broadcasters – gathered to celebrate the boundless summer of 1969 when man walked on the moon and the Washington Senators won 86 games.

In the midst of the pack huddled outside stood Keith Gallagher, a soft-spoken man with soulful brown eyes. In the dark first hours of the day, Gallagher drove from his New Jersey home to meet his childhood idol, Senators' first baseman Mike Epstein, to complete a mission of gratitude. Another fan, Jim Hartley, one of the privileged few inside the ballroom hobnobbing with the Senators, felt exhausted and ecstatic. With his cohorts in the Washington Baseball Historical Society, he worked for years to make this day possible. In 1969, when his rock band lost its gig at a Washington, D.C. nightclub, he filled his nights watching baseball at RFK Stadium. There, the Senators became his adopted family. As the doors burst open and fans scurried inside, Hartley looked around the brightly lit room, faux crystal chandeliers dangling from the ceiling like rays of sunshine, and smiled.

In one corner sat Dick Bosman. So obscure the Senators' opening day game program listed him as "Dave" Bosman, he finished the year with an eight-game winning streak and won the American League's ERA crown. Fifteen years later, his wife's candor helped the man who became the 1969 Senators' best pitcher make a life-altering decision.

Paul Casanova, the club's starting catcher and a fan favorite, missed the event due to a last-minute business commitment in Miami. His strong throwing arm and flamboyant playing style often ended in spectacular failure. In 1969, Casanova overcame trials that wiped away the colorful Cuban's perpetual smile and threatened to break him.

As fans met each player, happy sounds, like the cheer of children on Christmas morning, filled the space. At adjoining tables, Dennis Higgins, the tall, bespectacled, plain-spoken Missouri man and Casey Cox, the loud, boisterous, still blonde California surfer, traded war stories about Williams and the skull sessions he held with them on how to outwit hitters. In 1969, both gave Williams stellar pitching when the Senators needed it most. Both held regrets about their baseball careers after that storybook season.

The fans at Ed Brinkman's table erupted with laughter. The tall, thin shortstop graced the Senators infield for a decade until, on October 9, 1970, Washington's nefarious owner Bob Short sent Brinkman to the Detroit Tigers as part of the Denny McLain deal. Brinkman played the season of his life in 1969, complementing his fine defensive play with solid hitting. His contagious laugh and reputation for clubhouse antics cloaked a burning passion to win.

Brinkman's friend, Del Unser, reclined at an adjoining table. His companions conversed with the once fleet, young centerfielder who won so many games for the Senators with his feather-soft bunts, dramatic extra-inning home runs, unbelievable running catches, and pinpoint throws. For 12 seasons, his talents remained hidden on mediocre teams. Then, his career in twilight, his clutch pinch-hits helped bring ultimate joy to a town starved for a baseball championship.

In the back of the room, the 1969 Senators' quiet leader, third baseman Ken McMullen, enjoyed breakfast with his wife. He secretly signed autographs for the handful of fans at his table when the watchful eyes of the event's promoter (who wanted $10 per signature) looked

4

elsewhere. McMullen inspired his teammates with excellent hitting and fielding and creative practical jokes. When the Senators traded him to the California Angels early in the 1970 season, a vital piece of the team's heart departed.

Other fans traded salt shakers and tall tales with infielders Bernie Allen and Tim Cullen. Allen experienced twin pains in Washington, a catastrophic knee injury that lingered his entire career and disenchantment with Williams, his childhood idol. He used acerbic wit and disdain for team rules to provoke Williams' ire. Cullen, a classic glove man who struggled with the bat, endured his most embarrassing baseball episode on the happiest day of the Senators' season.

Scattered around the ballroom, Hank Allen, Arthur Lee Maye, and Ed Stroud traded stories with fans and posed for pictures. During his baseball career, Allen, the dignified former utility player, lived in the shadow of his younger, more talented brother Richie. At the reunion, he sang the praises of Williams, the colorblind manager who gave him opportunities to play that the previous regime withheld.

Maye, a smooth voiced doo-wop singer with a sweet left-handed swing, joined the Senators in mid-season and hit like an all-star. In September 1969, he slugged a grand slam that guaranteed Senators' fans the happiest season in Washington in 23 years. In the 1970s, Maye, an African American, felt the soul-draining pain of being denied a job he felt well-qualified to do – teach young ballplayers how to hit a baseball.

Stroud wore the broadest smile in the ballroom. His former teammates marveled at the fleet former outfielder's youthful looks, as if he could outrun time. "Did you see Eddie?" they said, "He hasn't changed a bit." The bliss of Stroud's simple, contended life after baseball kept the wrinkles at bay.

Stroud lamented just one thing, the absence of his old friend, pitcher Dave Baldwin. The studious, affable "Professor" taught himself a sidearm throwing motion to compensate for a college arm injury and years of poor performances in the lowest rung of the minor leagues. After baseball, Baldwin became a renaissance man. By day, he earned advanced degrees in genetics and systems engineering. After classes, he created numerous works of painting, sand art, and poetry and published his memoir. One example of his work was displayed in the hallowed place all baseball players aspire to reach.

Also absent was another intelligent pitcher, one of the Senators' most intense members. As his teammates engaged in earnest conversation with fans as waiters and waitresses scurried about, refilling water glasses and coffee cups, they reminisced about Notre Dame graduate and Washington's assistant player representative Jim Hannan.

Long interested in helping his fellow ballplayers with their finances, Hannan was one of the founding members of the Major League Baseball Players Alumni Association. Hannan's leadership, energy and passion helped the fledging organization grow into a stable, vibrant entity that serves more than 5,000 members.

Near Hannan, wily relief pitcher Bob Humphreys regaled fans with stories of his long career in baseball. A junk ball specialist, Humphreys became a mainstay in the Senators bullpen as soon as he joined the team in 1966. The most politically astute Senator, he worked for Virginia Congressman Richard Poff during the winter. After several years spent coaching in the minor leagues and college, Humphreys rekindled his love for baseball during an unexpected trip to Latin America.

Humphreys shared memories of his teammate, left handed pitcher Jim Shellenback. Few in the room remembered his struggle to rehabilitate himself and pitch again after a near fatal car accident in Pittsburgh in 1967. After the Senators acquired Shellenback from the Pirates in May 1969, he endured an emotional roller coaster. In July, four days after he married his sweetheart, he pitched one of the Senators' finest games of the year. A month later, his Uncle Frank Shellenback died. He was Ted Williams' first manager in professional baseball.

While players and fans dined and chatted, Williams' lieutenants, bench coach and confidant Joe Camacho, pitching coach Sid Hudson, and third base coach Wayne Terwilliger huddled together. They mourned the absence of two friends, first base coach Nellie Fox, who died in 1975 at age 48, and bullpen coach George Susce, the gnarled-fingered old catcher from Pittsburgh who doubled as the team's drill sergeant, forcing pitchers to run wind sprints until they dropped from exhaustion. Susce passed away in 1986, at age 78. Camacho, Hudson and Terwilliger waited for Williams, their leader and friend, hoping he could summon the strength to appear at the post-breakfast ceremony.

Eventually, conversation turned to others who missed the event such as Barry Moore and Joe Coleman. Moore, a flaky southpaw, never again pitched like he did the first three months of 1969. Traded to the Cleveland Indians in 1970, folks lost touch with the incorrigible country boy somewhere between RFK Stadium and a favorite fishing hole near his North Carolina home. Coleman, still learning to pitch in 1969, often clashed with Williams over his refusal to throw the slider. He harbored no warm feelings or memories about his two seasons playing for the Senators' legendary manager.

Another missing Senator, tough-talking, iron-fisted Brant "Bruno" Alyea, worked a dead-end job as a bouncer in an Atlantic City casino.

6

The big slugger from Passaic, New Jersey struck out far too often to last in the major leagues. Years later, Williams entered the gambling house where Alyea worked bearing a gift that moved the hardened man to tears of thankfulness.

Work commitments prevented Darold Knowles, a minor league pitching instructor, from attending. In 1969, Knowles returned to Washington on May 23 after a year-long stint at a United States Air Force base in Japan. With a week of practice, the best relief pitcher to don a Senators' uniform dominated American League hitters and stabilized a pitching staff on the brink of disaster. Few teammates knew how a military buddy in Japan worked out every day with Knowles to help him maintain arm strength and stamina. Four years after his all-star 1969 season, he stood on the mound in Oakland-Alameda County Coliseum, heart racing, one pitch from saving or losing a World Series championship for the A's.

The absence of the largest, most popular Senator, Frank Howard, created a void in the room and in fans' hearts. A prior commitment kept "Hondo," the gentle giant who won over Washington with his relentless hustle, prodigious homers, and abiding kindness, at bay. He met hundreds of fans at an autograph show the day before. Though they missed his massive physical presence, fans and players alike knew Big Frank remained present in story and spirit. In 1969, a spring training conversation with Williams transformed Howard from an undisciplined slugger into one of baseball's most patient and productive hitters.

Watching the room warm with joyful conversation, Ron Menchine closed his eyes and recalled Howard's finest moments as a Senator. His lips curled into a wistful smile. For three seasons (1969-71), none better than 1969, the erudite, smooth-voiced Menchine described Hondo and the other Senators' feats to listeners throughout the Washington Metro area on WWDC radio. He owned the privilege and felt the burden of broadcasting the Senators' last game in Washington. Though he performed his finest work on September 30, 1971, the melancholy, chaos-filled night baseball left the city, the team's departure for Texas marked the end of his dream job, the one he had longed for since childhood.

Like Menchine, the fellowship and affection of the morning energized these men, many seeing each other for the first time since they played together in Washington. For many, 1969 marked their best season in major league baseball. Two years later, nearly all retired or played elsewhere, the magic of 1969 gone forever. As morning gave way to mid-day, they stood straighter, walked taller, spoke louder.

7

The Senators selected Jim French to address the gathering. The pugnacious catcher's head barely peeked over the podium, a consequence of his squat 5' 8" stature. One of the club's least talented, but most popular players, he won the hearts of Washington's fans with his scrappy, hustling play. French spoke of the bonds he built with the 1969 Senators, a close team that fought valiantly together.

A whimsical smart aleck during his playing days, French convinced the photographer taking the 1969 Senators team picture to place him in the back row between Cox and Higgins, two of the team's taller players. With a devilish grin on his face, the top of his cap barely reached his teammates' shoulders. Throughout 1969, French teased and bantered with Williams in ways no one else dared. By then, French had resolved to fear no one. After baseball, he became a hyper-competitive securities trader and an attorney specializing in exposing securities fraud and guarding ranchers' rights to water on their land.

As French finished his speech, the room buzzed. Word spread that Williams resolved to make his way to the ballroom to speak. Soon, a door burst open and the 1969 Senators' manager, looking old and frail, appeared. The crowd stood in tribute, as Williams' son John Henry pushed his father's wheelchair onto the stage.

The proud, defiant baseball icon, swatted his son's helping hand away, stood up, hobbled to the podium and began to speak. From the first word, he captivated the audience with stories of his Senators. Over three decades, Williams' affection for the men he led grew. He said, pride swelling his booming voice, "I don't think anybody realized, or can believe it yet, how many really good players we had." Comfortable and delighted in the spotlight, he fielded questions from the awestruck crowd.

The memories and adulation enlivened Williams. His words rolled back time to the happy days of 1969 when, in the shadow of the Washington Monument and the reflected glow of the Capitol dome, Teddy Ballgame made an impossible dream come true. He turned the Washington Senators into winners and ordinary men into heroes.

The joy that filled the Westfields ballroom that wonderful Sunday morning in Chantilly stood in stark contrast to the mood 30 years earlier at the posh Statler Hilton Hotel in Washington, D.C. A grim Bob Short, who, in December 1968, purchased the Washington Senators for $9.4 million, prepared to address the Touchdown Club, a collection of Washington businessmen and sports fans, on the sorry state of his new acquisition.

1969 SENATORS REUNION
BREAKFAST

Sponsored by The Washington Baseball Historical Society
& Collector's Showcase of America

November 8, 1998 (7:30-11am)
Westfields Marriott
(Chantilly, Virginia)

GUESTS INCLUDE:

Bernie Allen	Johnny Holliday*
Hank Allen	Frank Howard
Rich Billings	Sid Hudson
Dick Bosman	Bob Humphreys
Ed Brinkman	Darold Knowles
Joe Camacho	Frank Kreutzer
Joe Coleman	Lee Maye
Casey Cox	Ken McMullen
Tim Cullen	Ron Menchine*
Mike Epstein	Ed Stroud
Jim French	Fred Valentine
Dennis Higgins	Shelby Whitfield*

*former broadcasters   ** special guests,
Steve Carlton & Warren Spahn.

Breakfast will feature speakers, doorprizes & memorabilia displays of the 1969 season. Following breakfast there will be autograph signings at the Capital Expo Center down the street.

TICKETS: $35.00*
Includes buffet breakfast, chances at doorprizes & discounts on admission to the Capital Expo Center and autograph tickets
FOR INFO CALL (703) 378-4673 or (703) 313-2302

1969 Senators Reunion Breakfast Flyer

9

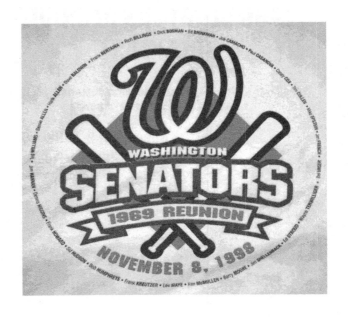

1969 Senators Reunion Breakfast Logo
Art by Ronnie Joyner (Used with Permission)

Washington Baseball Historical Society Logo
Art by Ronnie Joyner (Used with Permission)

1: Dismal

"The personification of acceleration."

-The Washington Senators' 1969 Press Radio-Television Guide's
description of owner Robert E. Short

The men of Washington's Touchdown Club awaited the luncheon address from the guest of honor, the Senators' new owner, Robert E. Short. Nattily dressed in the 1960s fashion staple, charcoal colored suit and thin navy blue tie, he picked at his steak and steamed vegetables and took a sip from his glass of water. Then, Short rose from his seat, strode to the podium, and removed his speaking notes from a pocket inside his suit jacket. The gray winter chill this afternoon in Washington, February 7, 1969, seemed to suck the joy from the occasion.

The gregarious, outspoken Short appeared perturbed and oddly quiet for a man who had just joined one of America's most elite fraternities, the 24 owners of major league baseball franchises. Most new owners treated their purchase as the fulfillment of a dream. With gleeful smiles they promise the moon – civic responsibility, savory concessions, reasonable ticket prices, and multiple World Series championships.

Not Short. With pursed lips and stern gaze, Short used dreary words to paint a picture of gloom for his dumbstruck audience. Describing his new franchise, he said "[Baseball in Washington] doesn't belong in last place in terms of a bankrupt club in a $20 million stadium in which people are afraid to watch games. I first recognized in December that when you are last in all respects – attendance, concessions, and the won-lost column – you are a dismal last, no matter how you measure it."

In a city desperate for a summer respite from lingering rage and fear in the aftermath of the riots and fires that occurred after when assassins killed Martin Luther King, Jr. and Robert F. Kennedy, Short offered nothing. He said his hometown friends from Minnesota thought him crazy to buy a miserable team that played in a "still-burning city" inside a stadium suburbanites felt unsafe attending.

His dramatic overstatement aside, Short did inherit a mess. The dreadful expansion Senators began operations in 1961, when American League owners approved two additional teams, the Los Angeles Angels

12

and a new franchise to replace the original Senators, a charter member of the American League. Calvin Griffith moved his Washington team to Minnesota after the 1960 season. The new Washington Senators played miserable baseball. From 1961-68, the club lost 768 games, an average of 96 per year.

Each horrendous season, attendance at D.C. Stadium, which opened in 1962, declined. It reached rock bottom in 1968 when 546,661 fans, by far the league's fewest, showed up. The area around the stadium resembled a war zone. As the city burned day after desolate day, President Lyndon B. Johnson dispatched members of the D.C. National Guard to protect the area. In the ranks stood Edwin Albert Brinkman, who spent his off-duty hours playing shortstop for the Senators. The brave souls who trekked to the ballpark walked past rifle-toting troops to get to their seats, praying their cars parked outside survived.

Short's players, save one, brought him cold comfort. In 1968, the team finished in last place in the American League with 65 wins and 96 losses. Washington batters struggled to hit. They finished seventh out of 10 teams in runs scored and ninth in batting average. Opposing teams feared just one batter, Frank Howard. His 44 home runs led all of baseball. Howard gave fans the only compelling reason to drive into the city to watch a game. Pitchers performed worse than the hitters. They surrendered the most runs in the league, had the highest ERA, and struck out the fewest batters. The future looked bleak as the club's two best players, Howard (32), and ace pitcher, Camilo Pascual (35) were also its oldest.

Well before he spoke to the Touchdown Club, Short made unpopular, but, in his mind, necessary changes. The Senators' 1969 Press-Radio Television Guide described Short as a "man on the move who is impatient of inefficiency, intolerant of intolerance, contemptuous of complacency, a stern foe of the status quo." He raced like a whirling dervish to shake the Senators "out of the doldrums." He fired manager Jim Lemon and General Manager George Selkirk. He would handle Selkirk's duties himself.

He changed the team's home uniforms, removing the navy blue pinstripes. Short preferred all white jerseys, with a brilliant red "Senators" written in cursive, the word angling in an upward arch across the front. He negotiated a new radio contract with station WWDC, ending the team's long association with WTOP. The change meant new broadcasters Ron Menchine and Shelby Whitfield would replace the popular team of John McLean and Dan Daniels.

Short voiced grave concern about the safety of D.C. Stadium, which Congress voted to rename Robert F. Kennedy Memorial Stadium

13

to honor the fallen statesman. Short asked the D.C. Armory Board, the organization that managed the stadium, for fenced parking with regular security patrols and brighter lighting in stadium parking lots and walkways. Inside the facility, he promised fans a better game experience, including warm hot dogs, salty peanuts and cold beer. Stadium concessionaires usually offered Senators' patrons the opposite.

During his speech, he hinted at his most controversial change, a plan to raise ticket prices. Two weeks later, he revealed the details. Short changed 15,000 formerly general admission sections into higher priced box and reserved seats, eliminating non-reserved seating from the stadium's lower bowl. All told, the changes increased the average Senators' ticket price from $2.14, the lowest in baseball, to $3.24, one of the highest. Box seats now cost $5, up from $4, general admission, $2 (formerly $1.50). *The Sporting News* studied ticket prices and named a Senators' game one of the most expensive nights out in the major leagues, pricier than seats at New York's Yankee Stadium. Short explained, "We have been selling bleacher tickets when we have no bleachers. The prices have been rescaled from an expert's point of view."

Short's actions rankled most of the Senators' small, but devoted fan base. Older fans who could barely afford the new general admission prices dreaded the long, uphill walk on RFK's switchback ramps to reach the upper levels. Once there, narrow, steep concrete stairs waited. Sales for season tickets numbered in the hundreds. Potential customers refused to pay premium prices for bargain basement baseball. Short claimed he made his changes because of the financial risk the franchise posed. He said, "I have my economic neck stuck out for miles."

Short's claim of fiscal hardship puzzled fans. He seemed wealthy enough and he paid a reasonable price for the Senators. Plus, he owned the Admiral-Merchants Motor Freight Company, at the time the largest trucking line west of the Mississippi. In 1968, Short's trucking interests grossed $40 million. He held controlling interests in Gopher Aviation, Inc., four hotels in downtown Minneapolis, and Los Angeles radio station KRHM.

Short enjoyed lucrative political connections as well. He served as Treasurer for the Democratic National Committee. He owned a Lear jet used to fly between Washington and his Minneapolis home. He spent weekdays in the District of Columbia, weekends in Minnesota. Short earned more handsome profits when he sold the National Basketball Association Los Angeles Lakers franchise to a California millionaire maverick, Jack Kent Cooke. Short purchased the Lakers while they played in their original home, Minneapolis. Two seasons later, he moved the franchise to Los Angeles. Washingtonians thought, "This man has money and knows how to get his hands on more." They resented a rich owner crying poor when the team still lacked a manager.

Short made Senators' fans uneasy. The man had political ties to Washington, but displayed no loyalty to or affection for the city. He attended Georgetown University Law School, served as an Assistant United States District Attorney in Washington, D.C., and worked for the Judge Advocate General's office of the Navy Department. But to local folks, he epitomized the out-of-town, carpetbagger owner. He knew precious little about the area's people, politics, history and culture, let alone its baseball.

Short insinuated that the Senators stood on shaky ground in Washington. He rejected fans' smug assurances that Congress would revoke baseball's twin jewels – its exemption from anti-trust laws and the reserve clause that bound players to their teams in perpetuity – should he try to leave the nation's capital. Short stated, "Congress does not keep baseball in Washington. Baseball keeps baseball here." He knew the team's lease with the Armory Board for the use of D.C. Stadium expired on September 29, 1971.

A marketing motive lurked behind Short's bleak tone and veiled threat to move the Senators to another city. Short understood human nature. He wanted to sow seeds of doubt and dissatisfaction in his target audience so he could sell them on his plan to make things better. Years before he bought the Senators, his silver tongue persuaded many people who first told him no to eventually say yes. Once he pursued something or someone, Bob Short refused to rest until he got what he wanted. For good reason, *Washington Post* columnist George Minot, Jr. dubbed Short the "Great Persuader."

The proper tone set, Short set his sales hook. Did he have a deal for Washington! Robert E. Short knew the simple steps to make the Senators whole again. First, he announced a team slogan, "It's a Whole New Ballgame in Washington in 1969!" He hired a promotions director, Oscar Molomot, to pitch season ticket sales in the business community. He concocted innovative giveaways like panty hose night to attract more women to the ballpark. He promised big trades, proclaiming himself a "swinger" eager to make blockbuster deals.

First, Short's fledgling team needed a manager. With spring training less than a month away, Short formed a search committee – himself – to find one. He scanned the Washington coaching staff and out of work former managers. He found solid baseball men available, like former Oakland manager Bob Kennedy and Senators' coach Nellie Fox.

15

Told Short considered him as a managerial candidate, Fox said, "I never dreamed I'd be considered. It's nice that someone thinks of you as managerial material." The two met the next day, but for Short, a humble man like Fox would never do. He found such men competent, but colorless, lacking the style and flair he craved. His forlorn team needed to make a splash on the Washington scene. He resolved to find a marquee manager, "the kind people dream about," he said.

While Short searched for his dream manager, a blockbuster sports story unfolded in Washington. On the front page of newspapers throughout the nation, the unmistakable gap-toothed grin of the greatest football coach in NFL history appeared. Vince Lombardi, one of the most respected, successful men in sports, somehow agreed to become head coach of the Washington Redskins, a team as bad as the Senators. All Washington rejoiced. Redskins' news dominated the headlines.

The story jolted Short awake before his first sip of morning coffee. In the blink of an eye, the Redskins – Lombardi's Redskins – had stolen the limelight and relegated Short's dismal team to the middle of sports sections and the back of fans' minds.

The Senators' owner contemplated his next move. It had to be huge and happen fast. After a few hours in deep thought, Short knew what to do. He needed a star and he set his sights on the brightest. Summoning all his business acumen, cunning, persistence and persuasion he set out to find the unattainable man he coveted. He called the Washington press together and announced to the world the sole target of his managerial search – the reclusive baseball legend, Ted Williams.

2: The Splendid Splinter Meets the Great Persuader

"His presence was awesome. He elevated our expectations and our ability."

-Ken McMullen, Third Baseman, Washington Senators (on Ted Williams)

Bob Short set out on his quest to land Ted Williams as the Washington Senators' new manager. Teddy Ballgame. The Splendid Splinter. The self-proclaimed greatest hitter of all time. Williams epitomized star power. Veteran sportswriters considered Williams, along with Joe DiMaggio (who served as a bench coach for the Oakland A's) as baseball's greatest living players. The mercurial man's man with the purest left-handed swing in baseball history, he studied the tiniest details of hitting and loved to talk about it for hours.

Since his last game in 1960, Williams stayed involved on the margins of baseball. He ran an elite high school baseball camp with Joe Camacho in Massachusetts. The camp recruited promising young ballplayers. A few, including Senators' pitcher Joe Coleman, became major leaguers. During spring training, he tutored Red Sox hitters in between fishing trips. The rugged individualist remained prominent in American culture through his role as national spokesman for Sears' sporting goods. He often appeared with host and friend Curt Gowdy on the Emmy Award winning television program "American Sportsman."

Williams enjoyed life on his own terms. He made his own schedule and guarded his precious privacy. With carefully selected friends, he took long fishing expeditions and safaris to exotic, secluded places around the globe. Nine years before, Ted Williams exhaled and put baseball's daily grind behind him.

Only Short thought Williams could be talked into managing major league baseball's worst team. Williams gave everyone who asked him, even Red Sox' owner and friend Tom Yawkey, the same emphatic answer – "No," with colorful cuss words he learned in the Marine Corps thrown in for emphasis. The great Splendid Splinter left baseball a hero. Why tarnish his legend directing a broken down club destined to lose 100 games or more?

Washington fans mocked Short's ridiculous crusade. They thought, "Five weeks before spring training and the fool is chasing Teddy Ballgame's fishing boat all over the world?" They felt Short was wasting precious time and their now more expensive ticket money on a

17

silly jaunt. Senators' fan Jim Hartley said, "When I heard Short was going after Williams, I thought, 'Yeah, right. What a jerk.'"

The Washington media wondered if Short had gone temporarily insane. The Senators needed a leader weeks ago. Why would a rookie owner seek a rookie manager, living legend or not, with opening day less than two months away? They dismissed Short's odyssey as a publicity stunt and a fool's errand.

Short pressed on. To convince Williams to manage the Senators, he first had to find him. The wandering sportsman could be anywhere in the world from the Florida Keys to a jungle in South America. With trademark doggedness, Short called American League President Joe Cronin, a friend of Williams, and cajoled him into coughing up the Splendid Splinter's unlisted phone number at his home in Islamorada Key.

With that phone call, Short got his first lucky break. Williams was home planning his next fishing trip. He answered the call and Short popped the question. Williams offered his standard reply.

The two men's first encounter encouraged Short. He achieved what all salesmen crave, a foot wedged solidly in the door. Rejection emboldened him. He called Williams again and received the same answer.

Short persevered. Calling on his best sales techniques, he changed tactics. He needed to somehow convince Williams to meet with him face-to-face. The personal approach would allow Short to employ his persuasive powers in ways cold phone lines thwarted. For one, he could show Williams a sample paycheck Short planned to offer him.

Short made two fabulous decisions to entice Williams to see him. First, he offered to meet on neutral ground in Atlanta, without notice to the media. Williams, in South Carolina to film advertisements for Sears, could book a brief flight south for the meeting. Second, Short told Williams he could fly him back to South Carolina in his state-of-the-art Lear jet.

The consummate salesman thoroughly researched his target. He remembered Williams served with distinction as a pilot and flight instructor in World War II and the Korean War. Modern commercial and military aircraft fascinated the former aviator. Short offered Williams the chance to inspect the plane and, maybe, take it for a spin before he returned to South Carolina – or perhaps, to Washington for a press conference.

Discussing airplanes instead of managing a baseball team, Short built a rapport with Williams and gained insight into his personality and desires. As the hours drifted by, the proud, confident, egotistical men grew comfortable with one another. Williams began to envision working with Short.

Williams continued to decline Short's entreaties, but each no seemed less emphatic. The Senators' owner knew it was time to make his best offer. He appealed to Williams' patriotism and his wallet.

Short offered Williams an arrangement unheard of in its generosity – a five-year contract worth a reported $65,000 a year, full say in choosing coaches and players, and partial ownership of the team. Williams' title would be Vice President-Manager. If the Senators' poor play drove him to distraction, he could move upstairs to the executive suite alongside Short.

Short also appealed to Williams' love for country. The nation's capital needed a unifying force. Who better than Williams to provide it? What better way to return to the game he loved than to fix the mess it had become in the city where the President of the United States lived? Williams and the Senators could salve the city's festering wounds, restore its lost pride.

After 12 hours together, Williams succumbed to Short's gold – and his silver tongue. Just days after Short's bold pronouncement, news broke that Ted Williams agreed to manage the Washington Senators. Only legal details remained before the formal contract signing and press conference to announce the deal.

During the wrangling over contract terms, which took more than a week to resolve and, for a time, appeared to fall through, Williams visited Yawkey. He sought his old chum's blessing before signing on the dotted line. Yawkey expressed unwavering confidence in Williams' teaching abilities. The legal and psychological hurdles cleared, Short, on February 21, 1969, announced Ted Williams as the Senators' new manager. Washington marveled at Short and celebrated the city's good fortune.

Williams said Short reeled him in with "the most fantastic offer I've ever received." He continued, "[Short] is a hard person to say no to. I never wanted a job as much as I wanted this one.

"The timing was just right. I've had eight years of fishing in Costa Rica and Peru and New Zealand and Alaska and New Brunswick and lately it was not much fun."

Hartley described the shock and joy fans felt when they heard the news. "What, he did it? How?"

Incredulous Senators' fans realized that their humble team now claimed the most famous skipper in baseball. Somehow, Short landed his promised marquee manager, a leader with as much brilliance and charisma as Lombardi, albeit without the experience or the championships. In three weeks, Washington changed from a sports backwater to the center of the nation's attention.

Now, Williams and Short faced the monumental task of rebuilding the Senators. While Short resumed lobbying for better stadium security and beer and hot dogs sold at the correct temperature, Williams learned the names and abilities of his players. With Teddy Ballgame on board, ticket sales jumped. Promotions Director Oscar Molomot sold more than 2,500 season packages.

The business partners flew from Washington to Pompano Beach, Florida to begin spring training. Washington and national media flocked to the Senators' spring training camp in the charming Florida town a few miles due south of Boca Raton to cover Williams' return to major league baseball.

Despite the distractions and hullabaloo, Williams remained calm. He exchanged friendly banter with reporters, signed autographs, and posed for pictures with fans. He beckoned those holding the cameras to move in close to get better shots of Washington's newest celebrity. Williams acted friendly and joyful, in complete contrast to the sullen, aloof personality he displayed during his playing days.

All Williams lacked in his idyllic world was baseball players. Only two from the Senators' major league roster, rookie utility infielder Rich Billings and veteran pitcher Phil Ortega, reported to camp to welcome their new boss. The rest, under the leadership of the Senators' assistant player representative Jim Hannan, honored players' union president Marvin Miller's request to strike for higher pensions and a reduction in the vesting requirement from five to four years. Hannan, who played a lead role in helping Miller formulate the union's demands, made it clear no other Senators would break ranks.

With new commissioner Bowie Kuhn's intervention, the owners and the union resolved the dispute after a week of negotiations. Kuhn rejected Short's idea to use replacement players to break the work stoppage. Under the new agreement, players received increased pensions, but less than they first demanded. In turn, the owners agreed to reduce the years of service needed to qualify to four seasons. Ten players on the 1969 Senators, Hank Allen, Brant Alyea, Frank Bertaina, Casey Cox, Jim French, Dennis Higgins, Barry Moore, Ed Stroud, Baldwin and Billings earned pensions thanks to the new rules.

The labor issues resolved, all but three Senators, Paul Casanova, Ken McMullen and Frank Howard, reported to Pompano Beach. Williams met with the team to proclaim his rules and set goals for the 1969 season. His ban on golf irked the players. His decree of a 15-minute post-game cooling off period before he opened the Senators' locker room to the media made sportswriters apoplectic. They petitioned the league and agitated the entire season, but Williams never wavered until the final game. Once Ted Williams made up his mind, no one could change it.

Next, Williams selected his coaching staff. He lacked knowledge about the mechanics of pitching and the intricacies of infield play and in-game strategy. To compensate, he chose a former major league pitcher and two former infielders. He looked for one other characteristic in his staff – backbone to stand fearless before Williams and fight for their ideas and suggestions.

He retained Sid Hudson, a tall, wiry former teammate, as his pitching coach. Nellie Fox, the former all-star second baseman for the Chicago White Sox and a holdover from Washington's 1968 staff, became his first base coach. Fox knew inside baseball in minute detail, from the best way to pivot on the double play to surreptitious ways to steal other team's signals. He was the consummate baseball man. Williams knew he needed help from his coaching staff in baseball nuances like giving and stealing signs, positioning infielders and outfielders and executing cutoff plays. He nabbed feisty Wayne Terwilliger, 1968 manager of the Senators' AAA farm club in Buffalo and a fellow Marine, for his third base coach. Like Fox, Terwilliger knew baseball's intricacies, but he lacked his fellow coach's talent. He could empathize with the humble journeymen on the Senators' roster. Throughout the season, Williams relied on Fox and Terwilliger for their sage advice on in-game tactical decisions.

To complete his staff, Williams added longtime Boston friend Joe Camacho as bench coach. Young Doug Camilli, 33, and ancient George Susce, 62, manned the bullpen. Camilli doubled as a player if catchers Casanova and Jim French fell injured. Susce forced the Senators into shape through his extreme, almost sadistic exercises and running program. "He was liable to kill us. Boy, did we used to curse him," Senators' pitcher Dennis Higgins said. Susce's unyielding strategy worked. The Senators completed spring training without a serious injury.

Williams' talented, experienced staff freed him to teach hitting and inspire and motivate his players. Constant failure wrung out the Senators' enthusiasm, a characteristic Williams possessed in abundance. After a week with his men, Williams said, "There is much raw talent on this team, but thinking in a baseball sense is foreign to many of the Senators. The main thing is, we need to improve. I think we will."

The comment revealed Williams' zeal as well as his penchant for frustration and anger. During his playing days, his temper sometimes overwhelmed his reason. Did Williams have the proper disposition to manage a poor, mistake-prone team? Did he have the patience to deal with repeated failure by players who lacked his talent and passion? Could he withstand writers' incessant second guessing of his line-up choices and unsuccessful decisions?

Williams knew his moody past cast doubt on his ability to lead. He acknowledged the silliness and sins of his youth. He insisted he had mellowed and matured. He promised to maintain self-control for the duration of his contract. He said, "People think I'll quit if we get off bad, but I'm in this thing to stay." Despite his past flaws, Ted Williams never quit. He left his shotguns and fishing rods at home.

Williams' intensity still flared, especially when it came to hitting. The Senators liked to goof off during spring training batting practice. Williams stopped those shenanigans. Ed Brinkman said, "You couldn't mess around. He was strictly business around the hitting cage."

While Williams worked on changing his team's baseball acumen and morale, Short inked players to contracts. In the days before free agency and guaranteed multimillion dollar deals, Short negotiated terms with each player at a picnic table behind the left field wall inside the Senators' practice facility, with no agents in sight.

Camilo Pascual, the Senators top starting pitcher, met with Short first. Pascual earned renown as a tough negotiator. The Washington media, always nearby, waited for the fireworks. A scant 20 minutes later, they watched dumfounded as Pascual smiled, shook hands with Short and left the table. He and Short agreed to a reported $45,000 deal.

Contract signings came fast and furious. Short talked Dave Baldwin and Brinkman into deals. He worked out terms with Hannan and Mike Epstein over the telephone. Ed Stroud signed and sprinted to the batting cage to work with Williams.

Casanova worked out a contract with Short during a long distance phone call. The Senators granted him permission to remain in Connecticut until he wrapped up some personal affairs and secured his family's belongings. The next day, McMullen signed a new deal. Howard, the only Senator Short failed to talk into the fold, conducted his annual spring training hold out.

Howard's teammates and veteran Senators' fans knew Hondo hated spring training. He wanted more time to relax at his Wisconsin home. Short, however, disliked people who dared spurn his charm and generosity. He placed Howard on the trading block. The Yankees and Indians made offers, but Williams convinced the piqued Short to avoid a rash deal. The poor Senators needed Howard, a hulking 6' 7" giant of a man, the club's leader, most reliable hitter, and sole drawing card.

Short and Howard used the newspapers to argue. Howard told *The Washington Post*, "I'll burn in hell if he expects me to call and tell him I've been wrong." Short refused to meet Howard's demand for a three year, $300,000 contract. On March 10, Howard declared an impasse saying, "We're miles apart." Short claimed he received a tempting offer for Howard from the California Angels.

Eventually, Short grew wise to Howard's holdout habit. He floated dubious trade rumors and let Howard stew. With everyone else in camp, Short waited for the giant Senator's call.

The club's early spring training play impaired Short's negotiating position. The Senators lost eight consecutive games. They looked hopeless in every facet of baseball. Williams remained calm until the final loss, an ugly defeat at the hands of the dreadful expansion Montreal Expos. His team looked feeble and incompetent.

Williams boiled over. He yelled at a pitcher, criticized his team's laziness and snapped at a reporter. People who doubted Williams shook their heads knowingly. They thought, "If this lousy team can get under Ted's skin after eight exhibition games, imagine what 162 real ones will do."

Short called off all trade talks and phoned Howard. The two antagonists compromised. On March 15, Howard reported to camp and signed a one-year agreement for a reported $90,000, making him the all-time highest paid Senator. A grinning Short claimed, "We were never close to trading him."

Howard, making a dubious claim he weighed a mere 255 pounds, began working himself into shape to earn his newfound fortune. His weight always involved guesswork, because he refused to let Senators' coaches weigh him. Even the strong, strapping 6'4" Hudson struggled to get Howard on the scale. Hudson said, "One day, I begged him and begged him and he finally got on and tipped the scales at 300 right on the button."

Howard recalled with a laugh, "Sid could never get me on the scale because I was always overweight."

As if on cue, with Howard in the line-up as the designated pinch-hitter for the pitcher, a spring training experiment in 1969, the Senators won their first spring game, an 18-5 rout of the Atlanta Braves. Williams said, "I'm glad to break that losing, losing, losing habit."

Howard and Williams were kindred spirits when it came to hitting a baseball. One day in batting practice, Howard made solid contact, where the bat feels weightless as it drives through the ball. Howard sighed and said, "That's the sweetest sound in baseball."

Williams replied, "That's the sweetest sound in life."

23

Howard's tardy, but fanatical work ethic won over Williams. He said of Howard, "He's the hardest working guy I've ever seen in spring training, bar none."

The long spring tested Williams' newfound patience. He grew weary of endless exhibition matches. He found solace between games as he labored to repair the Senators' broken approaches to the mental aspects of hitting and pitching. Del Unser, poised to begin his second season as Washington's centerfielder, described his manager's daily sessions with hitters. Unser said, "[Ted would] say, 'What pitch is important for the count? If you've never seen this pitcher before and he missed with his curveball is he going to throw you a fastball? What do you look for? You've got to look for the curveball. That's the only pitch you've seen.'"

He expected hitters to take more pitches, to look for pitches in exact locations depending on the ball-strike count and game situation. Players who failed to prepare for every possible hitting scenario felt Williams' fury.

He worked side by side with each player, emphasizing strengths to boost confidence. He found precise flaws for each hitter to correct. He told Howard to stop swinging at the first fastball he saw. Skinny shortstop Brinkman was under orders to forget swinging for home runs and to hit the ball "line drive down" to advance runners and get on base. Williams convinced Hank Allen to relax and use his quick wrists to drive balls to the outfield gaps. He directed Unser to shorten his stride and take a compact swing to pull more pitches to right field.

Williams spent ample time with Epstein, the left-handed power hitter he dubbed "my prodigy." He junked the crazy batting stance Epstein used in 1968, where he crouched low and cocked his head to one side. He allowed the insightful, intelligent slugger to experiment with stances until he found a comfortable one.

Williams held numerous skull sessions with his pitchers. He described a hitter's thinking in detail. Relief pitcher Higgins said, "Ted helped me tremendously. Listening to him talk about hitters helped pitchers, because it was on the opposite end of the scale; what a hitter's mindset was, what they looked for when they were facing certain situations. It gave me an idea of how to pitch to them. You knew what that batter was up there thinking and you worked around that."

Williams commanded his pitchers to throw more sliders, the pitch he found most difficult to hit. All obeyed, except Joe Coleman. The two argued over the benefits and drawbacks of the pitch all season long.

The most patient hitter of his era lectured his team on the importance of the walk. Williams wanted hitters to seek them and pitchers to avoid them. Years before Bill James and his ilk ruminated on the importance of on-base percentage, Williams understood its value. He knew walks increased pitch counts. Batters saw more pitches, while pitchers grew tired and vulnerable. In 1968, the Senators finished sixth in the league in walks and seventh in free passes allowed. He expected great improvement in those standings.

Two weeks before the season opener, Short's attempt to become baseball's trading swinger came up empty. Williams would battle his rivals with the same players from the dismal 1968 debacle. Under baseball's new two-division format, the Senators shared the American League East with the Detroit Tigers, Boston Red Sox, Baltimore Orioles, Cleveland Indians, and New York Yankees, the teams that finished in the top five spots in the standings the year before. Short expected Williams to achieve success with the same players that failed others before him.

Without new talent, Williams resolved to change the Senators' self-image. He demanded his club act and play like winners. He expected them to overcome talent deficiencies with hard work and heads-up play. He insisted on hustle at all times. No Senator ambled to the batting cage or strolled to and from his position during infield drills. During practices and games, he permitted one topic of conversation – baseball.

He posted former Yankees and Red Sox' manager Joe McCarthy's "Ten Commandments of Baseball" on the clubhouse door. Old Joe's list included clichés such as "Always run them out. You can never tell." The trite bromides presented a subtle message – winning depended on attitude as much as ability.

Williams worked hard to keep team morale and enthusiasm high. McMullen said, "His presence was awesome. He elevated our expectations and our ability."

As the end of spring training beckoned, the Senators kept losing and Williams stayed hard at his quest to instill winning behaviors. He accepted any request to take extra batting practice, working late into the evening to evangelize his men in the Ted Williams way. Williams hoped his players listened, learned fast, and caught his deep love and excitement for the game.

Out of respect for the funeral of former President Dwight D. Eisenhower, who died on March 28, the Senators canceled their final game in Pompano Beach against Boston. Williams and his former team would first meet on April 23 in Fenway Park.

The Senators packed their bags and prepared to break camp. One day before their scheduled departure, they heard bad news. Short moved two pre-season games on April 5 and 6, first scheduled for the Louisiana State Fairgrounds, to tiny 15,000-seat Turnpike Stadium in Arlington, Texas. He announced Head Groundskeeper Joe Mooney had inspected the Louisiana site and judged the grounds unplayable.

The Senators, after braving one of the coldest, windiest, and wettest Florida springs in decades, resented being forced to play two games in a dusty Texas town halfway between Dallas and Fort Worth. Short claimed he tried to move the games to a more convenient locale such as Milwaukee or Richmond, but found both sites already booked. Besides, the consummate businessman said, "We were told we'd have two sellouts in Dallas."

Williams and his players preferred two days off to relax before the pomp and circumstance of the Presidential Opener. Short refused to let his employees sit idle when they could barnstorm for profit on the way to Washington. He looked forward to the cash from two sell outs in Texas to offset the costs of spring training.

The tired, unmotivated club played listlessly in Texas and lost both games to the Pittsburgh Pirates. Combined, attendance for the two contests fell short of 9,000, far below Short's financial expectations and the promised 30,000 paid admissions.

The Senators left Texas and limped into Washington an exhausted team with a poor 8-19 pre-season record. Gamblers placed 100 to 1 odds on the Senators to win the American League pennant. In public, Williams set expectations low. He said, "I just hope we won't get slaughtered, but I think we'll be spoilers." Privately, he and his Senators intended to prove the detractors wrong by turning in a winning season.

Washington buzzed with activity to prepare for the Presidential Opener on Easter Monday. Cherry blossoms burst into full pink and white bloom. A new president, Richard Nixon, promised to throw the game's three ceremonial pitches from his honorary box seat behind the Senators' dugout. Mooney and his crew worked into the night to make the stadium's green field pristine. Fans clamored for tickets to the sold out event. Short refused to allow local television to air the game.

On opening day morning, April 7, 1969, a nervous Williams waited in his Washington apartment with his wife, Dolores, and baby son, John Henry. He prepared for the daunting task of transforming the wretched Washington Senators into a respectable baseball team. Fans waited with happy anticipation for Williams to make his splendid return to the national pastime.

At last the hour came. Williams kissed Dolores and John Henry and departed for RFK Stadium. Once there, he dressed in a brand new, gleaming red and white Washington Senators uniform, walked from the

26

locker room through the clubhouse tunnel and into the Washington dugout. He paced back and forth, waiting for the pre-game ceremonies to begin. A Senators' employee announced that President Nixon waited in the presidential box seat.

Removing his oversize warm-up jacket that hid the girth added to his midsection the past nine years, Williams gave a final word to his players and took a long, deep breath. With a few small steps, he emerged from the Senators' dugout, poised to make his giant leap back into baseball.

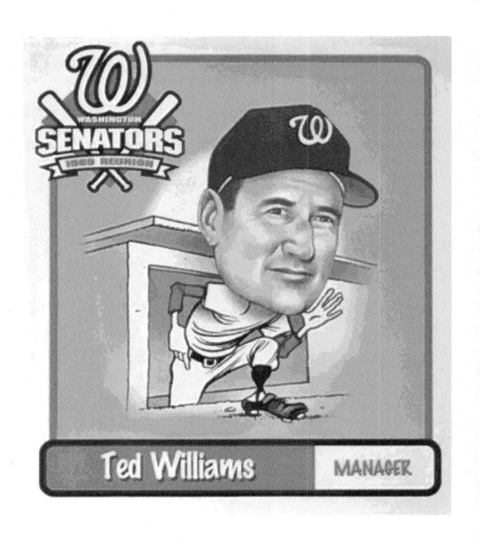

Ted Williams, Manager
Art by Ronnie Joyner (Used with Permission)

3: Twig: Born and Bred to Baseball

In March 1969, Ted Williams saved Willard Wayne Terwilliger from enduring hell on earth.

At the Senators' spring training facility in Pompano Beach, Florida, Terwilliger, known as Twig or Twiggy to all, hit countless groundballs to Washington's infielders – established veterans and youngsters alike. Williams knew next to nothing about the team that arrived in Pompano Beach two weeks previous. He looked around the field and saw strangers. Terwilliger, manager of the Senators' AAA farm team in Buffalo in 1968, knew the players' names, nicknames, bad habits, and, most important to Williams, talents.

Terwilliger recalled those early spring days. He said, "The [Senators] asked me to go to Spring Training, because I knew some of the players." A retired Marine who saw action at the battles of Saipan and Iwo Jima, Twig acted the role of good soldier. He worked those Washington infielders hard, all the while resigned to another year in Buffalo.

The Bison played in old War Memorial Stadium, nicknamed the Rock Pile because of its decrepit state. The faint of heart avoided the Rock Pile, situated in a dirty, crime-ridden area. Locker room robberies became commonplace. For safety's sake, the team moved most night games to nearby Niagara Falls.

Terwilliger expected to face this unhappy fate in 1969. Then, after infield practice one afternoon, Williams asked, "Do you want to be my third base coach?" "Well, you can imagine what a lift that was," Terwilliger said. Terwilliger's "yes" to Williams became a defining moment in his life. He escaped the drudgery of Buffalo for the thrill of Washington and major league baseball. It felt like going from an enlisted man's tent to the officers' club. Terwilliger, a humble journeyman infielder for the Cubs, Dodgers, Senators, Giants and Athletics during a 12-year major league career (1949-60), relied on knowledge of the intricate, inside details of baseball to survive. Williams, a regal slugging outfielder above such minutiae, knew he needed help from his coaching staff in baseball nuances like giving and stealing signs, positioning fielders and executing cutoff plays. Terwilliger explains, "Ted told [fellow coach] Nellie Fox and me at the start of the season, 'I don't know all these little intricacies. I know the game between the hitter and the pitcher.' That's the way he put it. If I wanted to put on a play, the hit and run, or something like that, I could do it. He didn't give me signs, per se, from the bench."

Terwilliger enjoyed the time of his life in 1969. He waved home 694 runners that season, the highest total in expansion Senators' history and the most for any Washington club since 1941. He said, "My recollections are all good from that season. If I had to pick one year out of all my years being in pro ball it would be 1969 coaching for Ted."

More meaningful than runs and victories, Terwilliger treasured the friendships he made with players and coaches alike. One friend, third baseman Ken McMullen, said "Wayne was a little crazy. He was just a kick to be around. I used to joke with him about his baseball card. You know how when you collect baseball cards you open up the packs and keep getting the same guy every time? I always seemed to get Wayne Terwilliger. I told him I had to put one of them in my bicycle spokes."

As the daily routine of the long baseball season progressed, Terwilliger and Fox built a deep friendship. Their conversations about baseball strategy, family and hometown friends, and the jokes and laughter transformed the game's daily grind into daily grace. Terwilliger still grieves the loss of his friend, who died in 1975. He said, his voice quiet in sad reflection, "Nellie and I became good friends. It started those years in Washington and we kept in touch until he died. When he died…that was a real shock to me. We were really good friends."

Terwilliger coached third base for Williams until Teddy Ballgame gave up managing after the 1972 season. By then, the old utility infielder loved coaching too much to ever stop. He coached for the Rangers' (1981-85) and Twins' (1986-94) and managed in the minor leagues. From 1995 – 2002, he managed the St. Paul Saints of the independent Northern League. In 2003, he jumped to another independent, the Fort Worth Cats of the Central Baseball League.

On his 80th birthday, June 27, 2005, Terwilliger joined Connie Mack as the second octogenarian manager in baseball history. The Cats gave away 1,500 Twig bobbleheads to honor the occasion. In September 2005, the old man managed the Cats to the league championship. After the season, to pay off a bet and keep a promise to his players, Terwilliger went to his local Wal-Mart, got his ear pierced, and placed in it a faux-diamond earring his wife chose. He said, "Cost me $29, but it looks pretty good."

In 2010, at age 85, Terwilliger retried from his job as the Cats part-time coach. He now works as a bagger at a grocery store in Willow Park, Texas. But from March to October, as long as he lives, Twig will, somehow, somewhere, be at a ballpark coaching, teaching, laughing, living, breathing baseball. Of his 62 years in baseball, 1969 remains closest to his heart: "I was out drinking a beer with Nellie Fox and I was coaching third base for Ted Williams and the club was winning – you couldn't ask for more."

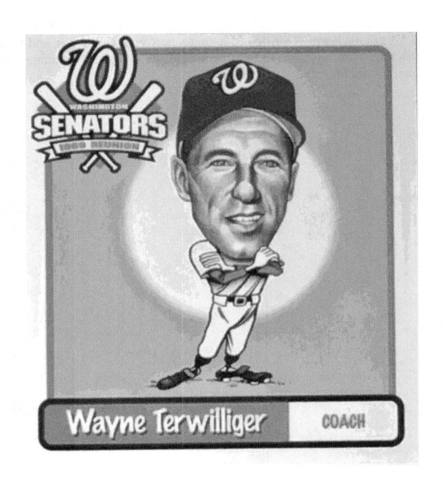

Wayne Terwilliger, Third Base Coach
Art by Ronnie Joyner (Used with Permission)

**1969 Opening Day; President Nixon throwing out ball
as Ted Williams, Ralph Houk, and Bowie Kuhn look on.**
(Richard Nixon Presidential Library and Museum)

Ticket to 1969 Presidential Opener
Private Collection of Rob Johnson (Used with Permission)

Opening Day Scoresheet – New York Yankees
Private Collection of Rob Johnson (Used with Permission)

SENATORS	1	2	3	4	5	6	7	8	9	10	AB	R	BH
UNSER	5³		D		S⁷	1⁶		4-3			5	1	3
STROUD	4-3	⑦			S⁸		②		S³		5	1	2
HOWARD	5-3	⑨		K		6-3		HR⁸			5	1	1
EPSTEIN	W		②	S⁷		1-3		3-1			4	0	1
McMULLEN / HIGGINS	1-3		4-3	6-4			K 4-3				5	0	0
BILLINGS		5-3	S⁸		S²		3	W			4	1	3
BRINKMAN	K		D⁷		S⁹		4-3	⑦			5	0	2
CASANOVA / HUMPHREYS	1-3	5-3		②		S³					4	0	1
PASCUAL		5-3									1	0	0
COLEMAN / BOSMAN				K	⑦		S⁹				3	0	1
	1/0	0/0	1/0	2/0	3/1	3/0	0/0	3/1	2/2		41	4	4

WASHINGTON

1 Cullen, if
2 McMullen, if
3 Alyea, of
5 Holman, if
6 Epstein, if
7 Allen, B. if
8 Casanova, c
9 Williams, Manager
10 French, c

11 Brinkman, if
12 Camilli, Coach
16 Hannan, p
17 Pascual, p
19 Dalton, p*
20 Coleman, p
21 Miles, p
23 Humphreys, p
24 Bertaina, p

25 Moore, p
26 Woodson, p
27 Bosman, p
28 Higgins, p
29 Cox, p
30 Unser, of
31 Billings, if
33 Howard, F. of
35 Allen, H. if

36 Stroud, of
37 Baldwin, p
40 Comacho, Coach
41 Hudson, Coach
42 Fox, Coach
43 Susce, Coach
44 Terwilliger Coach

* Disabled List

Opening Day Scoresheet – Washington Senators
Private Collection of Rob Johnson (Used with Permission)

36

4: Triumph of the Irregulars

"Greatness...there ain't a lot of it around, but Ted Williams was truly a great man."

-Brant "Bruno" Alyea, Outfielder, Washington Senators

The moment the opening day sell-out crowd of 45,113 saw Ted Williams set foot on the field, they rose as one. They cheered with vigor on that glorious spring afternoon to make the Senators' new manager feel at home in Washington. Head bent in humility and nervousness, Williams turned and ascended the steps to the presidential box where baseball commissioner Bowie Kuhn, New York Yankees' manager Ralph Houk, Bob Short, and President Nixon awaited. Williams shook hands with his fellow dignitaries, all in their first year on the job except for Houk, and climbed atop the Senators' dugout. The five posed for hundreds of pictures until the time arrived for Nixon to make his ceremonial pitches to open the 1969 baseball season.

For one afternoon each season, the Washington Senators basked in baseball's spotlight. With Ted Williams on board and baseball celebrating its 100th anniversary, the day brought unique joy to Senators' fans. The city decked the stadium in resplendent red, white and blue bunting. The front of Nixon's special seat bore the striking seal of his office. The bright white letters encircling the sign read "Presidnt of the United States." Tardy proofreaders noticed the error too late to correct it.

The rookie president tossed three pitches into the waiting crowd of Senators and Yankees bunched together in the infield. Washington's Hank Allen snared two balls. He asked Nixon to autograph both. "I kept one and gave the other to my mother," he said. Coach Joe Camacho also caught one of Nixon's tosses. Yankee pitcher Fritz Peterson, sporting an oversize fishing net, caught nothing.

During the pre-game ceremonies, Camilo Pascual, the Senators' starting pitcher, sat in the home bullpen and discussed the Yankee hitters in Spanish with fellow Cuban, catcher Paul Casanova. The 16-year veteran, the team's ace pitcher, felt relaxed. Pascual started presidential openers in Washington in 1956, 1960 and 1968. He fanned 15 Red Sox' batters in the 1960 opener, a brilliant complete game win. Back then, Pascual stood young and strong, a 5' 11", 170 pound fireballer poised to enter his prime.

Nine years later, the ruddy, handsome pitcher looked and felt older. Now 35, he ambled to the pitching mound. The familiar hill felt a bit unusual to him. In the winter, baseball owners ordered pitching mounds lowered from 15 to 10 inches and the strike zone reduced to encourage more offense. Pascual adjusted well to the changes in spring training. He felt strong and healthy.

Once the game began, Pascual lost command of his pitches. With the bright sun making the green field sparkle, Yankee hitters, even without recently retired star Mickey Mantle, battered the Senators' pitcher. In the 3rd inning, Jerry Kenney and Bobby Murcer hit solo home runs to drive Pascual from the game.

Bob Humphreys relieved Pascual and fared worse. In the 4th inning, the Yankees, thanks to two Senators' errors, scored three unearned runs. Williams replaced Humphreys with his mop-up man Dick Bosman. The young pitcher, the last player named to the Senators roster, skipped his first pitch to the backstop. Another Yankee scored to give New York an 8-0 lead.

Williams' first game looked like a fiasco, his team an embarrassment. Then, Bosman settled down and retired seven consecutive hitters. Washington batters, in a trait they displayed all season, kept battling. The Senators hit New York starter Mel Stottlemyre hard, but the crafty star dodged every jam. One of the finest pitchers in the American League, Stottlemyre worked special magic against the Senators. He had won nine of his last 10 decisions against Washington. Another victory looked certain. After eight innings, the Yankees led, 8-2.

The sole Senators' highlight was Williams' first argument with an umpire. Second baseman Tim Cullen chased and appeared to catch a popup in short right field. As he turned to throw, he dropped the ball. First base umpire Hank Soar ruled the batter, New York's catcher Jake Gibbs, safe.

Williams raced from the dugout to join Cullen's argument. The crowd and players on both teams watched in nervous anticipation. Would the world-famous Teddy Ballgame temper, Boston-style, erupt in his inaugural game? Williams pushed Cullen away and held an animated conversation with Soar. He balled his fists, frowned, waved his hands dismissively, and jogged back to the Senators' dugout. A few fireworks, but no out-of-control explosion. All season, Williams engaged umpires in animated arguments, but he never snapped and was never ejected. His team emulated their manager's intense, but self-controlled character.

With a victory unlikely, the crowd, including Nixon, lingered to see slugger Frank Howard's final at-bat. Fans wondered if the massive man would smash a homer into the upper deck or screw himself into the ground with a spectacular strikeout. Howard came to bat in the bottom

38

of the 9th inning with a runner on first base. Stottlemyre threw a fastball Howard liked. He took a mighty swing and the ball disappeared over the centerfield fence, 410 feet away. The crowd roared as Howard circled the bases. Nixon turned to one of the young boys sitting next to him and exclaimed, "Aren't you glad we stayed?"

Four batters later, Stottlemyre completed his 8-4 victory. Even in defeat, something seemed different about these Senators. They battled an all-star pitcher the entire game, belting 14 hits, the most Stottlemyre surrendered in a game all season.

The Yankees' ace felt the Senators' new vibe. He said he felt lucky to get hit so hard, yet win the game. While 1960s era athletes often spoke to the press with false humility, Stottlemyre showed genuine surprise at the Senators' grit.

Williams liked his team's persistence. He wanted his charges to battle every inning, every at-bat, every pitch. The Senators lost, but displayed a fire he hoped to stoke all season long.

After a day off to recover from the hoopla of opening day, the Senators and Williams faced New York again. Together, they shared one mission – get Williams his first win.

Starting pitcher Joe Coleman and Washington's hitters accomplished the task. Before 15,162 fans, the largest second-game crowd in expansion Senators history, Coleman gave a marvelous performance. He permitted seven hits and a walk in a complete game victory. In the 3rd inning, the Senators erased a 3-0 deficit with a pair of two-run home runs, one from catcher Paul Casanova, and another from Howard. The Senators won, 6-4.

Williams relished his first victory. When he opened the locker room to the media, he looked giddy with joy. He said, "It feels great, just great. It feels good to get that first one out of the way."

The following afternoon, April 10, the Senators and Yankees played the final game of their season-opening series. The contest marked the 1969 debut of Washington's Brant Alyea, the strapping 28-year-old chap from Passaic, New Jersey nicknamed "Bruno." Lou Piniella, Alyea's minor league teammate, invented the moniker. Alyea explained, "One day Piniella said to me, 'Bruuunooo!' Somebody heard it and I had a nickname."

Garrabrant Ryerson Alyea's baseball career started like a fairy tale. On September 12, 1965, he hit the first major league pitch he saw for a three-run homer. On a rainy April Thursday in Washington, April 10, 1969, Alyea experienced a second great beginning.

In the first inning, with Washington leading, 2-0, Alyea came to the plate with a new bat squeezed between his huge hands and Williams' philosophy drilled into his head. When the Senators' manager noticed his young slugger daydreaming in the dugout minutes before the game, he hollered, "Hey, Bush, you were swinging like an old woman in batting practice. If you want to stay in the big leagues, you've got to swing that quick bat."

Williams' motivational speech shocked Alyea into game-level intensity. On Yankee starter Fritz Peterson's first pitch, Alyea swung and made solid contact. The crack of the bat echoed through the damp, dreary stadium. The ball sailed deep into the Yankee bullpen in left field. The Senators led, 4-0.

Alyea's home run sparked a 16-hit barrage. Washington won the game, 9-6 and the season's first series, two games to one. In the first three games, the Senators scored 19 runs and posted a .361 batting average. Howard hit four homers. Alyea and his humble teammates hit as well as their manager in his glory days. The Washington newspapers already began to call Williams a miracle worker.

Alyea finished the game with three hits, two RBI and two runs. The tough-talking, big-boned, big-hearted good fella who spoke with a thick Jersey accent, off-color language and raw emotions traveled a long, hard road between his 1965 and 1969 first-pitch home runs. He spent most of his time in the minor leagues struggling to overcome a proclivity for swinging and missing the ball. He paced three minor leagues (Carolina League, Eastern League and Pacific Coast League) in strikeouts.

When Williams watched Alyea hit, he noticed many flaws. The young man's approach to the game, "hit the ball hard and hope for the best" made his manager grit his teeth in frustration. During lengthy sessions in the batting cage, Williams insulted, teased, and chided Alyea to motivate the young outfielder into overcoming his bad habits and weaknesses. He told Alyea to use a lighter bat and practice a more compact swing to cut down on strikeouts.

At times, Alyea struggled to adjust his hitting style and his confidence wavered. By the end of the spring, however, he grew to respect Williams' knowledge and methods. Alyea often sought extra help from his manager. He said, "I never wanted to miss something he would say, because it was so profound. When you're a hitter in the major leagues and you're having trouble, you get scared and you say, 'What am I doing wrong? Who can I talk to?' Well, when you're playing for the greatest hitter there ever was, you know damn well who to talk to. He'll put his philosophy in your head [and then] you'll know what to do."

Williams admired Alyea's pugnacious attitude and the two became friends. Alyea said, "He took a liking to me. [On road trips], he'd find me on the plane and say, 'come on over and sit down next to me, I want to talk to you.' We'd talk about the stewardesses, about hitting, about the future, about clothes, all kinds of things. He was just a fascinating guy and I guess I had enough B.S. to hold his interest."

When a men's clothier presented Williams, who favored the casual western look, with a closet full of flashy, colorful sport coats, he gave them to Alyea. An aficionado of 1960s "mod" styles, the young fashion plate planned to combine the new threads with his white leather shoes and loud, psychedelic ties.

Wardrobe differences aside, Williams enjoyed watching Alyea swing the bat during the first three months of the 1969 season. In 98 at bats, Alyea hit .296 with nine homers and 27 RBI. "I was having a tremendous season," he said.

In late June, Alyea's ability to hit deserted him. The more he struggled, the less Williams played him. His once fine season slipped into mediocrity and his statistics fell like a rock dropped from the Washington Monument. In his last 139 at-bats, he hit .216 with two home runs and 13 RBI. He finished his 1969 season with a .249 batting average (.746 OPS), 11 homers, 40 RBI, and 67 strikeouts in 237 at-bats.

His great-start, poor-finish performance exasperated Bob Short and the Senators' brain trust. At 29, Alyea no longer had time on his side. In 1970, when late spring injuries decimated the Washington pitching staff, Short traded Alyea to the Minnesota Twins for relief specialist Joe Grzenda and a minor league prospect.

The trade hurt Alyea, a sensitive man beneath his tough demeanor. He said then that, in trading him away, Williams "cut me deep." He praised his former manager's enthusiasm, but pronounced himself happy to leave Washington.

In 1970, Alyea played excellent baseball for the west division champion Twins. He hit .291 (.897 OPS) with 16 home runs and 61 RBI in just 290 plate appearances. Of course, his first game was his best; at the time the finest beginning to a season in baseball history.

In the Twins' opener, Alyea went 4-4, with two homers and seven RBI as his Twins crushed the White Sox, 12-0. The seven RBI established the record for a season opening game, since tied by Corey Patterson in 2003 with the Chicago Cubs.

After his fabulous game, media surrounded Alyea's locker. He recalled, "There were lights all around, like somebody set fire to the locker room. There were 20 writers and every one of them wants me to

41

rip Ted Williams. They said, 'I guess you showed him. What do you say to Ted now?'"

Alyea replied, in his thickest, toughest New Jersey accent, "I'll tell ya what I got to say. You see those four hits and those seven RBI? Thank God for Ted Williams, because he certainly played a part in it."

Remembering the scene, he continued, "They wanted me to rip him. Why would I rip him? The guy did nothing but help me. He's a great man. Greatness...there ain't a lot of it around, but Ted Williams was truly a great man."

Alyea followed his productive 1970 season with an abysmal 1971. He hit two home runs and batted .177. His problems at bat left him frustrated and confused. He never regained his 1970 form.

In 1972, Alyea bounced between Oakland and St. Louis. He started the season with the A's. Oakland traded him to St. Louis in May. After 13 games, the Cardinals shipped him back to Oakland. For a week in August, he played as the team's starting right fielder, filling in for the injured Reggie Jackson.

On August 14, 1972, a sweltering day in Baltimore's Memorial Stadium, Alyea hit a line drive to the right field gap. He rounded first, anticipating a double, but stopped hard when the Orioles' right fielder reached the ball. Alyea's spikes caught in the dirt. He felt a searing pain in his groin as he limped back to first base. The painful single represented Alyea's 214th and last major league hit.

Thoughts of what might have been still nag him. "Let me have a streak like Gene Tenace had [in the 1972 World Series] and the whole world would know me. But, what happens, happens," he said with a sigh.

In May 1973, Pawtucket, the Red Sox AAA affiliate, released Alyea. He retired from baseball and returned home to New Jersey. He landed a job bouncing drunks, cheats, and ne'er-do-wells out of Tropicana Casino in Atlantic City. When age finally robbed him of his fighting ability, Alyea parlayed the gift of gab he displayed with Williams into a job selling Volvos at a dealership near Philadelphia. He worked part-time there until retiring in 2014. Now fully retired, Alyea resides in New Jersey, near Philadelphia.

During his tenure at the Tropicana, Williams and fellow Hall of Fame member Mike Schmidt crossed paths with Alyea during an autograph and baseball card show. The three talked for hours. During the conversation, Williams looked at Schmidt and said, "You know, Schmidt, you could hit a ball a long way. So could I. This kid standing right next to you could hit it just as far as we could, but not quite as often."

Dismissing Schmidt, Williams pulled Alyea aside to talk in private. He put his arm around Bruno's wide shoulders and handed him a pristine, unused Ted Williams model bat. The Splendid Splinter signed the bat in big, bold letters – "To Brant, another great hitter, Ted Williams."

Alyea said, "When he gave me that bat, my eyes welled up with tears. I had to walk away. I couldn't believe it. Here's the greatest hitter of all-time calling me a great hitter. My God! Believe me, there's no price on that bat. It will be in my possession when I pass on. It shakes me up just thinking about it. When I'm feeling down in the dumps or I'm upset about something, all I have to do is reflect back to Ted Williams. I'm so lucky to have ever met him."

Brant Alyea, the man of great beginnings, found his happy ending at last.

The season-opening success Alyea and his teammates enjoyed against the Yankees faded fast. The Senators lost nine of the next 13 games. They managed to win three of eight games against Baltimore, but dropped four of five games with Detroit and the Yankees. The hitters, so potent against New York pitching, faltered. Five opposing pitchers threw shutouts against Williams' confused hitters. The Senators record fell to 6-10.

Win or lose, under Williams' leadership the team played competitive, hard-nosed baseball and started to develop confidence and camaraderie. Formerly unsung players began to flourish. Howard said, "[Williams] was tremendous with the guys who didn't play on a regular basis. I called them the irregulars."

In April, no irregular played better than Harold Andrew "Hank" Allen. Twenty games into the season, he boasted a .413 batting average, tied for fourth in the league with Minnesota's Rod Carew.

The hot streak gave Allen a respite from comparisons to his younger, more talented brother, the Philadelphia Phillies' troubled superstar Richie Allen. He grew tired of being called "Richie's older brother" instead of his own name. One teammate remarked, "He would tell people, 'I'm not Richie Allen's brother, I'm Hank Allen.'" He felt the incessant references to Richie tarnished his own accomplishments and robbed him of his dignity.

Further, his younger brother's outspoken ways and alleged poor behavior – the Phillies suspended him for part of the 1969 season for insubordination – tarnished Hank. People in the Washington organization told the press that they considered Allen a troublemaker. Senators' radio broadcaster Ron Menchine said, "Hank was a good guy.

43

I thought, because his brother was pretty much a head case, that he might not be an easy guy to get along with, but Hank was great."

One of eight brothers and sisters, Allen loved Richie, but knew he climbed to the major leagues on his own strength, facing down one most difficult obstacle. Allen felt his skin tone – he is African American – colored the Senators' decisions about where and how often he played.

In 1968, which Allen termed "a season of disaster," he often clashed with manager Jim Lemon. In Allen's opinion, the trouble with Lemon and the organization began during spring training. He recalled an extra inning game that left Allen as the last Senator available to pinch-hit. With the pitcher due up, Allen said Lemon looked at him with disdain and said, "Go on in there."

Allen delivered the game-winning hit, releasing everyone to Florida's springtime pleasures. He remembered his teammates congratulating him, but not Lemon. Allen said, "Generally when you win a ballgame, I don't care what game it is, the manager always congratulates everyone. So, then and there, I knew he was saying, 'I'm not going to use you. You might as well get it firmly in your mind you will not be on this club.'"

Allen appeared in 68 games in 1968, far less than the 116 he played under Gil Hodges a year earlier. He felt racial prejudice kept him and his fellow African American teammates off the field. He explains, "In spring training you had Ed Stroud, Fred Valentine, Sam Bowens, and me. We were all placed in right field. It was four of the black guys competing for one position. You were essentially eliminating yourself. All the guys talked about it. If it walks like a duck and quacks like a duck then it is a duck."

Other outfielders on the spring squad included Howard, Del Unser, Rich Billings, Cap Peterson, and Gary Holman, all white. No one competed with Howard in left field and Unser in center. Billings, Peterson and Holman vied for part-time or pinch hitting roles.

One former teammate said Allen's assessment was incorrect. He commented, "Hank was looking for the race card to be played on him and it really wasn't played." Both Unser and Howard had good seasons in 1968, while Allen struggled. He performed poorly at bat with a .219 batting average and a .265 on-base percentage.

Justified or not, the ordeal left Allen embittered and downcast. As soon as he met Ted Williams, everything changed. For all Williams' supposed faults, he possessed two virtues: generosity, through his gifts of time and money to the Jimmy Fund in Boston, and a total absence of prejudice. Williams' embodied both during his Hall of Fame induction speech in 1966. He implored baseball to enshrine former Negro League players when few in baseball even contemplated the notion.

As soon as he arrived in Florida for spring training, the Senators' new manager resolved to overcome any perceived racial obstacles. He started with his coaching staff. During a spring game against the Orioles, Frank Robinson began yelling at the home plate umpire from the Baltimore dugout. First base coach Nellie Fox responded with a borderline racist taunt, saying "Don't let big mouth get away with that stuff!"

The umpire ejected Robinson from the game, but Fox's antics angered Williams. He told Fox, "Shut up, Foxie, you're an agitator."

Williams' point in dressing down his coach and friend hit home with everyone on the team. The Senators' manager let results drive the teams' decisions. Allen said, "He gave you an opportunity to focus on what you did best and it was up to you to accept that opportunity. Ted's job was to get the 25 best players that he could, get them to compete, and get the most out of them. That's exactly what he did." Under the Ted Williams regime, performance alone mattered.

Allen recalled a pivotal spring training conversation with Williams while he was taking batting practice. He said, "I remember Ted standing behind the cage. He stated out loud where I could hear it, 'This guy, there's no reason in the world that he shouldn't be a better hitter than he is.' After I had my seven or eight cuts hitting, he kind of yelled it out, 'I'd like to know the reason. I really would like to know.'

"So, after I hit, he walked over to the side, put his arm around me and asked me, 'Well, what's the reason?'

"I said, 'Well, first of all it was opportunity.'"

Allen explained that sporadic playing time in 1968 kept him from developing the precision he needed to play well. Williams looked intently at Allen for a moment, and then said, "Could be. Could be."

Later, Allen hit a home run into the wind to win another extra inning game. Manager and teammates, black and white alike, embraced him. Allen gathered his belongings and started toward the clubhouse to shower. Williams stopped him. With dramatic flair, he said, "Buddy, I'm going to tell you something. They told me that I couldn't use you this year, but I can't do without you. You just keep doing what you're doing, bud, and you're on this club." After a .328 spring batting average, Williams held true to his word and placed Allen on the opening day roster.

On April 23, Williams and the Senators traveled to Boston to begin a two-game series with the Red Sox in Fenway Park. Ted Williams and Boston fans likely circled the games in red on their

45

calendars. These games marked the return of Teddy Ballgame to Boston, the town where he became an American legend. He came back in the road gray uniform of the Washington Senators, but in the eyes of Boston fans, the attire, for one, brief moment, morphed into the red, white and midnight blue of their beloved Red Sox.

Hank Allen
Art by Ronnie Joyner (Used with Permission)

5: Ted Williams and His Nasty Nats Invade Boston

"It was great. He'd stand in the middle of the locker room floor after an exciting victory, leading the "Nasty Nats" cheer, with his teeth out."

-Wayne Terwilliger, Third Base Coach, Washington Senators,
describing the antics of Frank Howard

When he met the Boston press before the game, Williams downplayed the upcoming match-up with the Red Sox as "just another game," a game his Senators knew he ached to win. Williams longed to show Tom Yawkey and Boston's fans that he had built a pretty tough team out of his ragtag Senators.

The night before the game, weather conspired against Williams and his club. Heavy rain forced officials to close Boston's Logan Airport. The Senators' plane diverted to Hartford and they rode a bus to Boston, arriving in Beantown just before 4:00 a.m.

The next day, Boston looked as gray and dreary as the haggard, iron-eyed Senators felt. The rain stopped, but Fenway Park's outfield resembled a quagmire, with pond-sized puddles everywhere. With a large crowd expected for the afternoon game, Boston officials examined the field and declared it playable. The tired Senators preferred naps, but played baseball instead.

Allen made the grueling plane and bus rides in considerable pain from a strained rib cage he suffered the night before against Detroit. Williams wanted his hot bat in the lineup, so he left the decision to play up to Allen. Allen's ribs ached, but, loathe to pass up playing time, he ignored the pain, fatigue and hazardous conditions and dressed for the game.

Williams, after getting directions to the visitors' clubhouse from a Red Sox attendant, donned his Senators' uniform, filled out his line-up card and, once again, set spikes on the sod of Fenway Park. The Boston crowd roared. Williams waved to friends in the stands. He embraced former teammate Bobby Doerr, a Red Sox coach and dear friend.

The longest, loudest cheers came when Williams approached home plate to exchange line-ups with Boston manager Dick Williams. The cries of 28,972 Boston faithful whirled around the hallowed stadium.

Williams smiled, but kept his head bowed, his pace even. Whatever internal feelings stirred, Williams, the old Marine pilot, focused on the task at hand – a game to win. He wanted his players to focus on victory, too. He recoiled from the day becoming a saccharine Ted Williams' homecoming. The closer game time beckoned, the more irritable he grew. He even shooed a gaggle of young autograph seekers from the top of the Senators' dugout.

Allen and his anxious fellow Senators soon fell behind Boston and their starting pitcher, Sonny Siebert, 1-0. Four of the first eight Washington batters struck out. Allen managed a single to right field for the first Senators hit.

Washington rallied in the 3rd inning. Howard hit an RBI single and Mike Epstein followed with a three-run homer. Allen singled, stole second, and scored when Bernie Allen's two-out single plopped into an outfield puddle. Allen's two hits pushed his average into Ted Williams-territory – above .400.

In the top of the seventh, Allen doubled and scored on Ken McMullen's three-run homer high over the Green Monster. The Senators led 9-3. Williams relaxed and enjoyed the pending victory.

To cap his fine hitting performance (3-5, 2 runs), Allen gave his happy manager one more pleasant memory. In the bottom of the ninth, young Boston slugger Joe Lahoud smashed a fly ball toward the right field foul pole. Splashing through puddles, divots and loose grass, Allen raced to the wall and made a leaping, home run-saving catch. His ribs crashed into Fenway's small right field wall, but Allen felt only joy. He starred in the game that gave his manager a stirring homecoming triumph. Washington won, 9-3.

The victory gave Williams an evening of bragging rights over dinner with his long-time Boston friends. Old Teddy Ballgame showed those ornery Boston writers he knew how to manage a ball club. He made winners and fighters out of a club written off as hopeless losers before the season began.

The post-game celebration in Boston marked the debut performance of the "Nasty Nats" chant. The song's bawdy locker room lyrics celebrated the Senators' new status as a winning team. Ed Brinkman usually ad-libbed new poems after every victory, while Howard, dressed in his birthday suit, directed the rowdy, off-key 25-man choir. Wayne Terwilliger recalled Howard's antics, "It was great. He'd stand in the middle of the locker room floor after an exciting victory, leading the Nasty Nats cheer, with his teeth out. Everybody loved him."

The Boston rains returned the next day, postponing the final game of the series. The foul weather gave Williams another day to savor the victory and Allen a night to rest his ribs. If Williams proved himself to Boston, Allen vindicated himself to his teammates and Washington's fans. Now batting .424, everyone saw what he could do with a fair chance. So long as Allen's bat and glove flourished, he played every day.

In early May, the Senators prepared to leave for a two-week road trip. Hours before their chartered jet's departure, the Senators' front office summoned Allen. He explained, "I came in one afternoon after a game and was getting dressed. Williams said 'Don't get dressed, Short wants to see you upstairs.'

"I thought to myself, 'What the heck is this?'

"I was kind of slowing around. Ted says, 'No, don't change your uniform. Go on up there just as you are.'

"So, I went upstairs. Team President Joe Burke was there. I waited outside his office thinking maybe I got traded. Burke invited me in and asked his secretary to bring a contract. He tore up my [old] contract and gave me a raise right then and there. I thanked him, signed a new contract, and came back downstairs to the clubhouse."

As soon as Allen returned to the locker room, a beaming Williams beckoned him over, shook his hand and said, "Didn't I tell you, you do what you've been doing, that I'd take care of you? Don't you worry, there's *more* where that came from."

For Allen, the day marked the zenith of his career. He slumped in June and July, his batting average falling to .271. He returned to a part-time role, starting in right field against left handed pitchers.

On the morning of August 16, Brant Alyea, Allen and five fellow Senators stood around the batting cage, waiting their turn to hit. Suddenly, Alyea took a full swing. He hit Allen's thumb, smashing it against the metal cage. The injury left Allen's thumb fractured. Unable to grip a bat, he spent a month on the disabled list. When he returned to in September, he could only pinch run and play the outfield. Alyea insists the mishap was accidental. He said, "I'd be [angry] if somebody did it to me, but, certainly, it wasn't on purpose. I'd never booby trap anybody to try to get in a game."

Despite the freak injury, Allen enjoyed the best season of his major league career in 1969. He overcame the bitterness of 1968 to become a versatile member of Ted Williams' bench. He played all three outfield positions, second base and third base. In 109 games, he stole 12 bases in 15 attempts, tied with Stroud for the team lead.

The fine season restored Allen's reputation and pride. He refused to let past unfairness or ill-fortune embitter him. His struggles made him a far better man than a ballplayer. Though Allen never again achieved success on the baseball field, he retained his dignity.

Early in the 1970 season, Washington traded Allen to the Milwaukee Brewers. He played sporadically, barely reaching 100 plate appearances. He united with Richie for the White Sox in 1972-73. In Chicago, Allen logged enough service time to earn a major league pension. After a brief stint in Hawaii in 1974, he retired from professional baseball.

After baseball, Allen worked training horses in Maryland. He spent 24 years at the job before retiring to a home in southern Maryland. In 1999, he returned to baseball, joining the Milwaukee Brewers' scouting department. In 2008, he moved to the Houston Astros, analyzing Houston's opponents when they play in Washington and Baltimore. He commutes to the ballparks from his home in Upper Marlboro, Maryland. He said, "I still love baseball, it keeps me young. I'll stick around as long as I know I'm contributing to the team."

During quiet mornings, he recalls his years playing baseball. He harbored few regrets. He said, "Your memories go back and you're happy. You'd go back and do it all over again. It was a defining time in your life when you were young and when you were doing the thing that you loved to do best of all. It had nothing to do about money, nothing to do about prestige. It was the best time of your life."

Allen and a team full of happy Senators left Boston, bound for Cleveland and a three-game series with the Indians. Washington enjoyed easy victories in the first two contests, improving their record to 9-10.

In the series' third and final game, a Sunday afternoon match, Al Dark's dispirited group of Indians, with one victory in their first 16 games, looked ready to crumble. The Senators jumped to an early lead, 6-2 thanks to starting pitcher Frank Bertaina's bat. The southpaw belted a three-run home run, the only one of his major league career.

Unfortunately, Bertaina's poor pitching jeopardized the lead. When Zoilo Versalles hit a homer in the 4th inning to make the score 6-5, Williams seethed. He ordered Sid Hudson to get Bertaina off the mound. On the way to the unhappy pitcher, Hudson tapped his right arm, the signal to bring Dave Baldwin in from the bullpen. The Senators' winning streak now rested on the strength and endurance of Baldwin's once prized right arm.

Baldwin empathized with Bertaina. He knew a steaming Williams lay in wait. Baldwin recalled, "The pitchers had mixed feelings about Ted and vice-versa. I remember being chewed out by him big time for something I threw or didn't throw to [Orioles' catcher] Elrod Hendricks. If you leave out all his bleeps there wouldn't be much conversation left.

51

He was pretty impressive anyway, but he overwhelmed you when he got mad."

On this day, Williams felt only joy when he watched Baldwin pitch. The right-hander retired the first two batters he faced to quell the Indians' rally and allowed only a single through the 5th and 6th innings. In the bottom of the 7th, with one out, Baldwin walked Max Alvis. When Alvis stole second base, Baldwin faced adversity for the first time in the game, but not in his improbable path to Washington and the major leagues.

He induced Cleveland's shortstop Larry Brown to hit a weak foul out. Baldwin needed to retire one more batter to escape the jam. Dark sent Russ Snyder, a left-handed batter, up to pinch-hit. Williams removed Baldwin, who sometimes struggled to retire left-handed batters, for Dennis Higgins. Higgins, who also threw right-handed, served as the Senators' top reliever until late May, when bullpen ace Darold Knowles returned from active duty in Japan. Higgins retired Snyder and stopped Cleveland in the 8th and 9th innings to give the Senators a gritty 6-5 victory. With 3 1/3 shutout innings, the official scorer named Baldwin the winning pitcher.

A veteran in the fourth season of his career, Baldwin traveled a long, hard road to pitch in the major leagues, a journey that tested his ability, attitude, patience and will. At first, everything came easy for David George Baldwin. Born March 30, 1938 in Tucson, Arizona, Baldwin grew into a fine natural athlete and became the local star, the smart, tall golden boy with the golden arm.

His manifest destiny beckoned him to stardom in the major leagues. By his sophomore year at nearby University of Arizona, he was a big man on campus, catching flirtatious smiles from gorgeous coeds and fielding generous offers from major league scouts. For Baldwin, victories came early, easy and often. He drank deep of the adulation. Fans told him, "You can't miss, Dave. You've got big-time talent in your strong right arm."

Then, in the middle of a college game, Baldwin felt a searing, life-altering pain in his right elbow. His arm ached, suddenly emptied of its natural talent. He recalled, "I snapped of a curve and my elbow just about fell off."

Baldwin thought, "So now what do I do? All that natural ability I've been gifted with, well, now I don't have it anymore."

To pitch again, Baldwin faced hard rehabilitation. The tougher part, the mental strength required to recover from a major injury, terrified him. His baseball career now depended more on the strength of his will than the gift of his genes.

He resolved to restore his arm and return to the ranks of elite pitchers through hard work. Dwelling on the injury drained him. The challenge to pitch again drove him. "The idea of a challenge is important," he said.

Time and effort healed Baldwin's right arm. In 1959, he led the University of Arizona to a second-place finish in the College World Series. When the season ended, he signed a contract with the Philadelphia Phillies and entered their minor league system. He pitched poorly (7.38 ERA) at Williamsport, Pennsylvania, his first stop in professional baseball. Worse, his arm started to hurt again. His pitches lacked power and explosion.

Philadelphia released him and Baldwin became a baseball vagabond, riding buses from Williamsport to Chattanooga, from Fort Worth to Durham. In 1964, the New York Mets and Houston Colt .45's, two of baseball's worst teams, cut Baldwin from their lowest minor league franchises. When the Durham Bulls let Baldwin go, they sat in last place, 40 games behind. The worst minor league team in organized baseball told Baldwin, "You can't help us. We don't need you."

After that spirit-crushing release, Baldwin fought the urge to give up. "There were a couple of times when I was pretty certain my career was over," Baldwin said. But he wanted one more shot. One team felt desperate enough to let him try, the lowly Washington Senators. On July 15, 1964 Baldwin signed Washington's offer to pitch for in its farm system.

The Senators assigned him to a Carolina League club in Burlington, North Carolina. There, Baldwin toyed with an experiment. Then 27-years-old, ancient for a minor league pitcher, Baldwin felt desperate. One day, while joking around before a game with his teammates, Baldwin noticed the pain in his right arm disappeared when he threw with a sidearm motion. Instead of bringing his arm over his head or to shoulder level, Baldwin moved his right arm far behind his body during his wind-up. He then thrust his arm forward with a downward, whip-like motion, snapping his wrist as he released the ball. The Senators' 1969 press guide described the delivery as "deceptive and wicked."

He decided to try his new pitching style in games. It worked wonders. When he followed the correct technique, the ball darted all over the strike zone. Hitters flailed in vain at his twisting pitches. He struck out 135 batters in 122 innings in Burlington. Late in 1965, the Senators promoted him to their AAA farm club in Hawaii. Baldwin reveled in his change of fortune – riding dirty buses in steamy North Carolina one day, relaxing on a beach in Honolulu the next. He said,

"Hawaii was the greatest place in the world to play, let me tell you. Those two years stand out in my mind."

When the 1966 minor league season ended, the Senators plucked Baldwin from the island paradise to his ultimate dream destination – a major league pitching mound. On September 6, 1966, Baldwin debuted with two perfect innings of relief against the Detroit Tigers in Tiger Stadium.

In 1967, Baldwin cemented his spot on the Senators' roster. He pitched 69 innings with a 1.70 ERA, the best season of his career. Baldwin said, "A great part of that was due to [manager] Gil Hodges and Rube Walker, our pitching coach. Hodges kept me out of any embarrassing situation. We had an outstanding bullpen. They saved my bacon and I hope I saved theirs."

The bullpen conversations with fellow relief pitchers Darold Knowles, Casey Cox and Bob Humphreys helped Baldwin cultivate strong friendships and gain valuable intelligence on hitters. "Surprisingly, a lot of the conversation that went on in the bullpen had to do with baseball. We're not talking about girls in the stands or something like that. You had to pay attention. You wanted to know what that hitter was up to that day."

Baldwin worked fanatically on his sidearm technique, but gave scant thought to how hitters approached the game – until Ted Williams arrived. He said, "I learned more about how hitters think from Ted than I had in ten years of pro ball before that. He was just a gold mine of information."

Baldwin savored Williams' knowledge, but bristled at his manager's penchant to remove him from tight, late-game situations against left-handed batters. Baldwin said, "A sidearm pitcher doesn't necessarily have trouble with batters from the opposite side."

Baldwin's statistics, however, show that lefty swingers bedeviled him. In 1969, right-handed hitters had a .200 batting average (.554 OPS) against him, while left-handers hit .328 (.955 OPS). For his career, right-handers earned a .208 batting average (.560 OPS) while left-handers hit .294 (.825 OPS). Baldwin felt some of the imbalance occurred because of his reluctance to throw the screwball to left-handed hitters. Late in his career, he threw the deceptive pitch to left-handers more often, with some success.

Overall, Baldwin pitched solid baseball for the 1969 Senators. He finished with a 2-4 record and four saves in 67 innings pitched, a regular in the Washington bullpen, albeit not for long. In December 1969, the Senators traded Baldwin to the Seattle Pilots, a financially strapped organization rumored bound for Milwaukee to become the Brewers. Baldwin felt ambivalent about leaving Washington.

He enjoyed the city, but not RFK Stadium in summertime. He said, "It was unbearable in that bullpen. We would sit there and just bake. All the heat funneled right to us. Your strength would be gone before you even got into a ballgame if you weren't careful. We'd go back underneath the stadium as much as we could. You couldn't watch the ballgame from back there, but it was cool. So we'd escape every chance we had."

Baldwin appeared in 28 games for the Brewers in 1970. He sported a fine 2.55 ERA, but Milwaukee sold him to the independent Hawaii Islanders three weeks before the 1971 season. The deal left Baldwin 37 days short of a major league pension. Now 35, age sapped his limited talents. Baldwin again summoned his courage and perseverance to pitch until he returned to the major leagues. He relied on guile and will power to last two seasons in Hawaii, a pleasant locale to try to save a career.

During 1973 spring training, the Chicago White Sox purchased Baldwin's contract from Hawaii and assigned him to their AAA team in Iowa. Late that year, Chicago manager Chuck Tanner and General Manager Roland Hemond learned of Baldwin's pension situation.

All the while, Baldwin pitched on, twirling sidearm fastballs, sinkers, and screwballs, and taking bus rides to towns all over the Midwest. He helped his Iowa club reach first-place in the American Association standings. In late July, his manager, Joe Sparks, asked to see him in his office. He gave Baldwin the good news – the White Sox had called him back to the big leagues.

Baldwin said, "The White Sox had so many injuries that year, they fell out of the pennant race. They called me up for the last 37 days. I've always been grateful for that. In fact, I still count on that pension pretty heavily."

Baldwin's final major league appearance took place in Chicago on August 7, 1973 at old Comiskey Park. He pitched two hitless innings against Cleveland. Then, he retired unnoticed, his career and his titanic struggle shrouded in obscurity.

Baldwin returned to his studies at Arizona. He earned a PhD. in Genetics and a Master of Science degree in Systems Engineering. Between classes, he painted works like "The Mockingbird Sings to the Relief Pitcher", "Cool Papa" and "Kid with a New Glove" that blend baseball, his southwestern heritage, and Picasso-like surrealism. One piece, "Fugue for the Pepper Players", hung on display in the Baseball Hall of Fame Museum in Cooperstown. Baldwin also wrote numerous articles on baseball and science and published a collection of poetry as well as his memoir, entitled "Snake Jazz", baseball slang for curveballs. Now retired, he lives in Yachats, Oregon and serves as the town's volunteer librarian. It's no wonder fellow Senators' pitcher Barry Moore said, "Just dressing next to him is an education."

Baldwin's April 27, 1969 victory sealed the Senators' three-game sweep over Cleveland and sent the team on a hot streak. Washington traveled to Detroit and split a two-game series with the reigning world champions. At home, the Senators defeated Boston to finish April with a winning record, 12-11.

Williams' team surged into May with three more victories to improve to 15-11. Stellar performances abounded. Howard hit nine home runs. Bosman pitched a one-hitter. Higgins earned seven saves. Everyone on the roster contributed to the team's unexpected success.

On May 4, 1969, a lovely Sunday afternoon in Washington, the Senators stood one victory away from a perfect 5-0 home stand. More than 24,000 fans filed into RFK for the game against the Cleveland Indians. Williams decided to give a rare start to his hard-driven, hyper-competitive back-up catcher, Jim French.

Richard James French, born August 13, 1941 in Warren, Ohio, a small town 15 miles west of the Pennsylvania line, never hesitated to work hard and take charge. He burned to achieve success in every situation. Assertive, head strong and bright – French held a bachelor's degree in Mathematics from Ohio University and a Masters' degree in Finance from the University of Indiana. Situations that frightened other people energized French.

All of 5'8" and 180 pounds, French stood tough, compact and thick in the middle, like a fire hydrant. Runners attempting to mow down French on close plays at the plate often stopped dead in their tracks. No one moved him against his iron will. He loved catching because "you run the game. You're in control."

French brought down men before whom others cowered. No one intimidated him. Not the great Ted Williams or the President of the United States. One afternoon, President Nixon visited the Senators' locker room. When he met French, Nixon said, "You're the one who hustles. I also know you're the team's best gin rummy player."

"I'm the best pinochle player," French corrected the Commander-in-Chief.

Small of stature and talent, but big on hustle and drive, Terwilliger, said of French, "He was the most competitive guy I ever saw."

On a lovely day in the nation's capital, French intended to make the most of his opportunity. In the 3rd inning, he contributed to the Senators small one-run rally with his second hit of the year. In the 7th, with the scored tied, 3-3, French walked. Williams decided to gamble.

He motioned to third base coach Terwilliger to give French the sign for the hit and run play. At first, French, a slow runner, thought about ignoring the sign, but decided to obey. "Baseball was different back then," he said. "If you wanted to play you did what you were told."

Cleveland pitcher Steve Hamilton threw a fastball as French broke for second. Unser swung and grounded the ball to the left side of the infield. With French running, the Indians' shortstop raced to cover second base. Unser's routine grounder skipped through the gap in Cleveland's infield for a single. French, running as fast as he could, reached third base. Brinkman followed with a line drive single to score French. Washington led, 4-3.

Catching his breath in the dugout, French conferred with Higgins, who relieved Washington starter Coleman in the 6th inning. French coaxed two scoreless innings from his tiring pitcher to preserve the slim lead. He willed Higgins through the 7th inning. After French and Hudson twice visited Higgins to calm his nerves, he induced Indians' slugger Ken Harrelson to ground into an inning-ending double play. In the 8th, Epstein's error put runners on first and second with two outs.

French walked to the mound and told Higgins to forget about the first baseman's miscue. French knew the right words to say during these impromptu conferences. He put the pitcher's mind at ease, sharpened their focus. Higgins retired pinch-hitter Chuck Hinton on an easy grounder to second base. French said, "As a catcher you need to be positive with your pitchers so they are confident." Williams rewarded French for his good work by removing him for a pinch-hitter, the fate of the humble back-up catcher.

He understood Williams' decision. The Senators needed an insurance run and, at bat, French struggled. In 1969, he hit .184. Over his career, he hit for a .196 batting average, with a mere 26 extra base hits. French did have one positive offensive skill, patience. In 1969, French had 41 walks in 158 at-bats, for a fine .348 on-base percentage. French said, "Baseball aficionados today like to point out I had a good on-base percentage, but I wasn't a good hitter."

Casanova replaced French, but the tough little catcher's influence remained. In the 9th inning, a self-assured Higgins snared a line drive and struck out the next two batters to earn his first win of the season. Baseball's hottest team improved its record to16-11, with 10 wins in 11 games.

In the raucous locker room party after the game, French figured prominently in the lyrics of the Nasty Nats cheer. Howard shared his post-game victory cigar with French. It made for a comical site, the diminutive French and the gigantic Howard, trading puffs on the cigar. French enjoyed the camaraderie and, above all, the victory. He and his teammates fought together, persevered and won.

French played in 234 games over seven seasons in the major leagues, excruciatingly few for a man who thrived on action, on controlling his destiny. He sums up his career, saying, without a trace of sentiment, "I was a part-time catcher who spent most of his time in the bullpen."

He took one valuable lesson from his baseball career. French played for two famous managers – Hodges and Williams. French said, "Gil Hodges was a quiet man, withdrawn. But I felt cowed around him, maybe because I was younger. I'm not saying anything negative about him, I just felt scared, nervous around him." The fear grated on French.

When the Senators announced Williams as their manager, French resolved to stand fearless before him. Williams tested that resolve. French said, "Ted Williams had the greatest presence of any person I've ever met. He could walk into a room of 500 people and you would immediately know that someone great had arrived. It was almost like the president walked in. He had magnetism."

The toughest of men fell silent before Williams. Former Senators said that Williams, when angry, frightened them. Not French. He said, "I knew Ted was a legendary figure, but I promised myself I would never again be cowed by a manager. I never argued with Ted, because arguments with him tended to be one sided, but we had a lot of discussions together about many topics. I always spoke my mind. Ted appreciated my candor. I never let myself feel intimidated in his presence."

More than any other Senator, French bantered with and teased Williams. His teammates watched, amazed, as the two engaged in frequent arguments, usually about men's fashions. French followed the colorful styles of the 1960s. He recalled, "Williams always made fun of my clothes. My retort was that he dressed like a bum – ratty sport coat, slacks and golf shirt. I always told him he must get his clothes free from Sears. He said, 'Yep! And all my fishing gear too.'"

Menchine said, "Williams would say, 'Frenchy, where'd you get that outfit?'

"French would reply, 'It's better than that million-miler you're wearing, Ted.'"

The banter often ended with Williams saying, "I wonder what the weather's like up in Buffalo (where the Senators AAA minor league team played) this time of year."

French stood his ground with Williams on baseball matters, too. Williams often mistreated pitchers, especially when they made mistakes. He screamed and yelled as the dejected hurler sat slumped in a folding chair. French often interrupted the tirade. "I'd say, 'Ted, I called it and he threw it, so blame me if you want to.'"

Williams muttered, "Well, he could shake you off," and walked away.

French's manager forgot that no pitcher dared shake off his signs for long. Each time he put down his fingers to call a pitch, French expected assent. If a battle of wills ensued, French intended to win – every time. He said, "I called the pitches, not the manager like they do today. It was my responsibility. Pitchers seldom shook me off and when they did I just called the same pitch again.

"My defensive skills were my strength. Part of that was being able to manage the game and call the best pitches to help the pitcher be successful that day. I knew his limitations and tried to work around them. Our pitchers trusted me. I knew what I was doing."

Washington pitchers appreciated their combative battery mate. Baldwin said, "French was great at calling the game. You knew [he] knew something the pitcher didn't know. I had tremendous confidence [in him]."

Bosman said, "[French] had a good feel for how to get the most out of a guy. He knew that some guys he had to lie to, some guys he had to get hard nosed with and when to do it."

Washington fans loved French as much as his pitchers did. On his rare extra base hits, French ran as fast as his short legs carried him and slid hard, tumbling into the bag in a cloud of dust and a heap of arms and legs. Once, he missed a game because he spiked himself running the bases.

After a daring dash to third or a headlong dive to catch a foul pop-up, French leapt to his feet, brushed himself off, removed his helmet, whisked the dirt from his flat-top haircut, and smiled. Fans cheered and chuckled at the same time.

French remarked, "I had a great rapport with the fans. I think they liked and appreciated me more than my ability warranted. Even the drunks were nice to me. One game I hit a triple and this drunk came out of the stands and kissed me. He was really lit up. I could smell the alcohol a mile away."

In Sept 1971, the Senators released French, bringing his seven year baseball career to an end. French said, "I was 30. I needed to start making money. I was glad I didn't leave baseball financially secure like today's players do, as long as they invest their money wisely. I enjoyed the fans, the friendships, and the memories, but you need to move on."

French put his education and thirst for competition to work. He landed a job as a securities trader at the Pacific Stock Exchange. French said, "I like competitive environments. I was one of the nuts on the securities exchange floor screaming and waving those little pieces of paper around. Those guys are a lot more competitive than baseball players. If you want to survive down there, you have to be willing to compete day after day," French said.

French eventually left the exchange floor and passed the bar exam. He became a securities attorney, representing investors' claims against firms accused of illegal practices. "It's often at the arbitrator's table instead of the courtroom, but we usually win," French said.

French still faces down giants. He lives on a 75-acre ranch in Aurora, Colorado. He represents his fellow ranchers, pro bono, in battles over water rights with ski resorts and oil companies seeking the precious water for snow-making and fracking.

Blocking the plate in 1969 or under tense cross examination now, French stands his ground. Armed with an intelligent mind, a steel-trap memory, and boundless energy, he battles in high-stakes competition day after exhilarating day.

He said of the 1969 Senators, "Our record was better than our talent. Williams made people better by the force of his personality. But maybe we were just lucky. Maybe the stars aligned for us that season."

Long ago, French shunned rocking chair reminiscences of past glory days. He said, "I've been much more successful at my careers in business and law than I was as a baseball player. I guess I'll retire some day, but not anytime soon. I love what I'm doing."

Hours after the Jim French-led victory over Cleveland, the club boarded an airplane bound for Oakland to begin a 12-game road trip against west division clubs Oakland, Seattle, California and Chicago. Only one of those teams, Oakland (82-80), finished above .500 in 1968.

Giving voice to his teammates' growing confidence, pitcher Jim Hannan predicted, "We'll do better than 50-50 against the west. I think we'll win three of the four series." It took all of two games to see how well such bravado inspired the Senators – and their opponents.

Jim French
(National Baseball Hall of Fame Library, Cooperstown, NY)

Jim French, Autograph Day, July 12, 1969
Private Collection of Mark Hornbaker (Used with Permission)

6: The Texas Gentleman

Sid Hudson, the 1969 Senators' pitching coach, looked impressive. A wiry, tall drink of water, he stood 6'4" and weighed 180 pounds, with long arms and huge hands. When Ted Williams laid eyes on him, he knew he wanted to keep Hudson, the pitching coach on Jim Lemon's 1968 staff, around – whether Bob Short liked it or not. Williams, the consummate hitter, understood the mental gamesmanship between batter and pitcher, but left the technique of pitching to practitioners.

After a few days of spring training, Williams decided his pitchers were in good, strong hands. Hudson remembered, "I enjoyed working for Ted Williams. [During spring training], he called me into his office and said, 'Sid, I've known you for a long time. You have all this experience. I'll just turn it over to you, and if I don't like what you're doing, why, I'll tell you so.'"

Hudson, a pitcher for Washington from 1940-52 (with 1943-45 dedicated to his nation to fight in World War II) and a teammate of Williams in Boston from 1952-54, taught pitchers the craft's every nuance. He knew the intricate details from running regimens between starts to the best way to grip a curve ball.

Hudson dedicated himself to assisting every pitcher on the club. He helped Dick Bosman develop consistency and pinpoint control. He said of Bosman, "He had a good attitude and he really worked at it. He'd try anything you suggested to him." Under Hudson, the 1969 Washington pitching staff performed with distinction. They turned in a 3.49 ERA, fifth best in the American League.

To everyone in the Senators' organization, however, Hudson's character surpassed his coaching talent. An encounter with Williams and relief pitcher Dave Baldwin exemplified his courage and honesty. A sidearm pitcher himself, he worked with Dave Baldwin to perfect the unorthodox style. At times, Baldwin struggled.

Hudson recalled one of those times: "We were playing in Baltimore. The game was tied going into the 9th inning and we brought in Baldwin to pitch against Boog Powell. I'd been teaching Baldwin to act like he was going to come sidearm and then come up over the top to fool left-handed hitters. I told him if you get ahead of Powell to try that.

"Sure enough he came up over the top and Powell hit it into the right field seats for a home run. When we got the clubhouse, Williams had Baldwin in there sitting in a chair. He was really giving it to him for making that mistake. I walked in said, 'Ted that wasn't his fault it was mine.' Williams didn't pay any attention, so I said it once more. He still didn't pay attention, so I said the heck with it and walked out.

"The next day, Williams called me into his office and he said, 'I caught you peeking at me yesterday, didn't I?'

I said, 'You sure did.'

"He replied, 'That's the way I like it.'"

The traits Hudson displayed to Williams flowed through Hudson's every action, every conversation. He took rookies and newcomers to the team, even radio broadcasters, under his wing, showing them the best places in Washington to rent an apartment and get a tasty, affordable meal. Radio voice Ron Menchine said, "Sid introduced me to the top restaurants in major league baseball." Everyone who met him felt like the affable, graceful man's close friend.

Del Unser called Hudson a "Texas gentleman."

Hudson appreciated the 1969 Senators' camaraderie and good humor. His favorite story involved Williams and first base coach Nellie Fox. Hudson said, "I used to throw batting practice to them. They'd argue with each other, and kid and carry on about what kind of hitters they were.

"Williams would always say, 'Fox, you little squirt, you can't even hit the ball out of the ballpark and so on. After a while, Nellie would just say, 'How many hits did you get, Ted?' (Fox finished his career with 2663, nine more than Williams). Boy, we had a lot of fun."

Hudson dedicated 56 years of his life to baseball, finally retiring in 1993. After Washington, he coached for Billy Martin in Texas and in the Rangers' rookie league where he guided future stars Juan Gonzalez, Sammy Sosa, Dean Palmer and Kevin Brown. He finished his baseball career coaching young pitchers at Baylor University near his home in Waco, Texas. Of his time at Baylor (1991-96) he said, "I had more fun in those six years, I believe, than any other time I spent in baseball."

Sid Hudson, one of baseball's elder statesmen, played and coached baseball with excellence and integrity. On January 3, 2008, he celebrated his 93rd birthday. A month earlier, he and his sweetheart, Marion, enjoyed their 65th wedding anniversary. Both passed away in 2008, Marion in May, Sid in October. A friendly, upright man, Hudson received a long, full, happy life as just reward for his kindness and generosity. Menchine aptly honored him when he said, "Sid was a classy guy all the way. He was one of the greatest men I ever met in my life."

Sid Hudson, Pitching Coach
Private Collection of Sid Hudson (Used with Permission)

7: S.O.S (Same Old Senators)

"Here I was a small boy and there's this 6' 4" guy coming at me in that road gray uniform with the bright red "Senators" on the front. My jaw just dropped."

-Keith Gallagher, Senators' fan, describing the first time he met Washington first baseman Mike Epstein

On the plane headed for Oakland, California to begin a 12-game road trip, Ted Williams leaned back in his seat and took stock of his team. The humble Senators 16-11 start put Washington in third place in the American League East Division, a game behind Boston and three back of first place Baltimore. The supposed worst team in baseball surprised other teams, writers and Washington fans with their fine play. The Senators left town with the cheers of Washingtonians like the wind at their backs.

The once lowly Senators walked tall. They felt far superior to the weaklings they flew west to conquer. In the spring, Williams worked hard to instill confidence in his players. He broke the team of its poor mental habits, a legacy of eight consecutive losing seasons. His methods worked wonders so far.

Now, Williams faced a new problem. Peering over his chair at the men seated behind him, Williams beheld an arrogant group, full of tough talk and swagger. This team thought it could simply step on the field and win. The young season still left many opportunities for his men to unravel. His players forgot last year, when they finished April with an 11-7 record before careening into last place. The worried Williams read his team correctly.

At the beginning of the trip, Washington dropped two contests in Oakland. In the second game, Del Unser's error with two out in the eighth inning allowed the eventual winning run to score. The Senators wasted two Athletics' errors in the ninth. The comeback derailed when Unser popped up a sacrifice bunt with two men on base. A 4-1 lead disappeared into a 5-4 loss.

The frustrating defeat set the tone for the entire trip. The Senators fared worse on their second stop, Sicks' Stadium in Seattle. They lost the opener 2-0 when the Pilots' Mike Marshall threw a two-hitter. The next evening, Williams' overconfident men endured the season's most humbling defeat.

The game started well for the Senators. Washington pounded five Seattle pitchers and led 11-3 after 5 ½ innings. Howard and Bernie Allen hit home runs as the Pilots' second baseman Tommy Harper kicked the ball all over the field, committing three errors. The cocky laughter from the Senators' dugout burned in the Pilots' ears.

Seattle wiped the Senators' smiles from their faces in the bottom of the 6th. The Pilots rocked three Washington pitchers, Camilo Pascual, Casey Cox and Dave Baldwin for eight runs, including a Rich Rollins grand slam to tie the game, 11-11.

An inning later, the Pilots scratched out another run to take a 12-11 lead. Now the chuckles came from the Seattle dugout. The stunned Senators woke up and battled back. In the 8th, Hank Allen and Ken McMullen stroked RBI singles to regain the lead for Washington, 13-12.

Williams turned the game over to Dennis Higgins, but wildness and poor fielding betrayed the Senators' reliever. Ed Brinkman's error, Higgins' wild pitch and two singles led to four runs. Somehow, some way, the Senators lost the game, 16-13.

The Senators' clubhouse steamed with frustration. Excuses reigned. Most focused on the sorry state of Seattle's sub-par ballpark, Sicks' Stadium. Built in 1938 for the minor league Seattle Rainiers, the park had poor lighting, inadequate seating, short fences (only 345 feet to both power alleys), and a rock-hard infield. The minor league facility posed as a major league ballpark until Seattle secured funds and a site for a domed stadium.

Ron Menchine named Sicks the worst stadium for fans, players and broadcasters by far. Frowning at the unpleasant memory, he said, "I've always liked a broadcast booth that was open, where you could soak up the atmosphere. In Sicks' Stadium, not only was the broadcast booth closed, but the visitor's broadcast from a booth where you couldn't see left field. It was absolutely the worst." Visiting players received shoddier treatment than the radio announcers. Poor water pressure in the park forced visiting teams to shower at their hotel after games.

The weather and Sicks' ancient aquatic infrastructure added to the Senators' misery. Toward the end of the game, the Seattle rains arrived and made the glum Senators cold and wet as the game slipped away. A smelly, muddy bus ride back to the hotel beckoned.

Dave Baldwin called the stadium and the game a "farce." His tired, dirt-caked teammates voiced similar opinions as they gathered their belongings and sat in their muddy uniforms. An apoplectic Williams refused to listen to the whining. His iron clad 15-minute cooling off period calmed none of his fury once the writers burst in. He said, "That was the lousiest ball game I ever saw in my life. It makes me so mad I could scream."

Mike Epstein reached the team bus first, about ten minutes ahead of his mates. While they sat in the locker room and contemplated a season beginning to unravel, the Senators' first baseman, always unique, some claimed contrarian, looked out his window. He noticed a heavy-set young boy, about 12 years-old, wearing a tattered Pilots cap, throwing pitches against a warehouse wall, fielding the ricochets with his beat-up baseball mitt. The rain grew heavier, but the soaked lad continued his game, full of joy. Epstein watched the boy "having the time of his life."

A loner whom one teammate called "different," Epstein found a silent kinship with the boy. His happiness cleansed Epstein's bitterness at the loss and turned his feelings from dejection to gratitude. A deep thinker – the Senators' press guide termed him "erudite and articulate" – Epstein, sitting in a wet, dirty uniform, suddenly felt grateful. The privilege to play professional baseball in front of boys like this helped him forget the night's stinging defeat.

As Epstein's dejected teammates boarded the bus, the boy stopped and gaped at the huge Senators, with, "worship in his eyes, just trying to see what they really look like," Epstein said. Epstein peered back at the child through drops of water running down the bus window.

The bus pulled away, bound for Seattle's beautiful Olympic Hotel with its lovely warm showers. Epstein kept staring out the window. He vowed the next time the Senators visited Seattle he would find that boy, put his arm around his round shoulders, and escort him to the Washington locker room to meet Williams and all the other Senators. Then, he would give the boy a baseball with his autograph on it.

The bus turned the corner at Rainier Avenue and headed down McClellan Street. The poignant scene faded from Epstein's sight, but remained deep in his memory. That awe-struck lad in Seattle reminded the Senators' first baseman of a boy he met in Yankee Stadium three weeks earlier.

Nine-year-old Keith Gallagher woke up with a stomach full of butterflies. In a few hours, Gallagher and his father were bound for Yankee Stadium so young Keith could see his first baseball game – the Washington Senators against the New York Yankees. Gallagher prepared for the big event. He grabbed his glove, a nice, new felt-tip pen and a pristine baseball. After a 25-mile drive northeast from his Garwood, New Jersey home, Gallagher and his dad entered the stadium, the hallowed House that Ruth Built.

They arrived at their box seats near the Washington dugout in time to see the Senators take batting practice. The choice tickets came courtesy of a friend, an Army colonel who happened to be Epstein's uncle. Epstein, born in the Bronx within walking distance of Yankee Stadium, often arranged for his extended family to attend Yankees games when the Senators visited New York. Work commitments prevented the colonel from attending, so he offered the tickets and a chance to meet his nephew to the Gallaghers.

He instructed young Keith to call out to Epstein after batting practice, "Hey Mike, the colonel sent me." When Epstein heard the signal, he walked over to greet them.

Keith Gallagher said, "Here I was [a small boy] this high and there's this 6' 4" guy coming at me in that road gray uniform with the bright red Senators on the front. My jaw just dropped. I had a ball in my hand and he autographed it right away and talked to me and my father. It was a real thrill. Ever since then, Mike has always been my favorite player."

The ball remained on prominent display in Gallagher's room until 1975, when a fire destroyed his home. He and his family escaped unharmed, but everything inside the house burned. Gallagher said, "When we went in looking for salvaging items in my bedroom, I looked for that Epstein ball and I couldn't find it. It was gone. That was the only thing I was trying to find that was really worth something to me."

A decade passed and Gallagher grew from boy to man. But the pain of losing the Mike Epstein ball in the fire remained etched in his memory. Gallagher decided to find Epstein's address and write to him. In the letter, he told his childhood hero the story of the lost ball and asked Epstein to consider sending a replacement.

If the people who played baseball with Mike Epstein knew what Gallagher did, they might have cringed. They did not know him as a kind, sentimental man. The moody left-handed slugger refused to conform to the role most athletes played during the 1960s: give innocuous comments to the press, listen to your manager, and play where the organization sends you.

Epstein often did the opposite. When he played a good game, whether his team won or lost, he told the writers so. When Williams benched him against left-handed pitching, Epstein questioned the strategy. When people complained he struck out too often because he always swung for the fences, Epstein replied, "Sure I go for home runs. I'm not getting paid for my glove."

He offered candid commentary on the plight of baseball players. In 1970, he noted that Curt Flood had put baseball "on the right track so far as the reserve clause is concerned. [It] needs to be changed and will be and it won't be detrimental to baseball. If there were some way to work around the reserve clause, a kid wouldn't just have to die on the bench."

The man who quit the Baltimore Orioles' minor league club in Rochester and declared himself a free agent in 1967 felt secure in his non-conformist ways. He said, "I don't think it's a question of popping off. I prefer to think of it as an expression of an individualist."

A month after he mailed the letter, Gallagher received a reply. The enclosed letter, from Epstein's wife, said Mike found the story genuine and touching. She told Gallagher to look for a package in the next few days.

A week later, Gallagher received a parcel with a new Mike Epstein autographed ball inside. The forlorn boy inside the man found his lost treasure at last. Gallagher gently turned the ball in his hands to admire the signature from every angle. He traveled back in time to the wonderful afternoon with his dad at Yankee Stadium, the day he met Mike Epstein. He said, "I was just reliving the whole thing over again."

Over the next decade, Gallagher and Epstein became pen pals of sorts. Gallagher said, "I've written back to him. I've gotten many photos and books with his picture in it. He's always been very accommodating with signing the autographs for me."

The items Epstein signed are precious keepsakes in the Gallagher household. He said, "I wouldn't trade any of it for a Joe DiMaggio, Mickey Mantle, anything like that. That's what it's all worth to me."

When he learned Epstein planned to attend the 1969 Senators' reunion in November 1998, Gallagher resolved to go, too. He drove from his New Jersey home to Chantilly, Virginia to meet Epstein face-to-face again and to say, "Thank you." When the two met, Epstein welcomed Gallagher, and, 30 years later, fulfilled his promise to the spiritual brother of that happy, baseball-playing boy in Seattle.

Epstein turned in a fine 1969 season, with a career-best 30 home runs and 85 RBI. He hit his share of tape measure home runs into RFK Stadium's right field upper deck. The team painted the seats blue to remember his prodigious blasts.

Little went right for Epstein the next season, 1970. He fell into a prolonged slump and hit 10 fewer home runs than in 1969. He struck out 117 times, far too many for Williams.

In May 1971, the Senators traded Epstein and Darold Knowles to Oakland for Frank Fernandez, Don Mincher and Paul Lindblad. Though it received less attention, the deal tilted as heavily in Oakland's favor as the ill-fated trade of Joe Coleman, Jim Hannan, Ed Brinkman and Aurelio Rodriguez did for the Detroit Tigers.

Epstein played consistent, intelligent baseball for the 1972 World Champion Oakland A's, World Series winners. He hit 26 home runs, with 70 RBI. Five weeks later, Oakland's owner, Charlie Finley, traded Epstein to the Texas Rangers. He played his final two years, 1973-74, with Texas and the California Angels.

Epstein played 10 seasons in the big leagues. He earned a World Series ring and hit 130 home runs. He enjoyed a long, successful career in business and now owns a baseball instruction business, "Mike Epstein Hitting" with his son, Jake in suburban Denver. But he made his best contribution to the game after he retired, when he restored Keith Gallagher's lost childhood heirloom and fulfilled his own life-long quest of gratitude.

On May 11, 1969, the afternoon after Epstein's epiphany on the team bus, the Senators lost to Seattle again, 6-5. Baldwin surrendered a game-ending home run to Mincher. The Pilots' sweep left the reeling Senators 0-5 on the road trip.

At the next stop in Anaheim, against the California Angels, Washington won one of three taut contests. The winning team won each by a single run. Paul Casanova's RBI single in the 10th inning of the series' second game gave the Senators their lone win in eight games.

Two more frustrating losses greeted the Senators as they began a four-game series against the White Sox in Chicago. The White Sox won the first game 7-6, in spite of three home runs from Epstein and five Senators round trippers overall. The next night, unheralded White Sox' hurler Gerald Nyman, who had pitched one inning the entire season, threw a one-hitter for the second and last shutout of his brief major league career. Chicago won, 6-0.

The Senators left Washington expecting their trip west to vault them into pennant contention. After nine losses in 10 games, Williams' deflated team needed to sweep a Sunday doubleheader in Chicago just to salvage a shred of dignity.

As the defeats mounted, Washington fans knowingly shook their heads and thought, "Same old Senators." They cringed with every pitch, waiting for the team to fall apart like they did every summer. Williams' doubters waited for him to snap as his team crashed from the heights of 10 wins in 11 games to the depths of nine losses in 10. They felt sure he would soon humiliate a player in public, berate a writer, embarrass the Senators with some sort of outburst, and then retreat to the Florida Keys, fishing rod in hand.

Williams hated losing, but he hated quitting, too. The rookie manager showed more patience than anyone expected. Teddy Ballgame had more than enough intestinal fortitude to withstand one bad road trip. He focused the Senators on their upcoming Sunday doubleheader in old Comiskey Park.

A cold, rainy day made Chicago's rickety ball field bleaker – and emptier – than usual. Only 6,274 hearty South Siders showed up. The White Sox contemplated canceling the games because of the wet weather, but insisted on playing. They savored the chance to kick the poor Senators when they were down. After an hour delay, the rain subsided. The umpires inspected the field and declared "play ball."

In both games this dreary Sunday in Chicago, Washington placed their hopes on the strong right arm and narrow shoulders of Dennis Dean Higgins. Higgins, a humble, plain spoken sort from Jefferson City, Missouri, began to feel at home in the hero's role. He had already saved the Senators and their undermanned pitching staff from disaster many times in 1969. Higgins won or saved 12 of the Senators' first 20 victories, including the club's sole win on this miserable road trip.

The first game went into extra innings tied 2-2. The Senators took a 3-2 lead in the top of the 10th on Mike Epstein's RBI single. Sid Hudson phoned the bullpen and ordered, "Get Higgins hot."

When the Senators' rally ended, Higgins jogged in from the bullpen, warm-up jacket draped over his right arm, head bent down. He projected humility, not confidence. With his huge spectacles and gawky gait, Higgins looked quite un-athletic. With his wide blue eyes peering behind the thick, round glasses, he seemed to say, "How in the heck did I get here?"

Yet, this man now held the game in his large, uncertain hands. Higgins pitched poorly, uncorking nervous, wild pitches. A walk, sacrifice bunt and wild pitch put the tying run at third base with one out.

Higgins paced around the mound. Hudson visited his unsteady pitcher to review the plan for Chicago's next batters, Luis Aparicio and Bill Melton, two of the club's finest hitters. The speedy Aparicio, an all-star and excellent bunter, readied himself. The Senators infield moved in, anticipating the squeeze play.

Higgins kicked the dirt on the mound and tugged his glasses tighter on his prominent nose. He knew his teammates and Williams needed him to escape this jam. Before he threw his first pitch to Aparicio, Higgins remembered spring training, when Williams told his pitchers he expected them to think like hitters, especially in game-deciding situations. The memory calmed Higgins.

On Higgins' first pitch, Aparicio swung away. He popped a shallow fly ball to right field. Ed Stroud raced in and caught the ball, hit too shallow for Chicago's runner at third base, Woody Held, to try to score. Higgins had one out to go for the win.

As Melton entered the batter's box, Higgins remembered another conversation with Williams in Pompano Beach on the many virtues of the slider. Higgins decided to throw the pitch to Melton, but he left the ball high in the strike zone. When Melton's bat hit the ball, Higgins cringed. His hard-hit ground ball skidded on Comiskey Park's new artificial turf, but Brinkman, positioned perfectly, corralled the baseball. The Senators' shortstop made a strong, accurate throw to first base to retire Melton and preserve Washington's thrilling 3-2 victory.

In the second game, the Senators jumped to a 3-1 lead, but the White Sox rallied in the 8th inning. A Chicago walk and single put runners on first and third with one out. Williams called on Higgins again. He surrendered a sacrifice fly, but struck out Buddy Bradford to preserve Washington's lead, 3-2.

In the 9th, Chicago's Carlos May and Walt Williams hit one out singles, putting the tying and winning runs on base. Once again, Aparicio batted, with Melton on deck. Higgins and Aparicio battled to a full count. When Higgins threw the next pitch, both Chicago runners took off. Aparicio swung and missed. Casanova sprang from his crouch and fired the ball to Ken McMullen at third base. McMullen snapped his glove downward and tagged May just as he reached the base. The thrilling game-ending double play gave Washington another 3-2 win and the doubleheader sweep they coveted.

Happy teammates rushed to the mound to congratulate Higgins. Williams offered a firm handshake and hearty slap on the back to the weary pitcher. The Senators entered the day 17-20 and sinking. Now, they stood one game under .500 and headed for home. Thanks to Higgins, everyone in the Washington organization stepped a little lighter. The plane ride home to Baltimore's Friendship Airport felt shorter. The peanuts and beer tasted great.

The two saves gave Higgins nine for the season, tops in the American League. In 30 innings pitched, Higgins sported a 1.80 ERA, the league's lowest. On May 20, Higgins won the Senators' first game back in Washington, a 6-5 squeaker over the Pilots. The victory restored the Senators record to an even 20-20.

Pitching in his third game in two days left Higgins unfazed. "Back then, you didn't just pitch an inning here or there like they do today. You went in at the 7th inning – sometimes earlier than that – and finished the game, if you could," he said.

The down-to-earth, 6' 3", 180-pound relief pitcher allowed little to bother him. He took a matter-of-fact approach to tight situations, the epitome of the baseball bromide "don't get too high or too low." He often whiled away the first hour of games in placid conversation with Darold Knowles, a fellow Missourian.

Higgins said in his classic Show-Me-State accent, "Darold and I were brought up about 50 miles apart, so we'd reminisce on some of the old guys back home and shoot the breeze until it was time to get mentally ready to pitch. That's the advantage of being a reliever. You got about six innings to get yourself organized before you have to worry about anything, until the phone rings."

A workhorse, Higgins pitched in 17 of the Senators' first 39 games. He performed nightly heroics in an underwhelming manner. He stumbled through games walking batters, flinging wild pitches, giving up rocket line-drives, loading the bases and driving Williams crazy. The pitchers whose leads Higgins often jeopardized paced back and forth in the dugout, dodging teammates' nervously spitting tobacco juice on the dugout floor. Somehow, Higgins usually escaped the jams just in time to earn a win or save. The Missouri pragmatist said, "I just got the job done."

Higgins finished 1969 with 10 wins, nine losses and a team-leading 16 saves despite walking 56 batters and throwing 15 wild pitches. His combined 26 wins and saves placed him in company with Knowles (9-2, 13 saves) and top firemen Sparky Lyle (8-3, 17 saves) and Rollie Fingers (6-7, 12 saves). Higgins remembered with pride, "I was pretty high up in the [Rolaid's ®] Fireman's Race for awhile. If I could have continued at the pace I started, I'd have been in great shape."

The 1969 season ended Higgins' stay in Washington. In the off-season, the Senators traded pitchers Higgins and Barry Moore to Cleveland for utility infielder Dave Nelson and pitchers Horacio Pina and Ron Law. Higgins pitched often for the Indians, with four wins and 11 saves in 90 innings, but his earned run average increased by half a run (3.48 in 1969 to 3.99 in 1970) and he still walked too many batters. Of pitching in Cleveland's and its cold and cavernous stadium, hard by the shores of Lake Erie, Higgins said, "I hated it."

In 1971, Cleveland gave up on Higgins and sold him to the St. Louis Cardinals for cash. Higgins appeared in 18 games for the Cardinals over the next two seasons. He pitched his last major league game on August 26, 1972. He hurled a scoreless 9th inning to save a victory for Bob Gibson.

Higgins regrets the downward spiral his career took after 1969. He said, "Part of that was my fault." He lowered his head, the pain of falling short of his own expectations still palpable. He preferred to discuss the good times in Washington when he became one of the team's unsung heroes.

"Great town. We played .500 ball and drew darn near a million people. Best place I ever played. I wouldn't trade it for the world. I miss those days. I really enjoyed that summer," Higgins said with a wide smile.

After he retired from baseball, Higgins enjoyed his post-baseball years. He opened a sporting goods store in Jefferson City where he and his sons worked hard to make it a thriving business in the local community. In 2013, he was inducted into the Missouri Sports Hall of Fame. He still makes his way to the family store most days. He works a little, living the life of the semi-retired.

The locals who visit and sit for a spell at the store's entrance, letting the day pass on by, might hear Higgins spinning a yarn or two about the happy times he spent long ago with Ted Williams and his bullpen buddies way back east in Washington, D.C.

Higgins' clutch pitching stopped the tailspin, but the Senators stumbled at home against the league's two new arrivals. After Higgins' win, Washington dropped the next five, including three to the Kansas City Royals. The losing streak left the Senators with a 20-25 record and an unfathomable eight losses in nine games against the two expansion teams.

On May 26, Billy Martin and his Minnesota Twins pounded the demoralized Senators, 7-1. Williams' team left the field to the noise of Martin's derisive laughter and unhappy fans popping wax paper cups in RFK Stadium's upper deck. Minnesota's win gave the Senators a 4-15 record in their last 19 games.

The heady days of April gone, Williams slumped in his office chair and collected his thoughts. How could he inspire his team to play winning baseball again? The answer stood closer than he realized. For this night marked the first game of the season for a man who would make Washington's pitching staff whole again. Darold Knowles had returned from across the sea.

Dennis Higgins
(National Baseball Hall of Fame Library, Cooperstown, NY)

Mike Epstein, Autograph Day, July 12, 1969
Private Collection of Mark Hornbaker (Used with Permission)

8: Darold Knowles: A Cavalry of One

"I stood out there and I remember thinking, 'Boy, don't mess up.'"

-Darold Knowles, Relief Pitcher, Washington Senators, on pitching with two outs in the bottom of the 9th inning in Game 7 of the 1973 World Series

United States Air Force Sergeant Darold Knowles collected his thoughts as he sat aboard the C-130 transport headed west to Andrews Air Force Base, six miles southeast of Washington, D.C. Soon, Knowles would be home, state side, doing what he felt born to do – pitch a baseball. The moment his feet touched the ground, he longed to wear his Washington Senators uniform once again and warm up his left arm in the bullpen at RFK Stadium.

Since July 1968, Knowles had lived and worked at Itazuke Air Force Base in Japan. He served as a clerk/typist on the base the Air Force used to fly reconnaissance missions and give air cover to American ships sailing in the Sea of Japan, the Gulf of Tonkin, and the South China Sea.

A month remained in his enlistment, but he was home. The next morning, he sped to the Senators' clubhouse. Knowles walked into a bleak situation. Sportswriters and fans alike agreed that Williams' nice little April had dissolved into the Senators' annual collapse. The descent from a 16-11 to a 20-26 record evoked breakdowns in 1961 (30-30 to 61-100), 1967 (58-58 to 76-85) and 1968 (11-7 to 65-96). Why should 1969 be any different?

To his downcast teammates, Knowles rode into town like a cavalry of one. The Washington pitching staff suffered from injuries and, under Ted Williams' wrath, frayed nerves. Dick Bosman nursed an injured shoulder. Williams publicly lambasted ineffective starting pitchers Jim Hannan, Joe Coleman and Camilo Pascual, banishing each to the bullpen until they corrected their flaws.

Fellow relief pitcher and Missourian Higgins rejoiced at Knowles' return. "Darold was the best relief pitcher we had," Higgins said. In Knowles' absence, Higgins and Casey Cox pitched bravely, but their arms ached. The two logged 75 innings in the 46 games the Senators played without Knowles on the roster.

Knowles wanted to pitch right away, but Williams and his coaching staff preferred that Knowles work out for a week to master command of his pitches and strengthen his left arm. Bosman's injury, which sent him to the disabled list, changed the plan. On May 25, with no reliable pitchers available in the minor leagues, the team added Knowles to the roster to replace Bosman.

The next day, Knowles pitched a perfect mop-up inning in the Senators' 7-1 loss to the Twins. It was his first major league action since July 12, 1968, more than 10 months previous. The first batter Knowles faced was Harmon Killebrew, nicknamed "Killer" because he destroyed unprepared pitchers. Knowles remembered Killebrew's at-bat. "He hit a line drive, just a sharp hit. It was a bad pitch. He should have hit it out of the ballpark. Instead, it was a line drive right at somebody. That kind of got my feet wet."

For the next three days, the Senators resisted the urge to use Knowles in a game while he prepared on the sidelines. On May 29, an off day, everything clicked for the Senators' most reliable relief pitcher. Knowles' pitches cracked into bullpen coach George Susce's glove. His breaking balls danced. Williams and Hudson marveled at his accuracy, strength and stamina.

Neither man knew about Knowles' fanatical exercise regimen while he served in Japan. Knowles prepared for his return to the pitcher's mound from the moment he dragged his duffel bag through Itazuke's iron gates. He said, "One of my fellow servicemen, a friend of mine from Toms River, New Jersey [named] Bob Fiocco, used to catch me. We'd play catch three or four times a week. We would go play handball and work out. So I stayed in shape and was ready when I got back."

Knowles' second appearance of the season came on May 30, in the 9th inning of the first game of a doubleheader against the White Sox. Unlike his token appearance against Minnesota, the outcome hung in the balance. Chicago led 4-3 and had a runner on first base with one out. Williams entrusted Knowles to hold the visitors scoreless and sustain hope for a Washington rally. Standing on the RFK Stadium mound, kicking at the dirt around the pitching rubber to make it just right, a grateful Knowles felt at home, doing what God created him to do.

From his childhood, Darold Duane Knowles, born December 9, 1941 in Brunswick, Missouri, yearned to throw a baseball. He pitched in high school, for one season at the University of Missouri, and for five years in the Baltimore Orioles' minor league system. By 1969, his fifth season in the major leagues, Knowles had become a master craftsman of pitching. He knew every nuance of a baseball, how the seams felt in his hand, how to grip each pitch, how to adjust for the weather, the batter and the ballpark.

Knowles threw a fastball and an assortment of breaking pitches – sinker, slider, change-up and palm ball. He specialized in teasing hitters to take huge swings as the ball danced under their bats. If the batter made contact, the ground ball usually ended up in the glove of a sure-handed Senators' infielder for an easy out. Left-handed batters found the southpaw Knowles especially difficult to solve.

On the Memorial Day afternoon, the first game of a single admission doubleheader, Knowles faced Chicago's catcher Ed Herrmann, a left-handed batter. He grounded a sinker ball toward second base. Tim Cullen fielded the ball, stepped on second, and threw to Howard at first for an inning-ending double play. Knowles' shrewd pitching gave the Senators a chance to win.

In the bottom of the 9th inning, Frank Howard's two-out single tied the game, delighting the crowd, more than 21,000 strong. In the 10th, Knowles held Chicago scoreless again. In the Senators' half of the extra frame, with two out and Mike Epstein at second base, Ed Stroud chopped a swinging bunt in front of home plate. He sped down the first base line as Epstein broke for third. Herrmann grabbed the ball, but, with the blazing Stroud running, rushed his throw. The ball skipped past Chicago first baseman Tom McCraw and rolled into short right field. An alert Epstein sprinted home to give Washington a stirring 5-4 victory, Knowles first win since June 1, 1968.

When public address announcer Sherm Brody proclaimed Knowles the winning pitcher, the crowd roared with joy. It made for a perfect story: the returning veteran wins his first game in 364 days on Memorial Day. Knowles rejected the sentimental story line. He felt his long deployment threatened his baseball career. He blamed the Air Force's refusal to reduce his overseas tour on military red tape and petty politics.

A month later, with time and perspective, Knowles softened his view. He pointed out his good fortune to serve in Japan, far from the fighting, misery and death in Vietnam. He lost time and money, but not his life. Thirty days with his teammates cleansed his contempt. "If I went around bitter," he said, "the only one I'd hurt is myself."

Knowles' victory gave the Senators a third consecutive win and raised their season record to 23-26. For the next 12 games he pitched nearly flawless baseball. In 21 innings his ERA stood at a perfect 0.00. He surrendered one unearned run. Knowles said, "It was one of those things where you get in a zone and everything seems to go right. I was just so happy to be back and so confident. It just kind of snowballed and turned out extremely well."

Knowles' fine pitching helped restore the good old days to the Senators' bullpen. He renewed friendships and slid into baseball's pace and rhythm. He said, "We all kind of ran together. I probably spent more time with Jim French and Bob Humphreys than any of the others. We're still close today."

Dave Baldwin remembered how Knowles helped his fellow pitchers relax with his good-natured teasing of Susce. "George and Darold were just a great combination, because George was of the old school and Darold wasn't. Darold just ribbed George all the time. George had been catching for centuries by that time and his fingers were all gnarled. He had broken every finger several times and his fingers went in all directions. Darold would say things like, 'George, don't pick your nose, you'll put your eye out,'" Baldwin said.

Knowles' streak of games without giving up an earned run ended on June 23 when he gave up five to Baltimore. By then, Knowles' excellent pitching caught the eye of Detroit's manager Mayo Smith, who would soon choose the American League All-Star's pitching staff.

The storybook beginning to Knowles' season continued throughout 1969. He finished with a 9-2 record, 13 saves and a 2.24 ERA in 84 innings pitched. He appeared in 53 of the 117 games he spent on the Senators' roster. His presence strengthened the pitching staff and the entire team. Washington enjoyed a 66-51 record once Knowles came on board. He said, "It was a pleasure being back and all of a sudden we were winning. That was the big thing. The fans got caught up in it and it was such a thrill."

Frustration filled his remaining days in Washington. In 1970, he earned a glittering 2.04 ERA and 27 saves in 119 innings pitched. Yet, Knowles lost 14 of 16 decisions. Rarely did such a stellar performer suffer so much undeserved punishment. He said, "I had a [great] year. It just didn't show."

In 1971, Knowles escaped Washington for Oakland as part of the trade that also sent Epstein to the A's, a budding dynasty. Thanks to Bob Short, the proud, talented pitcher left a poor team bound for oblivion to join a club poised to win five straight division titles and three consecutive World Series.

At first, Knowles disdained the trade. He said, "I was kind of upset, because I enjoyed my time so much in Washington. I enjoyed the people, the fans. I had a home there. All of a sudden I'm traded. And I wasn't going to be the closer. It was about a month before I realized that the guy down there with the handlebar mustache (Hall of Fame pitcher Rollie Fingers) was pretty damn good and we had a chance to win the

World Series. Eventually, I understood that I was a spoke in a big wheel and it was great."

Knowles got a taste of playoff baseball with Oakland in 1971. He gave up a double and threw a wild pitch that let a runner score in Game 3, the last contest of the 1971 American League Championship Series (ALCS). In 1972, after he pitched the best season of his career (1.37 ERA in 66 innings pitched), Knowles broke his thumb in the final week of the regular season. He missed the A's championship run.

The unfortunate injury spoiled Knowles' first taste of being a champion. "You play your whole life and that's what you want to do, pitch in a World Series. A lot of guys play their whole career and never have the opportunity. Even though I got the World Series ring, it was a downer for me because I wasn't able to pitch," he said.

In 1973, Oakland made the play-offs again. This time, Knowles was healthy. As each game played out, he sat in the bullpen and waited. The series took the full five games to resolve, but Knowles never appeared in the A's win over Baltimore. He stewed inside, lamenting the prospect of sitting idle for another post-season. He had one chance left, the World Series against the Cinderella New York Mets.

In Game 1 Oakland held a 2-1 lead in the 9th inning. With one out and a New York runner on first base, Mets' manager Yogi Berra put in Rusty Staub, a left-handed batter, to pinch hit. Dick Williams came out of the A's dugout to remove Fingers and signal for Knowles. Soon, he would throw his first pitch in a World Series.

Berra removed Staub for right-handed pinch hitter Jim Beauchamp. Knowles calmed himself. As elated as he felt, he knew an A's victory depended on him. He ignored the cameras, the bunting, the commissioner, and the celebrities. He focused on the catcher's target and threw the best pitches he could. Knowles retired Beauchamp on a pop out and the next hitter, Wayne Garrett, on a fly ball to right field. Knowles, in his World Series debut, saved Game 1 for Oakland.

In every one of the first six games of the tight, excruciating series, Williams called on Knowles. He pitched brilliantly, allowing a single unearned run in Game 4. Knowles recalled, "It wasn't even mentioned that no one had ever pitched in all seven games until the morning of the seventh game. There was just some little quote [in the newspaper] that if Knowles happens to get in this game, he'd be the only man to ever pitch in all seven. I was just hoping I'd get in one game, I never dreamed I'd get in seven."

In Game 7, with the A's one out from the championship, Knowles had not appeared in the game. He explained, "Of course we go to the 9th inning and I always thank Gene Tenace, because he made an error with two out in the 9th or I wouldn't have gotten in there."

Tenace's miscue made the score Oakland 5, New York 2 and left two Mets' runners on base. Garrett, a left-handed hitter, came up, representing the tying run. With Fingers in his fourth inning of work, Williams replaced him with Knowles. The fate of the Oakland A's depended on Knowles' left arm.

As he prepared to face Garrett, Knowles struggled to calm himself. He said, "In the 15 plus years I pitched in the big leagues that is the only time I can really say I felt the pressure. I stood out there and I remember thinking, 'Boy, don't mess up.'

"I didn't think about it until later, but, man, that was pressure. I put in on myself. Other than that, I was always extremely confident."

Wiping his perspiring left palm on his pants, Knowles, the master craftsman, set about finishing his greatest work. On his second pitch, he induced Garrett to pop out to A's shortstop Bert Campaneris. Lost at the bottom of the jubilant infield pile-up, Knowles rejoiced. He said, "Getting the last out of the World Series, of all the years and games I pitched in the big leagues, that was absolutely the greatest thrill I ever had in baseball and still will be until the day I die."

Knowles pitched for Oakland in 1974 and earned his third consecutive World Series ring, but he did not appear in the post-season. Knowles was 33 and appeared past his prime. His 1974 ERA was the highest of his career, 4.22 and he pitched only 53 innings. Six days after the final World Series game, the A's traded Knowles to the Cubs.

In Chicago, Knowles suffered through the worst season of his career. In 88 innings, he managed 15 saves, but finished with a 5.81 ERA. The sub-par performance put his career at risk. The 1975 season haunted Knowles. "My dream was to finish my career with an ERA under 3.00. But my first year in Chicago, when we played all the day games, I had a lousy ERA. Other than that year, I would have done it. I wound up 3.12 or something overall and I'm proud of that. But [a career ERA under 3.00] was just something I wanted to do and it didn't happen," he said.

In the off season Knowles resolved to pitch better. He worked harder on conditioning to withstand the long, hot day games at Wrigley Field. Knowles said, "I was very determined. The next year I came back and had a good year. The ERA was under three (2.89 in 72 innings pitched) in 1976."

Knowles' dedication and determination carried him for three more seasons in the major leagues. He bounced from Chicago to Texas (1977) to Montreal (1978) and, finally, to St. Louis (1979-80). When he retired in 1980, Knowles had pitched in 765 games, at the time the most appearances by a left-handed pitcher in baseball history. Sparky Lyle took the title from Knowles the next season and many pitchers have broken it since.

Knowles pitched his final game for the Cardinals on April 18, 1980, exactly 16 years after his major league debut. When he retired, only two other 1969 Senators remained in the league, Del Unser and Toby Harrah.

In retirement, Knowles' passion for baseball endured. He coached for the St. Louis Cardinals in 1981 and remained on the staff through the club's three World Series appearances in the 1980's (1982, 1985 and 1987). In 1993, he coached for the Philadelphia Phillies, who lost the World Series to the Toronto Blue Jays. All told, Knowles sports seven World Series rings, albeit three for losing efforts.

Since 2008, Knowles has served as the pitching coach for the Dunedin Blue Jays, a Florida League (Class A) affiliate of Toronto. He says, "The game's a little bit different now then it was back when I played. I played five years in the minor leagues. I think I saw *a* pitching coach one day."

Few of the young Dunedin pitchers realize the accomplishments of the old man teaching them. He says with a sigh, "I was there a month before people realized I had pitched in the big leagues. Many people say I remember you and they can quote my career [statistics] which is a very nice feeling, but it's usually the older generation."

With his durable left arm and meticulous work habits, Knowles, the pitching craftsman, became a champion – a word associated with few who played for the Washington Senators. With nearly 50 years in the game, the fire to pitch still burns. He said. "I'm proud of my career, the fact I was durable, lasted as long as I did, and had some success. I'd have probably made a few dollars today. I wished I'd pitched in more games, because I just wanted to be out there. Wish I could do it today. I'll tell you, if they move that mound up 15 feet, I'll make a comeback!"

Knowles' Memorial Day triumph in 1969 failed to jump start the Senators. In the nightcap of the May 30 doubleheader, Washington lost, 8-5. The club's record fell to 23-27.

The next morning, a hot, humid Saturday, Williams and catcher Paul Casanova worked together in an extended batting practice session. Williams usually focused on players' mental approach to hitting, but with Casanova in a season long slump, he corrected bad technique. He moved the catcher's feet closer to the plate. He made Casanova work until he learned to shift his hips faster when he swung to generate more power.

Casanova hoped the session with Williams might help him end a three-year spell of poor hitting. Born December 21, 1941 in Colon, Cuba, he suffered through a miserable season in 1968. To add to his misery, Casanova weathered a nasty rift with the Senators' organization. In June, 1968, disgusted with his poor performance and alleged slipshod work habits, George Selkirk, Washington's general manager at the time, demoted Casanova, a member of the American League All-Star squad in 1967, and his .181 average to the minor leagues. Selkirk told Casanova he would remain in the bush leagues until he adjusted his batting eye and his attitude.

The bitterly disappointed Casanova refused to accept the demotion. He termed the Senators' move unfair. In Casanova's opinion, the Senators made him the scapegoat for the team's poor performance. The two sides exchanged barbs in the Washington newspapers, but, with no other real choice, Casanova relented. He returned to the team three weeks later and finished 1968 with a .196 batting average (.462 OPS), the worst season of his career.

Casanova's misery continued in 1969. His numbers heading into the May 31 game looked awful – batting average, .185, on-base percentage, .246, slugging average, .258. Casanova's defense suffered as well. With lightning-quick reflexes and a powerful arm, "Cazzie" – fans and teammates' affectionate nickname for the Senators' catcher – made fools of runners who dared to attempt a stolen base or strayed too far from their stations. For his career, Casanova threw out runners on stolen base attempts 41 percent of the time. In 1969, his success rate dropped to 33 percent, a career worst. Casanova's outward demeanor mirrored his on-field performance. He played baseball with his emotions laid bare. The wide, friendly smile that captured fans' hearts rarely appeared.

Senators' rooters loved Cazzie because he played with flamboyance and flair. In 1967, fans voted Casanova, not Howard, the team's most valuable player. In the book *Clemente: The Passion and Grace of Baseball's Last Hero*, author David Maraniss wrote that the Pittsburgh superstar played baseball with "beautiful fury." Casanova, a wiry 6'4" and 180 pounds, played with enthusiastic futility. He matched Clemente's fire, but achieved less lofty and often comical results. Paul Casanova made failure entertaining and memorable.

He swung the bat so hard he sometimes toppled head first into the dirt. Often lost on the base paths, he started slides twenty feet shy of the base he was headed toward – or retreating from. He seemed to run in both directions at once before an opposing player, suppressing a smile, tagged him out in a tangle of arms and legs and dust.

Casanova expected his pitchers to play with the same enthusiasm. If a pitcher struggled to throw strikes or his intensity waned, Casanova rose from his crouch, stepped onto the grass in front of home plate, and fired the ball back to the pitcher at laser-beam speed. The ball cracked into the offending pitcher's glove, echoing around RFK Stadium. The pitcher frowned and turned away to prevent Casanova from seeing him wince, the hand inside his glove burning.

One of Casanova's victims, Bob Humphreys said, "Cazzie had a gun. He would throw it back harder to you than you threw it. He did it to try to wake you up on the mound. Knowles, Cox and I said among ourselves one day, 'Hey, let's bare hand one of those.' But none of us had the guts to do it. He liked to show off his arm. You can do it if you've got it and he had it."

As a small crowd filed in for the afternoon contest, Casanova put on his catcher's gear and warmed up Joe Coleman, Washington's starting pitcher. He thought about Williams' tips that morning and looked forward to hitting against Chicago's pitcher, Tommy John.

In his first at-bat against John, Casanova singled to center and his confidence grew. The next time up, he lofted a sacrifice fly to give the Senators their first run. The trace of a smile appeared.

Coleman and John battled to a 3-3 tie after 6 ½ innings. In the bottom of the 7th, Tim Cullen led off with a single. Casanova hit next. He tapped the dirt from his spikes and entered the batter's box. He moved close to the plate as Williams taught him that morning. John threw a fastball and Casanova swung with a violent uppercut. He smacked the ball into the Senators' bullpen for a two-run homer. He rounded the bases at full speed, a wide grin on his face.

In the 8th inning, the White Sox tied the game, 5-5, when Knowles allowed two runners to score. During the Senators' turn in the 8th, Casanova came up to bat with the bases loaded and two out. Chicago's relief pitcher, Wilbur Wood, threw a ball, then two strikes. Everyone knew Wood's next pitch was the knuckleball, untouchable at its fluttering best.

Casanova prepared for the perplexing pitch. It wafted through the air and seemed to stop when it reached the middle of the plate. Casanova snapped his wrists and lined a single to left-centerfield, driving in two game-clinching runs. His three hits and five RBI gave Washington a 7-5 win and raised his batting average to .205. After the game, a happy Casanova told the press, "Mr. Williams has been very patient with me."

The 1969 season included few such highlights for Casanova. He finished with a .216 batting average (.536 OPS), a disappointment to himself and the team. In 1970-71, Casanova, despite a Herculean effort, failed to overcome his hitting deficiencies. Always eager to swing, pitchers took advantage of his impatience. He never managed 20 walks in a season. His on-base percentage hovered around .250, much too low for an everyday player. After the 1971 season, Washington traded their long-time starting catcher to the Atlanta Braves.

Casanova played his final three seasons (1972-74) as a light hitting, good fielding part-time catcher for Atlanta. There, he befriended Hank Aaron and helped him cope with pressure and racist threats as Aaron pursued Babe Ruth's home run record. While watching from the Braves' bullpen, Casanova caught homer number 716.

On March 28, 1975, at the end of spring training, the Braves released Casanova. His 10-year baseball career was over. After baseball, Casanova lived a nomadic life. He traveled between South America and the U.S., pursuing various business interests. In the 1970s, with Pat and Leroy Kelly as partners, he opened a discothèque in Caracas, Venezuela. Later, he moved to Miami and owned a youth baseball academy for Cuban expatriates.

In July 2017, at the Major League Baseball All-Star FanFest in Miami, Casanova, despite being in poor health, captivated a large audience of fans and retired Latin baseball players. A month later, on August 12, Casanova died. Still beloved in Washington, the Nationals held a moment of silence for him before their game that evening.

Wherever he wandered, Paul Casanova took along the warmth of fans who watched him play baseball with his unique blend of vigor and jubilance. During the 5th inning of the Senators' last game in Washington, Williams sent Casanova up as a pinch-hitter. When they heard his name, the fans stood and cheered their beloved Cazzie with a passion that matched his zeal for baseball and the city. Only Howard received more cheers that sad evening. Casanova loved Washington and the city's fans loved him.

The 1969 Senators said goodbye to May with a victory and a 23-27 record thanks to Casanova's fine performance (3-3, 5 RBI). Williams inspired Casanova and his teammates to play respectable baseball again. The Senators' enthusiastic manager refused to let himself or his men falter.

Washington needed a win to finish their 13-game home stand with a 6-7 record, a nice recovery from the 1-6 start and get June off to a good beginning. Fortunately for the Senators, Williams placed the ball in the capable hands of the team's best starting pitcher during the first two months of the season – a lollygagging left-hander who drove his coaches crazy.

Darold Knowles
(National Baseball Hall of Fame Library, Cooperstown, NY)

Paul Casanova
(National Baseball Hall of Fame Library, Cooperstown, NY)

9: The Subtle Pain of If

"If I had the choice, if I could go back in time and do the whole thing again, there's a whole lot of things I'd do a whole lot different."
-Casey Cox, Relief Pitcher, Washington Senators

With two outs in the 9th inning of the Senators June 1 game against the Chicago White Sox, left-handed starting pitcher Barry Moore let a sly grin cover his face. The Senators led 9-2 and Moore had starred in the team's pending triumph. His complete game win, in a tidy one hour and fifty minutes, improved Moore's record to 4-1 and the Senators' to 24-27.

The excellent nine innings of work maintained his miniscule 2.02 ERA, second best in the league behind Jim Palmer's 1.85. Out of the blue, Moore became the Senators' ace. By the end of the 1970 season, his career dissolved in injury and failure.

When he first joined the Senators in 1965, Robert Barry Moore brought the slow, country ways he learned in his hometown of Statesville, N.C., to the big city of Washington, D.C. He liked to hunt and fish. He avoided hard work and shunned the limelight.

Moore played the stereotypical role of the easy going, slightly daft southpaw for the Senators. During spring training, he announced he traded his regular, full-size cigars for a new, smaller brand to "improve my wind." Williams and his coaches tried again and again to light a fire under Moore. He sometimes forgot about wind sprints and side throwing sessions. Even Williams' infamous wrath failed to change Moore's slowpoke habits. "It's just the way I am, I guess," he said.

In his next start, Moore injured his ribcage. He attempted to pitch through the pain and injured his shoulder. The rest of the season, except for a masterful complete game, four-hitter in July to defeat the Red Sox, his performance suffered. In 76 innings after June 1, his ERA more than doubled to 4.30. Williams lost confidence in Moore and dropped him from the starting rotation. Nevertheless, he persevered through the pain to finish 1969 with a 9-8 record, his only winning season in the major leagues.

The Senators traded Moore to Cleveland in December 1969, part of the same deal that sent Dennis Higgins to the Indians. In June 1970, Cleveland traded Moore to the White Sox. He pitched poorly for both teams, finishing the year with a 3-9 record and a 5.30 ERA. He pitched his last game in the major leagues on October 1, 1970.

90

Once he retired from baseball, Moore disappeared. Washington Baseball Historical Society President Jim Hartley said, "Moore is the Dorian Gray of the 1969 Senators."

Moore never recaptured the magic he performed during the first three months of 1969. His brief, but excellent work stabilized a starting pitching staff teetering on the verge of collapse. Now, presumably, he relaxes in North Carolina's great outdoors, hunting and fishing to his heart's content.

Moore closed out the Senators two-week stay in Washington with a flourish. The upbeat club traveled to Kansas City and Minnesota for a six-game road trip. Williams' scrappy club won three of the first five to improve their record to 28-29. The trip's last game pitted Camilo Pascual against the Twins' wily veteran, Jim Perry.

Minnesota slugger Harmon Killebrew's three-run homer in the bottom of the 8th inning erased a 5-2 Washington lead. Bright thoughts of a return to a .500 record (29-29) vanished. In the bottom of the 9th inning, Knowles struck out Killebrew with two runners on base and two out. In the 11th inning, with Senators' reliever Casey Cox pitching, the Twins had runners on second and third with two out. Williams ordered Cox to intentionally walk Tony Oliva.

The curious decision meant Killebrew stepped to the plate with the bases loaded and the game again in the balance. Teams that gave Killebrew two chances to beat them usually regretted the largess. Cox faced a difficult, but simple task – retire one of baseball's best hitters or lose the game. All eyes looked to him.

Fortunately for Washington, Joseph Casey Cox rarely shunned the spotlight. He liked to draw attention to himself. The 6'5", 200-pound handsome, blond surfer boy from Long Beach exuded strength and self-assurance. Cox lived life with carefree exuberance. He looked like the young, cocky built-for-speed young men folks imagined when they listened to the Beach Boys. With his deep, melodic voice, Cox even sounded a little like the group's baritone, Mike Love.

By the time he faced Killebrew this June 8 afternoon in Minnesota, Cox had pitched in 22 games, all in relief. He sported a 3-1 record and 2.37 ERA. He loved the heavy workload. "I was capable of pitching a lot and strong. I liked to have the ball in my hand," Cox said.

The versatile Cox could relieve for one inning or eight. "He seems to thrive on work," Hudson said. The tireless pitcher hurled more than five innings in relief four times during 1969. He won all four games.

Cox's long relief masterpieces filled him with confidence, but he faced a hitting machine on this cool, clear day in Minnesota. The play-off bound Twins boasted a roster full of strong hitters like Killebrew,

Oliva, Rod Carew, and Rich Reese. Manager Billy Martin's men could destroy any pitcher's self-assurance.

Killebrew, the American League RBI leader at the time, carried his huge bat to the plate and stared toward the pitcher's mound. Cox steeled his nerves. The bases full of Twins, Cox had no place to put the massive slugger, Minnesota's Casey at the Bat.

From the Twins' dugout, Martin razzed Cox with his yap-yap-yap Chihuahua style of bench jockeying. Cox ignored him. Taking its cue from Martin, the crowd of 20,486 roared as Cox's first two pitches sailed wide of the strike zone. "Two more bad pitches," they thought, "and our Twins taste victory."

Cox battled Killebrew, working the count full. He now faced a seminal moment in the Senators' season and his career. The tall, handsome pitcher peered in for the sign from catcher Paul Casanova. He threw only two pitches, a sinking fastball and a slider. He knew Killebrew expected the fastball. Cox recalled the lazy days of spring training when Williams revealed how good hitters think. Cox said, "If you turn around everything he says, if you go 180 degrees, well, you're taking advantage of what he's saying against the hitters. That's the way I looked at it."

He decided to throw the slider. The ball dove toward the plate, hard and heavy, with a sharp downward spin. A good pitch, but destined to break below Killebrew's knees for ball four. To the Twins' slugger, though, the pitch looked too good to resist. He swung just as the ball darted under his bat. The mighty Killebrew struck out. Cox prevailed.

In the 12th inning, Unser pulled a two-run home run down the right field line. With the help of a double play grounder, Cox and the Senators prevailed in a heart-stopping 7-5 victory. Washington reached .500 at last.

For Cox, the victory over Minnesota, their all-star slugger, and their annoying manager, proved Williams could trust him to win big games in the major leagues. He said, "[Striking out Killebrew] gave me a lot of confidence. And I just went from there."

On June 9, he stood in fifth place in the league ERA race with a glittering 2.29. He shared space in *The Sporting News* league leaders section with all-stars Palmer, Blue Moon Odom and Mike Cuellar. For the next month, Cox dominated. By July 13, he enjoyed a 7-1 record and a 1.78 ERA, the American League's best.

Soon, Washington's first fan, the President of the United States, noticed Cox's excellent performances. Richard Nixon, an ardent baseball fan and occasional visitor to RFK, met Cox in July 1969, during a post-game tour of the Senators' locker room. Nixon introduced himself and said, "You're leading the league in earned run average aren't you?"

Cox nodded and stammered a humble, "Yeah," but he treasured the moment. "For the President, as busy as he had to be, to comment on that," he said, shaking his head in wonder. Cox saved an autographed picture of Nixon at a Senators game to remember the glorious night when the president waited to speak with him.

When injury, poor performances and a string of eight games in five days left Williams rotation in tatters, he gave Cox a new assignment – starting pitcher. A relief pitcher his entire major league career until then, Cox performed well in the role. He pitched complete games in four of his 13 starts. His durability placed him third on the Senators' staff with Moore, behind Joe Coleman (12 complete games) and Dick Bosman (5).

In his final start of the season, Cox surrendered five earned runs in three innings to Boston's potent lineup. His season-worst outing increased his ERA to 2.78, the sixth-best mark in the league. His 12 wins tied Coleman for second best on the Washington staff. For the first time, Cox felt he belonged in the exclusive club of good major league pitchers.

Cox enjoyed helping the Senators become winners, too. He said, "It was fun to be on a winning ball club. And it was just a thrill [to play] for Ted."

Cox fondly remembered spring training with Williams. After hours talking about hitters and how they think, the manager herded his pitchers to a practice field for a game of pepper. They played in the waning hours of spring training, the sun setting in radiant splendor behind the Pompano Beach coastline. Cox recalled, "Ted would start hitting line drives at your ankles. He had such great bat control. A lot of little things you remember."

Cox's fine pitching and magnetic personality made him a popular speaker on the Washington banquet circuit. His laugh line: "A kid came up to me, started asking me for autographs on a baseball card. The kid had me sign 10 cards.

"I said, 'Why do you want so many?'

"He said, 'It takes 10 Casey Coxes to get one Sonny Jurgensen.'"

Cox never again pitched like he did in 1969. He earned a regular spot in the 1970 Senators rotation, but squandered it with a 4.45 ERA and 27 home runs allowed in 192 innings pitched. He pitched poorly in 1971-72 as well. On August 30, 1972, Texas traded him to the New York Yankees. After Cox pitched one game for the Yankees in 1973, they released him. At age 31, the major league career of one of the 1969 Senators' top performers was over.

Looking back, Cox wondered if he celebrated success a little too much and took his position in baseball for granted. He still wrestles with regret. In 1998, he said, "I didn't have the good years after [1969]. That was my fault, because I probably didn't work as hard as I should have. I wish I'd have worked harder, done a lot of things differently. If I had the choice, if I could go back in time and do the whole thing again, there's a whole lot of things I'd do a whole lot different."

After working in the insurance world for several years, Cox retired and now lives in Greater Largo, Florida. He served as the president of the local Republican Club until 2016. The city of Long Beach, California elected him to its baseball hall of fame in 2007.

But in 1969, Williams and the Senators toasted Cox and sung his praises for vanquishing Killebrew and the Twins. The club returned home after their successful road trip with confidence restored. Instead of falling apart, as many predicted, Washington had won four of six and nine of their past 12 games. Together, they set a new goal – become the first expansion Senators team since 1961 to achieve a winning record beyond June.

The quest started badly. Oakland won the first series, two games to one. The California Angels visited next. In the series' opener, the Angels started Jim McGlothin, a right- handed pitcher. The Senators' veteran, left-handed hitting second baseman Bernie Allen smiled. With a right-hander on the mound, he knew Williams had penciled him into the starting line-up. Allen and Tim Cullen formed the Senators' second base platoon. Cullen, a right-handed batter, played against lefties. Allen looked forward to the action. In the past week, he broke out of a hitting slump with five hits in 10 at-bats.

In the 3rd inning, Allen bounced a ground ball RBI single to right field to give the Senators a 3-1 lead. In the 6th, Allen crushed a long drive over RFK's right field scoreboard against Angels' reliever Pedro Borbon. The homer, Allen's second in three games, gave the Senators a 4-1 lead. For the light-hitting Angels, the three-run deficit proved insurmountable. Allen singled again in the 7th inning to complete a 3-4 night. The Senators won with ease, 6-2.

Yet, before the game ended, Williams put a blemish on Allen's successful night. Before the Senators took the field for the 8th inning, Williams told Allen to take a seat. His night was over. Tim Cullen, a better fielder, replaced him. Being removed from games frustrated Allen. He felt Williams owed him an explanation for such decisions, but he received nothing. "He just said, 'This is the way it's going to be and that's it.'

"It just about drove me crazy, not getting to play for no reason. Nobody knew how to take him. I don't think he should have been a manager. You have to know how to handle people when you manage."

Like many boys who grew up in the 1950s, Bernard Keith Allen idolized Ted Williams. Born April 16, 1939 in East Liverpool, Ohio, Allen mimicked Teddy Ballgame's swing as closely as he could during neighborhood sandlot games with his childhood friend, Lou Holtz. As an adult, Allen's awe and admiration for the Splendid Splinter endured – until he met his idol face-to-face in Pompano Beach during spring training.

When the two met, Allen received Williams with childlike enthusiasm. He told Williams he read his book *The Science of Hitting* and everything else Williams wrote about baseball. After shaking hands, the Senators' manager wasted no time squashing his second baseman's wide-eyed reverence.

"Williams came up to me and said, 'I really like your swing. I like how you stand in against left-handed pitching,'" Allen recalled. Williams then said, as he walked away, "By the way, I'm not going to play you against left-handers."

Teddy Ballgame kept true to his word. Allen made a mere 35 plate appearances against southpaws in 1969. The strategy stunned Allen. "He complimented me, and then he pulled the rug right out from under me. I don't like to rip people, but things happened that I wasn't happy with," he said.

The unhappy first meeting set in motion a steady deterioration of the two men's relationship. Allen's frustrating run-ins with Williams made it difficult to concentrate on playing baseball. Allen said, "Williams didn't communicate with anybody."

Williams, a Marine veteran and child of an earlier generation, expected his players to respect his unquestioned authority. According to Allen, Williams told his team at spring training, "We're going to do things around here in a good way – my way."

Allen's generation coined the phrase "question authority." The saying became a mantra for hippies, flower children, opponents of the Vietnam War, and unhappy baseball players. Each time Allen mouthed a zinger, like "Oh, we're not trying to win tonight?" when Williams left him out of the starting line-up, he dug himself deeper into Williams' doghouse.

Williams and Allen had polar opposite personalities. Williams thrived on boisterous enthusiasm and old school military leadership. He

95

liked loud chatter at batting practice and in the dugout. He wanted his players to demonstrate a visceral passion for victory.

Allen internalized his intensity. As his desire to win grew, he became more contemplative. He concentrated harder. His approach stemmed from his success in college football. He earned All-America honors playing quarterback, kicker and defensive back with Purdue University. In 1960, he led the Boilermakers to a stunning upset of top-ranked University of Minnesota. He defeated Notre Dame three times. In 1999, Allen was elected to the Purdue University's Hall of Fame.

In football, a quarterback's calm leadership meant composed teammates. If Allen ran around screaming his head off, the whole offense would follow and fall apart. Quiet fervor, not gung-ho, rah, rah leadership, worked for Allen. Not so Williams. Allen said, "Williams was very talkative, enthusiastic and I was quiet. I think Williams took it as I was not interested in playing. That irritated me. I was always a fierce competitor."

Allen enjoyed two outlets for his dissatisfaction with Williams, winning and coach Nellie Fox. Allen said, "I didn't enjoy Williams, but as long as the team was winning, I didn't care. I'd talk to Nellie Fox a lot. I did blow up now and then. He'd calm me down. I knew Nellie and respected him. We hit it off well, but he couldn't explain to me why Williams did those things."

If victories and Fox helped him cope with Williams, Allen faced another obstacle – constant pain – alone. Few teammates realized Allen played baseball with one good knee.

On June 13, 1964, at RFK Stadium, Allen, then with the Twins, started to turn a double play. He explained, "Don Zimmer hit me with the cross-body block while my foot was on the bag." Zimmer and Allen collided as Allen's throw sailed over first baseman Bob Allison's head. Allen crumpled to the ground. "My knee collapsed. I lost my anterior cruciate ligament (ACL) and my medial collateral ligament," he said.

His left knee a twisted mess, Allen's teammates carried him off the field. Senators' team physician, Dr. George Resta, an orthopedic surgeon, examined Allen's knee and wanted to operate immediately. Twins' owner Calvin Griffith, a man who one former player said "tossed around nickels like they were lead weights" preferred to delay the decision until the Twins' team doctor, a general practitioner, examined Allen. Griffith's man reached a different conclusion than Dr. Resta. He recommended eight weeks of rest and a week or two of rehabilitation.

With little choice, Allen followed his team doctor's advice. He returned to action, but his knee gave way every time he tried to turn a double play. Griffith still refused to permit surgery.

96

Desperate, Allen sought other doctors for help. "On my own, I went to see the team doctor with the Minnesota Vikings on the sly, but he couldn't help me." Allen returned to the Twins' doctor. He told Allen the best orthopedic surgeon in the country, Dr. Don H. O'Donoghue, worked for the Department of Orthopedic Surgery at St. Anthony's Hospital in Oklahoma City.

O'Donoghue knew more about the repair of knee injuries than anyone else in the country. In July 1973, he published an article, "Reconstruction for Medial Instability of the Knee, Technique and Results in Sixty Cases" for the *Journal of Bone and Joint Surgery*. From 1960 to 1970, O'Donoghue performed 335 knee ligament operations at St. Anthony's, including the repair of Chicago Bears' middle linebacker Dick Butkus's wrecked knee.

Against Griffith's wishes, and with his own money, Allen traveled to Oklahoma to see O'Donoghue. The doctor examined Allen and recommended immediate surgery.

O'Donoghue reconstructed Allen's left knee using a technique his journal article termed a "salvage procedure" and a "last chance." If successful, Allen faced a long recovery before he could perform everyday activities such as jogging and climbing stairs. For the week following the procedure, he lacked feeling in his leg.

The doctor's article read, "If reconstruction is to be successful, the patient must be healthy, well-motivated, and able and willing to carry out an extensive rehabilitation program." O'Donoghue told Allen his knee needed three years to recover its full strength. He gave Allen a 50-50 chance of playing a recreational sport like golf or bowling and no chance of returning to major league baseball.

Allen refused to accept the doctor's dim assessment. He began a torturous, daily exercise program to restore the knee. He dreamed of once again taking his sweet left-handed swing and driving a pitch out of the ballpark and making a graceful pirouette to complete a double play.

His knee required constant attention. Allen said, "It took a lot of hard work behind the scenes. Only the trainer knew. I had to work out in the off-season. I had to work with weights. I worked every day like that to be able to play. I was just determined to play again even though my knee still hurt and wasn't stable."

In 1966, Allen arrived in the Twins' spring training camp, ready to go. Griffith had a thank you gift waiting – a salary cut from $12,000 to $10,000 per year. An incensed Allen said, "I was bitter at baseball for awhile. That's when all the problems started. I learned to fight for myself. I knew I had to fight back in baseball to survive. That's why I became the Twins' player representative. Once you become the player rep, you knew you would get traded."

Allen played 101 games for the Twins in 1966, but the club wearied of his complaints and advocacy for his fellow players. In the off-season, Minnesota traded Allen and Camilo Pascual to the Senators for pitcher Ron Kline.

The hard-working second baseman remained with the Senators for five seasons, through 1971. He played with constant pain in his knee and regular fights with Williams over playing time. Allen felt Williams left him chafing on the bench far too often. "It drove me crazy. I didn't know what my role was," he said.

In 1969, despite his troubles with Williams, Allen turned in his best performance since his rookie season (1962). He hit nine home runs, walked 50 times in 365 at-bats, and managed to steal five bases, a career high. He finished the year with a .247 batting average (.726 OPS).

Allen's tense relationship with Williams worsened over the next two seasons. He attempted to annoy the Senators into trading him. Allen said, "I started saying a few things in D.C. to upset people, because I wanted out. I tried and tried to get out, but they wouldn't trade me."

His teammates persuaded him to ask Williams to relax his ironclad rule against playing golf during the season, including off days. The inflexible manager fined violators $1000 for setting foot on the links.

Allen recalled, "They told me, 'Bernie, you're the player rep, go talk to Ted.'

"I didn't want to run in there, but I did it."

Allen entered Williams' office and made the request. Williams said, "You shouldn't be playing, it hurts your swing."

Allen replied, "Ted, it won't hurt me. I swing left-handed, but I play golf right-handed."

"What would you do a stupid thing like that for?" Williams replied.

Allen answered, "I don't want to ruin my golf swing."

A dumbfounded Williams stared at Allen in silence. The loose-tongued ballplayer left the room with a smile, but Williams had the last laugh. The ban on golf stood.

When Denny McLain arrived in Washington in 1971, Allen joined the incorrigible pitcher's mutinous clubhouse clique, the Underminers, dedicated to driving Williams batty. McLain enjoyed sneaking off to golf courses in every American League town, with Allen as his regular accomplice.

Allen fondly recalled one incident, "Denny knew all the golf pros in the U.S.," he said.

"One day [McLain] told me, 'C'mon Bernie, we're playing golf this morning at eight."

Allen continued, "Williams' coaches would try to catch us. It was like cops and robbers. We walked through the [hotel] lobby and Joe Camacho and George Susce were sitting there. They saw us get in a cab. They got in the next cab and followed us.

"McLain told the driver to take us to some place in downtown Kansas City. We got out, walked through a building and into a cab on the other side. We got away and called a bunch of golf courses until we found one where we could get a tee time.

"Camacho and Susce ran around to every course and asked if Bernie Allen and Denny McLain were playing there. The golf pro always said he didn't know anyone with those names. Then, Denny would give them tickets to the game."

Allen remained with the Senators through their final season in Washington. He finally got his wish in December 1971. The Senators traded Allen to the New York Yankees. He said, "My manager [in New York], Ralph Houk, told me, 'Bernie, you must have really pissed off Ted. We tried for years to deal for you, but he wouldn't talk to us.'"

Thirty-three-years-old, his aching knee slowing him down more every day, Allen struggled to give anything of value to the Yankees. In 1972, thanks to Yankee Stadium's short right field porch, he hit nine homers and nine doubles, but drove in a paltry 21 runs. His batting average plummeted to .227 (.687 OPS). He hung on for one more season, splitting a handful of games between the Yankees and Montreal Expos. Allen played his last game for Montreal on September 19, 1973 at Chicago's Wrigley Field.

After baseball, Allen co-owned a sporting goods store, sold industrial ceramics, and did part-time color commentary for the Indianapolis Indians, Cleveland's AAA affiliate. He also had a brief stint as a part-time minor league instructor for the Montreal Expos. Now retired, he enjoys the company of his wife and 12 grandchildren. He still sneaks off – from his wife rather than his manager – to play golf every chance he gets.

In his 12-year major league career, Allen most enjoyed playing for Washington, despite all the run-ins with Williams. Of the many memories, he most enjoyed the time he left an entire stadium laughing. On a cold April evening, the Senators played the Baltimore Orioles at RFK Stadium. A light mist fell, making the infield slick.

Allen used a special shoe to protect his bum knee. He said, "After I got injured, I started wearing an Adidas® shoe with blunt spikes, like a golf shoe. I had to get special permission from the league to wear it. My knee was not strong enough to support regular spikes."

When Baltimore pitcher, Tom Phoebus, hit a slow bouncing ball over the pitcher's mound, the blunt spikes betrayed him. Allen recalled, "I went to my right to get the ball, planted my feet, and my [left] foot slid from under me. I flipped over, landed on my head, bounced twice, and rolled over. I was really seeing stars. Brinkman came over to me laughing and said, 'OK, Bernie, what do you do for an encore?'

"I said, 'Eddie, lift up second base so I can crawl underneath it.'

"I couldn't see the dugout, but later everyone told me they grabbed towels to put over their faces so they could laugh without Ted seeing them. One guy said it looked like someone sneaked up behind me and tied my shoelaces together. Nellie Fox told me, when we were alone and out of earshot of Ted, that in 26 years it was by far the funniest play he'd ever seen in baseball.

Orioles' radio broadcaster, Chuck Thompson said, "Folks, that was funny. Bernie Allen might not have thought it was funny, but it was."

"The next day at the park, a kid asked me for an autograph. He said, 'Mr. Allen, I loved your trick play last night.' I wanted to say to him, 'Shut up, you little brat.'"

Comedy and tragedy alike, Allen cherished his years in baseball. He said, "I was told I would never play again and I played nine more years. I got to do something most people dream about. And I loved it. I was one of the lucky ones who got to compete. I had more luck than most – except for my knee. I wish I knew what I could do if I hadn't got hurt."

The Senators struggled in the mid-June contests that followed the Allen-led victory over the California Angels. Washington lost four consecutive games to fall to 31-35. The home stand ended in failure, two wins and six losses. Dick Bosman's return from his arm injury provided the only morsel of good news.

Short worried the Senator's upcoming schedule might break them and end the city's budding interest in his franchise. His team played 16 of the next 20 games on the road against Detroit, Baltimore, Cleveland and Boston. Summer training camp for Lombardi's Redskins loomed one month away.

In his RFK office, Williams sat in deep thought. The trading deadline passed with swinger Short again sitting idle. After the deadline, the club acquired veteran outfielder Arthur Lee Maye from Cleveland, but what difference could a 34-year-old well past his prime make?

The road trip began in Detroit on June 20. On the last day of spring, the weather turned wintry in Detroit. Fans and players huddled in blankets to battle the biting wind and frigid night air. The Senators played with grit and determination. Knowles threw $3^{1/3}$ innings of shutout relief. Ken McMullen broke up a potentially inning ending double play in the 10th, enabling the go-ahead run to score. Brant Alyea followed with a three-run blast. Washington earned a hard fought victory, 7-2.

The Senators won three of four games in Detroit. At their next stop, Baltimore, the Senators dropped the series' first match, 5-3. On June 23, 1969, Washington's record stood at 34-37, tied for fourth place with the Yankees.

The next day at Baltimore's Memorial Stadium, the Senators suffered their most teeth-gritting loss since the May 10, 16-13 implosion in Seattle. The stinging defeat tested Williams and his men's mettle. The season had reached its turning point.

It was all an umpire's fault.

Barry Moore, Autograph Day, July 12, 1969
Private Collection of Mark Hornbaker (Used with Permission)

Casey Cox
Art by Ronnie Joyner (Used with Permission)

Bernie Allen, Autograph Day, July 12, 1969
Private Collection of Mark Hornbaker (Used with Permission)

10: Del Unser: Handsome Young Oriole Slayer

"You're going to hit some home runs someday."

-Ted Williams to Del Unser, Centerfielder, Washington Senators, during 1969 spring training

Ted Williams looked into the hazy evening sky and held his breath. In the bottom of the 11th inning, score tied 3-3, he watched as Frank Robinson's fly ball rocketed deep into the Baltimore night. As the ball flew toward the Memorial Stadium bleachers, Williams followed the majestic blast as it sailed to the foul side of the left field foul pole this humid summer evening in Charm City, June 24, 1969. Williams exhaled. If pitcher Jim Shellenback could retire Robinson, the Senators still had a chance to win.

As he drew his next breath, Williams heard the crowd roar. The flabbergasted Senators' saw a flock of celebrating Orioles as three Birds circled the bases to complete a 6-3 victory. Seconds earlier, Williams saw third base umpire Hank Soar start to lift both arms to signal "foul ball." While Williams looked away, Soar changed his mind.

Enraged, Williams raced from the dugout to confront the indecisive arbiter in a foot-stomping, dirt-kicking, arm-waving, hat-throwing tirade. Unmoved, Soar stood by his call. The game over, the umpires retreated to their clubhouse, leaving a still livid Williams alone.

With no one left to berate, Williams trudged off the field. On his way to the visitors' locker room, Williams rued the squandered opportunities to defeat the first place Orioles. In the 7th inning, the Senators had a runner on third base with one out, but could not score. They put runners on first and third with no one out in the 9th and one out in the 11th, but came up empty. With each failure, Williams' blood pressure notched higher. His players seethed in the visitors' clubhouse, cursing their ill fortune, the blind umpires and the annoying writers poised to make them re-live a game they wanted to forget.

The jarring defeat dropped the Senators record to 34-38. Their season again teetered on a precipice. The next evening, June 25, the Senators fumed. In batting practice they chanted "fair ball, fair ball" anytime a Washington hitter smashed a long fly ball near the left and right field foul poles.

Once the game began, the Senators unleashed their wrath on Orioles' starting pitcher Mike Cuellar. After 2 ½ innings, the Senators led 6-1, driving Cuellar from the game. Baltimore responded with two runs in the bottom of the 3rd against Washington starter Joe Coleman. By the end of the 5th inning, the Orioles had tied the game, 6-6. With a bullpen tired from extra work the night before, Williams reluctantly replaced Coleman with Humphreys.

The Senators needed a hero to avoid another heartbreaking loss to their northern neighbors. He was a handsome, brown-haired, blue-eyed young man who vanquished foes with his bat, arm, legs and glove. The Senators needed Del Unser, their smooth left-handed hitting centerfielder.

As the Baltimore fans celebrated, expecting victory, Unser sat in the Washington dugout with his dejected teammates. With the left-handed Cuellar on the mound, Williams, a proponent of platoons, started reserve Sam Bowens, a right-handed batter, in center field.

In the 6th inning, with right hander Jim Hardin pitching for Baltimore, Williams sent Unser up to pinch-hit for Bowens. Anxious, Unser swung at Hardin's first good pitch and flew out. But the Senators regained the lead, 7-6, on a Paul Casanova RBI ground out.

Unser came to bat again in the 7th inning against a new Baltimore pitcher, Dave Leonhard, with two Senators on base and two out. The crowd – and both teams – sensed the game had reached its pivotal moment. If Unser failed, a Baltimore comeback win likely followed.

A calm, relaxed Unser watched a few of Leonhard's pitches, gauging their speed and break. He remembered Williams' hitting seminars in the spring. His manager asked one question over and over – "What are you going to look for next pitch?"

He recalled his baseball pedigree. Delbert Bernard Unser, born December 9, 1944 in Decatur, Illinois, grew up in a baseball family. His father, Al Unser, played four seasons in the big leagues (1942-45) for the Detroit Tigers and Cincinnati Reds. Unser said, "I [was] raised in baseball. I was exposed to an awful lot that most kids weren't. Like my Mom putting four or five kids in a one-seat car and driving it from Illinois to California by herself to go join my Dad, who was playing with the Hollywood Stars at the time. This is the way we were raised, so it wasn't any big deal to me." With Del Unser's background, so called pressure situations like the one he faced in Baltimore, left him unfazed.

Unser also faced Leonhard with a lighter bat and a renewed approach to hitting, thanks to Williams. When Unser joined the Senators in 1968 he used a 36 inch, 36 ounce war club. He applied the teachings he learned from Harry "The Hat" Walker in the Senators' instructional league – bunt, slap the ball to left field, and run like the wind to beat out grounders. Williams, who engaged Walker, the 1969 Houston Astros' manager, in a series of spring training debates on hitting, scoffed at his colleague's philosophy. Williams believed Walker's way ignored the benefits of walks and power. He told Unser, "You've got a good stroke to left field and I don't want you to lose it, but you're going to hit some home runs someday. You've got enough power to pull the ball once in awhile when you get your situation and your pitch." With a bat light enough to whip through the strike zone, Unser pulled inside pitches to right field and the hits came in bunches. Unser said, "There were a lot of cheap hits, because the infielders were misplaying me for about a month or two. For a long time I got a lot of hits to right-center. Then word gets around," he said.

By the time he faced his crucial at-bat in Baltimore, Unser had raised his batting average from .234 on May 1 to .268. Ahead in the count against Leonhard, Unser correctly guessed the Baltimore pitcher would try to jam him with an inside fastball. The Senators' fleet young outfielder took a lightning-quick, compact swing. The bat's sweet spot met the ball dead-center. The screaming line drive whizzed past Robinson and carried over the right field wall for a game-changing three-run homer, just the fourth of Unser's career. A gaggle of happy and relieved teammates greeted the Senators' latest hero at home plate.

After Unser's blast, the Orioles scored two more runs, but Darold Knowles escaped 8th and 9th inning jams to save Humphreys second win of 1969. Washington defeated Baltimore, 11-8, a satisfying victory over a tough foe that erased the previous night's bitter taste.

In the clubhouse after the game, Unser found his teammates in high spirits. A 24-year old in his sophomore season, Unser joked and laughed with his more senior teammates like Ken McMullen, Ed Brinkman and Frank Howard, all established veterans. His fellow Senators set a tone of joyful professionalism, an atmosphere that let Unser loosen up and play his best baseball day after day. Unser enjoyed his mates' banter. He said, "You get a bunch of boys together in one room and you know you're going to get a little mischief. It was just like a high school locker room, guys ragging on guys, tons of guys teasing people. Bus trips from the ballpark to the airport were special. There was always something going around. Of course, if Frank Howard said two words, they were all wrong and everybody would bury him for it, especially Eddie Brinkman.

"It was like some of the winning teams I played on late in my career. They knew how to divorce themselves from the game and have fun."

During games, the Senators prided themselves on playing sound, hustling baseball. "They were serious on the field. There was so much pride and respect for the game. You just didn't go out and mess up," he recalled.

Unser took to heart the lessons he learned from his veteran teammates. A rookie of the year candidate in 1968, he performed even better in 1969, with a .286 batting average, a 56-point improvement over his 1968 mark. He matured into one of the Senators' most versatile offensive weapons to complement his fine play in the field. By 1969, opposing teams knew not to test the strong left arm that led American League outfielders in assists and double plays in 1968. Senators' pitchers appreciated Unser's ability to stop runners in their tracks and chase down fly balls in the gaps, especially with the slow-footed Howard in left field.

Unser recalled, "They always used to tease him that if the ball was 10 feet to his left he'd yell 'Del! Del! Del!' [It wasn't] quite that bad. He always hit his cutoff man. He hustled. He was all about giving his best on the baseball field."

A 6'1", 180-pound centerfielder, Unser remembered the one time he failed to respect Howard's booming voice. He said, "My first spring training in Pompano Beach one afternoon somebody hit a ball to the gap in left center. I'm going to impress them, show them I can fly. Well, the wind is blowing the wrong way. I don't hear Frank Howard call 'I got it.' I hit him running full speed and it was just like Sylvester from the cartoon strip hitting a wall. I mean I just slid down his left side. From then on, when I got over in that neighborhood, I was going to be darn careful."

After the 1971 season, the Senators dealt Unser to Cleveland. While he hated leaving his Washington teammates, he felt little love for sweltering RFK Stadium. He said, "The humidity is incredibly thick. We had some games where some of our pitchers didn't get the ball down and it's gap to gap to gap. You need oxygen out there in the outfield."

Unser spent his next seven seasons playing for a collection of mediocre clubs in Cleveland, Philadelphia, New York, and Montreal. The constant losing shrouded his talent in obscurity. By the time he played for the Expos (1977-78), Unser had reached the twilight of his career. The part-time role he played in Montreal frustrated him. "I played almost no time because they had [Warren] Cromartie, [Andre] Dawson and [Ellis] Valentine coming up. I was pinch-hitting a lot and I was terrible at it." He managed three hits in 38 at-bats as a pinch-hitter in 1978. For the entire season, he hit just .196.

Unser termed his time in Montreal an "agonizing purgatory. I wasn't playing every day. I was probably feeling sorry for myself." With the 1979 season about to begin, the Expos had little use for a 34-year old outfielder who could barely hit his weight.

Unser became a free agent and took up racquetball to stay in shape. While playing in a tournament in Las Vegas, he called Philadelphia's General Manager Paul Owens seeking a job as a reserve left-handed hitting outfielder and first baseman. Owens jumped at Unser's offer. He told Unser, "You can't get in shape for baseball playing racquetball. Get your ass down here."

Unser said, "I flew back to my home in California that night, packed up, and took a red-eye [to the Phillies' spring training camp in Clearwater, Fla.]. He saw me the next day and couldn't believe it. I said to him, 'When you need a job you don't waste any time.'"

Unser landed a job as a back-up on the Phillies' 1979 squad. He played in 95 games and made 54 appearances as a pinch hitter, hitting .304 with three consecutive pinch-hit home runs, tying Lee Lacy, who set the a major league record the previous season. Unser had molded himself into a reliable pinch hitter through hard work and a changed attitude. He said, "You learn by just banging your head against the wall and saying – 'You know, this isn't the way to approach it.'"

Unser renewed ties with Philadelphia hitting coach Billy DeMars. DeMars helped him adjust–his swing, making Unser a consistent hitter again. Unser said, "To me Billy is one of the best hitting coaches of all-time." Their hard work paid off in the 1980 post-season.

In the 8th inning of the fifth and final game of the National League Championship Series, Unser's Phillies trailed Houston 5-4 with runners on the corners and two out. With pitcher Ron Reed due up, Philadelphia manager Dallas Green called on Unser. Four outs from a trip to the World Series, the Astrodome crowd buzzed.

Unser prepared the entire series for such a moment. When the club arrived in Houston, he badgered DeMars until he agreed to enter the Astrodome's dark, dingy, rodent-infested tunnel to help Unser practice hitting. "Houston had a horrible tunnel. You wouldn't want to go down there," Unser said. He told DeMars, "I don't feel right. If I get in here I don't want to leave any stone unturned."

With the game in the balance, Unser's preparation paid off. He lined a game-tying RBI single to right field. He said, "I really believe that's one of the reasons why I got a hit."

The Phillies added two more runs, but the Astros tied the game 7-7 in their half of the 8th inning. Unser came to bat again in the 10th and pulled a double down the right field line. He scored the series-clinching run on Garry Maddox's two-out double. For the first time in 30 years, the Phillies reached the World Series.

In the Fall Classic against the Kansas City Royals, Unser contributed a clutch pinch-hit in Game 2 and a 9th inning, game-tying pinch-hit double in Game 5. He eventually scored the winning run on Manny Trillo's infield single. The Phillies won their first-ever championship two days later in Veterans Stadium. To this day, the name Del Unser brings smiles to Philadelphia baseball fans. "Those fans are great in Philly, I don't care what anybody says," Unser noted. "If you ever win a World Series they never forget you."

Unser relished the 1980 season, the year he at last played for a champion. He said, "It was terribly exciting to be a part of the many reasons why we won. You just take that to the grave with you. It's that special and I'm very thankful for it."

The Phillies retained Unser for two more years, but he played sparingly. In June 1982, the Phillies gave Unser his unconditional release. After his playing career, Unser coached and scouted for several teams, finally settling in with the Phillies for more than 20 seasons. He remained in the Philadelphia organization until his retirement in October 2017. He served as hitting coach, farm director, and scout. He takes great satisfaction in his 40-year tenure with the Phillies' organization, including a World Series title in 2008.

Unser is equally proud of the four seasons he played in Washington. He said, "We really prided ourselves in how we played the game. We played it right. We always battled and never quit. I respect that about that team a lot. When you look at the individuals on that team, quite a few of them were big-time winners in life."

In a happy confluence for Unser, the first game the new Washington Nationals played took place in Philadelphia on April 4, 2005, the Phillies home opener. To throw out the ceremonial first pitch, the Phillies searched for the best person to honor baseball's return to the nation's capital and to celebrate the 25th anniversary of Philadelphia's 1980 World Series championship. They sought a person who performed heroic deeds on the baseball field in both cities, a winner in baseball and in life. The Phillies chose Del Unser. Baseball fans in Philadelphia and Washington alike agree they made a perfect choice.

Unser's heroics in Baltimore on June 25 inspired the Senators to play winning baseball again. In a four-game home series against Boston, the Senators won the last three, two in thrilling fashion. On June 28, Washington won 4-3 on McMullen's lead-off home run in the bottom of the 10th inning. The following day, in the first game of a doubleheader at sweltering RFK Stadium, the gritty club overcame 100 degree temperatures and a 4-2 Red Sox' lead in the 9th inning. Ed Brinkman scored the winning run on a dash home from second base after Boston's catcher made a wild throw attempting to complete an inning-ending double play. A boisterous crowd of 28,631, hailed the hustling shortstop and his never-say-die teammates. The inspired Senators romped in the nightcap, 11-4.

The 38-39 Senators traveled to Cleveland and won the first three games of the four-game series. On July 2, the club's record read 41-39, the first time a Washington team enjoyed an above .500 record in July since 1960. A loss to Cleveland in the series' finale and a split of consecutive road doubleheaders with the Red Sox on July 4 and 5 placed the Senators' record at 43-42.

With a single game left on the 20-game stretch that many, including owner Bob Short, thought might ruin their season, the Senators triumphed in 12 of 19 games. Short said, "Before the last road trip, I could envision us finishing in last place, and that could have knocked me out of baseball. People were ready to say Williams was a flash in the pan."

Eight games in the previous five days, however, left Williams with an exhausted pitching staff. They desperately needed a complete game from their best pitcher. Four months earlier, no one dreamed that an unproven young right-hander named Dick Bosman would be the best man for the job.

Del Unser
(National Baseball Hall of Fame Library, Cooperstown, NY)

11: Dick Bosman: Out of Nowhere

*"...having the Presidential Opener because you pitched for Washington;
that meant you were the main man."*

-Dick Bosman, Pitcher, Washington Senators

At the beginning of the 1969 season, Dick Bosman merited so little regard
that the Senators' opening day program listed him as "Dave" Bosman. He
recalled, "I was just a young kid scuffling to make it. I didn't have a very
good year the year before. I was 2-9. We weren't a good club and I didn't
pitch well either."

In spring training, Bosman struggled to make the team. He worried
Williams' low opinion of pitchers and unfamiliarity with the Senators'
staff might hurt his chances. Bosman said, "It almost makes it a tougher
job to make a club, because you got a guy that doesn't know you at all.
Sometimes that works for you, sometimes it doesn't. In this case it did,
because I worked hard. I was certainly eager to learn, especially from a
Hall of Fame guy."

Williams watched Bosman get hit hard in early spring training
games. The manager told his struggling young pitcher, "You've got a
chance to be pretty good, but you've got to learn to use what you've got."

Bosman replied, "When do we start?"

He learned Williams' lessons well enough to win a roster spot as a
long reliever and spot starter, the last man chosen for the Washington
pitching staff. Bosman believes the time he spent with Williams in the
spring helped form him into a successful, cerebral pitcher. He said, "Most
of what I know about the mental part of pitching, the cat and mouse game,
so to speak, between the pitcher and the hitter, is what I've learned from
Ted."

Washington teammate Lee Maye agreed. He said, "Ted got Dick
Bosman to believe he was a great pitcher. He listened to everything Ted
told him."

Bosman burst into the Washington spotlight the evening of May 2
when he pitched a one-hitter against the Cleveland Indians in front of an
amazed home crowd. Sid Hudson said of Bosman's shutout win, "A
masterpiece. A man can't pitch much better than that."

The groundbreaking game filled Bosman with confidence. He
said, "That game really defined what the year was going to be about. It
was like, 'Shoot, I can do this. I can do it more than once in awhile.'

That is how pitchers are born. They gain confidence from having success."

Bosman faced a more difficult test on July 6, a warm Sunday afternoon in Boston. The Senators' budding ace usually pitched every five days, but, with four doubleheaders in the last week, Williams needed Bosman to pitch on three days rest against the powerful Red Sox line-up, stocked with polysyllabic power hitters like Yastrzemski, Petrocelli, and Conigliaro.

Early in the game, Bosman dominated Boston's hitters. His fastball, slider and sinker hit Paul Casanova's mitt with pinpoint accuracy. Boston's sluggers pounded easy ground balls to Washington's sure-handed infielders. Bosman threw what hitters called a heavy ball, nearly impossible to hit in the air when the ball broke low in the strike zone. After six innings, the Red Sox had managed two hits. A long string of zeros appeared after the bright white-lettered "BOS" on Fenway Park's hand-operated scoreboard.

Entering the 8th inning, the Senators enjoyed a comfortable 5-0 lead. Bosman, a weak hitter, chipped in with an RBI single.

With a five-run lead, Bosman breezed through the 8th inning and retired Boston's first two batters in the ninth. One out from a shutout, he started to falter, his arm and body's strength depleted. Yastrzemski, Petrocelli, and Reggie Smith singled to load the bases. Conigliaro batted next. Bosman peered toward the Senators' empty bullpen, and then into the silent, still Washington dugout.

Bosman knew he must finish the game. He wiped sweat from his brow, grabbed the rosin bag to dry his fingers, and summoned the perseverance that enabled him to make the opening day roster. He called on the self-confidence he gained from his May gem against Cleveland. Bosman remembered, "I had Conigliaro with two strikes and I threw him a sidearm curve ball. He hit a little check swing ground ball up the first base line that I ended up having to cover the bag on. It was a tough, bang, bang play at first base to get him."

Bosman took Frank Howard's throw and stepped on the bag just ahead of Conigliaro's foot. The umpire bellowed, "Out!" and the Senators celebrated another victory, their 44th of the season and 13th in the last 20 games. An exhausted but elated team sang the Nasty Nats song, showered, packed and boarded a bus bound for Logan Airport and a jet ride home. The Senators played the next 11 games in Washington.

In an extended stretch of road games expected to break them, the Senators played thrilling baseball. They won four of the 13 victories in their final at-bat and had the winning run at the plate in three of the defeats. The drama enthralled the Senators' fans. When the team's airplane landed at National Airport, more than 1,700 fans roared in joy to welcome them home. They hailed their new heroes' arrival with handmade signs that read "Welcome Home, Team." They chanted "Hondo, Hondo, Hondo" and begged for autographs. One elderly fan stated, "It's the first time I've been really excited about them since the days of Walter Johnson and Joe Cronin."

After years of futility, baseball fever gripped the nation's capital. Fans throughout the Washington Metro area cheered the Senators. Del Unser recalled the evening he and his wife Dale, together with several teammates and their wives, attended the musical "Damn Yankees" at Burn Brae dinner theatre in Silver Spring, Maryland. At intermission, the stage manager announced the presence of some real Washington Senators in the audience. The patrons responded with a standing ovation.

While he signed autographs for admiring fans on his way out of the airport, Bosman's thoughts returned to his virtuoso performance in Boston. The game calmed his fears about the health of his arm. Six weeks earlier, Bosman's shoulder ached. He pitched six strong innings in a victory over the White Sox, but his shoulder felt miserable. Bosman recalled, "[We] came back on the red eye and we had off on Monday. I got up in the morning and told my wife Pam, 'there's something wrong here.'"

Bosman met with trainer Tom McKenna and team doctor George Resta. He recalled, "The doc came in and took some x-rays. He looked at them and said, 'It isn't anything real serious, but you've got a deltoid muscle here that's strained pretty good. I'm going to shoot you up with some cortisone and put you on the disabled list.'"

The injury frightened Bosman. He knew he needed a complete season to establish himself as a bona fide major league pitcher. He said, "It was the first time I'd ever gone on any disabled list. I sat around on that DL for 30 days and did a bunch of rehab and heat packs and a lot of deep massage. I started throwing again and it still hurt.

"You have a lot of doubt. Here you are coming back after your arm is hurt. Your mind plays tricks on you. I mean, guys blow out here and there and you think, shoot, I could be next."

A wary Bosman told Resta of his lingering pain. The doctor assured the concerned pitcher that the soreness came from minor scar tissue in his healing shoulder and was normal. He advised Bosman to pitch through the pain. He began with gentle side sessions and pre-game batting practice. Hudson and Williams watched and decided their young pitcher needed more intense rehabilitation before rejoining the big league club.

The Senators sent Bosman to their AAA team in Buffalo for 10 days. Bosman reluctantly agreed to the assignment. He said, "It was

115

rough. You were in the old Rock Pile, a bad ballpark. It was certainly a bad club."

Bosman pitched one game for Buffalo. His arm felt strong and he wanted out of the dilapidated ballpark and depressed city. "I left the Buffalo club right after the game," Bosman said. "Hector Lopez was managing the club. He said, 'Where are you going?'

"I said, 'I'm getting out of here. I'm going back to Washington.' I pretty much held them to their word, because you got everything to lose and nothing to gain. I knew I was ok, so I recalled myself."

Bosman joined the Senators again on June 17 after a 29-day stay on the disabled list. That night, Bosman pitched a flawless, pain-free inning of mop-up relief in a Senators' loss to Baltimore. The successful outing erased Bosman's fears. He said, "I remember striking out Don Buford with a back door slider. It was a nasty, sharp slider. I thought to myself right there, 'I'm ok, I'm ok.'"

Bosman returned to the Senators' starting rotation on June 22. He missed a start on July 20 when his shoulder soreness returned, but the three-day All-Star break gave him enough rest to return to full strength.

When August arrived, Bosman became invincible. The Senators won 12 of his last 13 starts. He went 8-0, including a two-hitter to defeat the New York Yankees' ace and Senators' nemesis Mel Stottlemyre. In that game, Bosman came within five outs of a no-hitter.

After victory, writers and cameras surrounded Bosman's locker. No one called him Dave. Bosman said, "Writers asked me, because it was my first good season and I was just kind of kicking around before that, 'How are you doing this?'

"My only comment at the time was, 'Don't wake me up.' Because I didn't know how I was doing it, other than I knew my concentration was very, very keen every time I went out there. In the past, I wasn't throwing the right pitch at the right time. Now, I knew what I wanted to do and I was getting it done."

Bosman completed his out-of-nowhere stellar season with a 14-5 record. The 14 wins doubled his previous career total. His ERA, 2.19, bested Palmer (2.34) and Mike Cuellar (2.38) for the American League title. "It was my breakout year as a pitcher," Bosman said.

During the 1969 season, Bosman, a detailed note-taker, wrote down the insights he learned during his dream season. He captured in well-organized notebooks information on opposing hitters, his pre-game routine, and his pitching patterns. As he wrote, he recalled the words his father spoke to him when he first left Kenosha, Wisconsin to begin his professional career.

116

"He would always say, 'Use your head. Be smart,' Bosman said. "As things started to come together in '69, [his words] were beginning to take on a new meaning. My Dad was always my biggest booster and my first coach. His belief in me was something that he always reinforced," Bosman said.

When the 1970 season began, Bosman used spring training to study his notebooks and hone his game, not scuffle to make the club. Williams dubbed Bosman his number one pitcher, the man entrusted to start the traditional Presidential Opener. Pitching with an aching hamstring, Bosman walked nine batters in a nightmarish losing effort against the Detroit Tigers. He longed for another opportunity.

He got his chance the next season. "I wanted the ball," Bosman said. "The Presidential Opener, from the time I can remember, was huge. Being the opening day starter anywhere was big, but having the Presidential Opener because you pitched for Washington, that meant you were the main man."

On the strength of his 16-win season in 1970, Williams again named Bosman the opening day starter in 1971. Bosman faced the Oakland Athletics and their 21-year old superstar, Vida Blue. On that glorious spring day in Washington, the Senators' final opener, before 45,061 thrilled fans, Bosman stole the spotlight from Oakland's young upstart. He pitched a complete game shutout, while the Senators drove Blue to the showers in the 2nd inning. Bosman's 8-0 victory filled Washington with joy. Young boys throughout the region replayed the game for weeks in their back yards, taking turns being Dick Bosman.

Bosman remained with the club when it moved to Texas. He turned in a respectable 8-10 season in 1972 for the awful Rangers, losers of 100 games. In May 1973, the rebuilding franchise traded Bosman to the Cleveland Indians. Bosman's career neared its end, but a good season and one unforgettable outing remained in his aging right arm.

In Cleveland Stadium, the infamous Mistake by the Lake, on July 19, 1974, Bosman pitched a no-hitter against the Oakland A's, a baseball dynasty poised to win its third consecutive World Series. Bosman's own error ruined an otherwise perfect game. The A's remembered Bosman's masterpiece. In May 1975, Oakland traded former all-star John "Blue Moon" Odom to the Indians in exchange for Bosman and Jim Perry.

Bosman pitched excellent baseball for the A's and eccentric owner Charles O. Finley. He won 11 games, with a 3.52 ERA. He helped Oakland grab its fourth straight West Division title. The Boston Red Sox ended the A's three-year championship reign in the 1975 American League Championship Series. Bosman joined Oakland one year too late to pitch in the World Series.

117

The next season, 1976, good hitters began to maul Bosman's best pitches. He made too many early exits from his starting assignments. As the 1977 season dawned, Finley cut the 33-year-old pitcher. The late release left Bosman with little time to make another team's roster. He said, "I felt that I still had some good years in me, but it wasn't to be. I left like most players. You leave kicking and screaming and they take the uniform right off your back."

Bosman settled down in Northern Virginia with his children and his wife, Pam, whom he wed in 1969. "God bless her," Bosman said. "She's a tremendous reason why I am where I am." Eventually, Pam Bosman, watching with a loving spouse's insightful eyes, helped Bosman make a crucial career decision.

In 1977, Bosman met Johnny Koons and began selling cars for the Washington area automobile empire. Koons asked Bosman to coach his sons' Little League team. The man who pitched a no-hitter and started two Presidential Openers stooped to show 10-year-old boys how to throw fastballs and change-ups. He told wide-eyed lads stories about Hondo, the great Teddy Ballgame, and his lesser known Senators compatriots.

Coaching baseball came naturally to Bosman, the studious note taker and analytical pitcher. The boys' enthusiasm rekindled his love for the game. He said, "Johnny Koons gave me a chance to come out and work with the kids. That's how I began my apprenticeship as a coach. Well, those Little League kids grew up. As they grew, we coached them through Babe Ruth League, high school and American Legion ball, and then college. I ended up at Georgetown University coaching young men." All the while, Pam noticed her husband's joy and talent for teaching others.

In the winter of 1986, the Chicago White Sox called Hudson, seeking his recommendation for someone to fill a vacancy on its major league coaching staff. Bosman said, "Sid was the first pitching coach I ever had. When I got traded to Washington in 1965 from San Francisco, he was the roving minor league instructor. Sid came into York, Pennsylvania and that's the first time I met him. He taught me a lot of the physical parts of pitching. How you spin a curve ball. How you make this ball sink. He would catch [me] a lot." The two men developed a lasting friendship. Hudson pictured Bosman, the intense, hard-working young man with all those notebooks. He remembered Bosman's patience, fortitude and attention to detail while the two worked together in the minor leagues and in Washington. Hudson phoned White Sox' General Manager Ken "Hawk" Harrelson and suggested Harrelson's club hire the former Senators' ace. A few days later, Harrelson called and said, "We want you to come back."

118

The offer surprised Bosman. He had already signed a contract to coach baseball at Flint Hill High School. He aspired to build a dynasty much like Stu Vetter's basketball program at the elite Northern Virginia private school. Flint Hill promised to build a new baseball field for Bosman's soon-to-be invincible team.

At a crossroads, Bosman asked the White Sox for three days to ponder the offer. "I didn't aspire to [coaching]. I had been out of the game for nine years. I watched my kids grow up. I wasn't making a ton of money, but we were doing ok," Bosman said.

The evening before his decision, he told Pam, "I don't think I'm going to do this."

Pam looked into her husband eyes and said, "Well, you signed a professional contract to be a baseball player and you ended up playing 11 years, darn near, in the big leagues. Now, you have somebody that wants you to come back and coach and you know you're really a better coach than you ever were a player."

The next day, Bosman called Harrelson and accepted his offer. He coached in Chicago for two seasons. In 1992, Johnny Oates, manager of the Baltimore Orioles, hired Bosman as his pitching coach. In his first crack at the job, Bosman received rave reviews. He tutored a rookie right-hander, and eventual hall of famer Mike Mussina, who became one of the top pitchers in baseball.

When Baltimore fired Oates, Bosman followed him to Texas to serve as the Rangers' pitching coach. He held the job for six seasons (1995–2000). The Rangers' captured A.L. West Division titles in 1996, 1998 and 1999 during Bosman's tenure.

In 2000, the Rangers' pitching collapsed and Texas fired Bosman. Despite the blow to his professional pride, Bosman's passion to teach others remained. He has held a variety of minor league coaching positions, joining the Tampa Bay Rays organization in 2001. From 2008-2018, he served as the minor league coordinator for pitching for the Rays. Bosman announced his retirement at the end of the 2018 season, looking forward to his first summer vacation with Pam and his family in 33 years.

Thanks to his wife's candor, Bosman enjoyed a long, happy association with the game he loves. He taught the Sid Hudson way to throw a curve ball, the Ted Williams rule for confusing a hitter, and the Dick Bosman path to excellence he learned from his dad so many years ago in Kenosha.

In more than 50 years of service to baseball, Bosman played a multitude of roles – struggling young pitcher, staff ace, aging veteran and dedicated coach. Senators' fans who saw him pitch from 1969-71 knew Washington had a fighting chance when Bosman took the mound. His career statistics look mundane – 11 seasons, 82 wins, 85 losses, 3.67 ERA. Yet, during the final seasons the Senators played baseball in Washington, no one pitched better.

When the Washington Nationals played their last game at RFK Stadium on September 23, 2007, the club asked Howard to throw the game's ceremonial first pitch. Hondo demurred. He knew the man who most deserved the honor – the last ace of the Senators, Dick Bosman.

Bosman's July 6 victory in Boston and the warm reception from the adoring fans at National Airport sparked the Senators. Back home in RFK Stadium, the grateful club played its most inspired game yet. Washington defeated Cleveland, 7-2, with a multitude of great performances. Cox relieved Jim Shellenback in the 3rd inning and pitched 6 $^{2/3}$ innings of perfect baseball. Howard hit two home runs, one 486 feet into the outer reaches of the upper deck. Mike Epstein added a round tripper of his own.

Brinkman saved two runs in the 3rd with a diving stop of a Hawk Harrelson's ground ball. Bernie Allen and Unser made outstanding plays in the field. In the delirious locker room following the game, Jim French said, "This is the best game I've ever played in. It had everything – great plays, good execution, great pitching. We all did our part."

Washington split the next six games, two with Cleveland and four with the Yankees, to bring their overall record to 48-45. The last victory, a 10-1 drubbing of New York on July 13 in the second game of a Sunday doubleheader, included a fairytale come true.

The Senators' starting pitcher, Shellenback, married his sweetheart three days earlier in Alexandria, Virginia. Marriage agreed with the Senators' southpaw, acquired from the Pittsburgh Pirates in May. He enjoyed a baseball pedigree, being the nephew of Frank Shellenback, the Splendid Splinter's first professional baseball coach.

As his new bride watched her groom pitch, Shellenback bamboozled Yankee hitters. He pitched around six Yankee hits and three of his teammates' errors, limiting the New Yorkers to a single run. Howard punctuated the victory with a towering home run, his 33rd of the season, a shot into the upper deck in left centerfield. More than 31,000 fans, the Senators' second largest home crowd of the year, joined Mrs. Shellenback in a standing ovation as her husband limped off the field with a complete game victory. With five days to wait before his next start, the newlyweds began a delayed, but blissful honeymoon.

Two years earlier, Shellenback lived a nightmare. He sustained multiple serious injuries in a car accident on September 30, 1967. The accident left Shellenback with a compound fracture in his right leg, a fractured rib, internal injuries, a sprained wrist, facial cuts and a tongue laceration. He returned to baseball after a year-long recovery, but still

120

dragged his right leg as he walked. He lived in constant pain, but learned to ignore it while on the pitcher's mound. The Senators benefited from his determination, but the 25-year-old pitcher developed those character traits at a high cost.

In 1969, Shellenback finished the season with a 4-7 record and 4.04 ERA for the Senators in 30 games, 11 as a starter. Shellenback pitched for the Senators and Rangers until 1974. After 1974, he toiled in the minor leagues before playing his final major league season with the Twins in 1977. Shellenback remained with the Minnesota organization. In 1983, he served as the Twins' pitching coach and then returned to several scouting and minor league assignments. From 2008-2012, his final year in professional baseball, he served as pitching coach for the Appalachian League's Elizabethtown Twins. In 2019, Shellenback was named to his hometown Riverside, California Sport Hall of Fame.

Washington followed Shellenback's fine effort with two victories over Detroit. On July 14, Coleman struck out nine Tigers in a 3-0 victory, his second consecutive shutout. The next evening, with President Nixon in attendance, the Senators defeated the Tigers, 7-3. Nixon praised the Senators' fine effort, taking special pleasure in the home run the light-hitting Cullen smacked down the left field line. A triple play Detroit turned in the 5th inning merited only light applause from the chief executive, an unabashed Senators' fan.

The win raised Washington's record to 50-45. Williams' overachieving team trailed second place Boston by a scant 1 ½ games. Since 1952, a different time in a different world, no Washington baseball team had performed this well so far into the season.

The Senators' resurgence thrilled Washington area baseball fans. They flocked to the ballpark in unprecedented numbers. It seemed possible 900,000 or maybe even one million fans would come and see the Senators. Short took notice. He said, "This team is on the move. The manager is on the move and the fans are coming out. We're going in the right direction."

The Post's William Gildea wrote, "Natsomania is infectious and spreading. The place to catch it is RFK Stadium." Future Washington Baseball Historical Society president and author Jim Hartley found he could no longer buy a general admission ticket and sneak past unsuspecting ushers to his favorite seat in Section 421. He said, "I thought, 'Now wait a minute, I've been here before.' After school let out, everybody caught on. Big crowds became the norm rather than the exception."

For Hartley and his growing band of fellow Senators' aficionados, things were about to get even better.

121

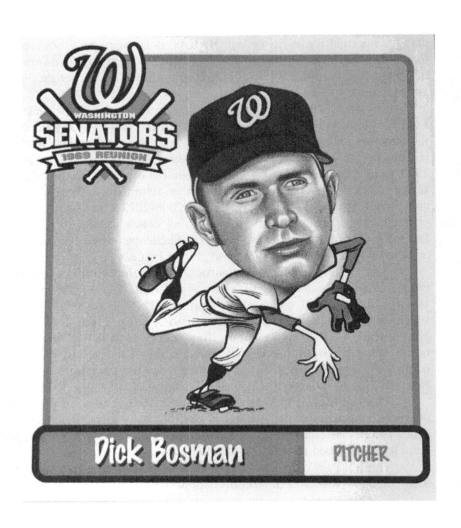

Dick Bosman, A.L. ERA Champion, 1969
Art by Ronnie Joyner (Used with Permission)

12: Stargazing in Washington

"Anytime you get a chance to perform in a premiere event like that in front of your people, Washingtonians, your fans, it's one of the highlights of my career."

-Frank Howard, Outfielder, Washington Senators, on the 1969
All-Star Game, held July 23, 1969 in RFK Stadium

In mid-July, the Senators added more bounty to fans' astonishing cornucopia of baseball pleasures. The club announced the public sale of 20,000 tickets to the All-Star game. The night before the announced 9:00 a.m. sale, fans lined up outside four designated ticket windows, two each at RFK Stadium Gates A and B. The sale offered the chance of a lifetime to see baseball's greatest stars.

The 1969 All-Star game marked the coup de grace of baseball's centennial celebration and the second time in eight seasons that the nation's capital hosted the Mid-Summer Classic. Baseball planned special events to rekindle waning interest in the game. It helped that the national pastime was enjoying an unexpected rebirth in Washington.

Commissioner Kuhn invited every living member of the Hall of Fame, along with several other dignitaries and guests, to attend a gala banquet at the luxurious downtown Sheraton Park Hotel. There, Kuhn planned to announce baseball writers' selection of all-time teams, baseball's greatest player, and the greatest living player. The following afternoon, President Nixon invited 400 baseball icons, including Williams, to the White House for a pre-game formal reception.

While waiting for the ticket windows to open, fans dreamed of game programs full of Hall of Fame members' signatures and a seat at RFK Stadium to view the world's greatest baseball players. Weary men, using precious vacation time while waiting in line, dreamed of seeing, in person, old favorites like Willie Mays, Hank Aaron, Ernie Banks, Roberto Clemente, Harmon Killebrew, Brooks and Frank Robinson, and Bob Gibson as well as new stars Tom Seaver, Reggie Jackson, and Johnny Bench.

The clock struck nine. Ticket sellers opened their windows and prepared for the throng waiting peacefully in the muggy morning air. Suddenly, windows clicked open at eight locations, not the announced four. The crowd broke ranks and the placid scene became a donnybrook.

Frantic fans at the back of the line raced to beat earlier arrivals to the new locations.

Without barricades to mark the lines, Senators' employees to distribute numbers and information, or police to keep order, a near-riot ensued. Fans, fast friends trading stories of Howard's tape-measure home runs, became bitter rivals, pushing and shoving one another to get to the windows first. No one emerged from the Senators' offices to quell the fiasco. Frightened, harried salespeople sold the tickets as fast as they could to customers pressed hard against the booths by the restless mass behind them.

Once the final ticket sold, workers closed and locked the windows and huddled inside, waiting for the crowd to disperse. Poor souls who waited in line for more than six hours went home with nothing, not an apology from Short or any team official. *The Washington Post* called the club's performance "stupid, miserable, incredible and insulting."

On the field, the Senators took their cue from the bumbling front office. They dropped five of their remaining six games for a 51-50 record at the All-Star break. Even with the recent downturn, Washington's record represented considerable improvement. In 1968, the Senators won their 51st game on August 28. The same players worked comparative wonders under Williams' magic touch.

Washington lost the final game before the break in New York, 3-2 in 11 innings. Senators' players forever remembered the contest's enduring image – more than 30,000 New Yorkers rising in silence and then singing "God Bless America" upon hearing the news that the Apollo 11 lunar module, with astronauts Neil Armstrong and Edwin "Buzz" Aldrin safe inside, had landed on the moon. The next morning, July 21, 1969, Armstrong and Aldrin set foot on the lunar surface. At one with the entire country, Washingtonians gaped at the sight of two American astronauts' grainy, ghost-like images walking on the moon. At that moment, any dream seemed possible – racial harmony, an end to the Viet Nam war, the New York Mets in the World Series, and a winning season for the Washington Senators.

A joyful nation looked forward to the 40th All-Star game. American League players, whose votes determined the league's starters, chose Howard as the team's left fielder. Manager Mayo Smith selected Knowles for his pitching staff and Williams as a coach.

The night before the game, baseball's brightest stars entered the Sheraton Park Hotel for the Centennial celebration. A gaggle of photographers snapped rapid-fire photos as 37 tuxedo-wearing Hall of Fame members arrived with their guests, hurrying inside to escape the sticky, steamy Washington night. Kuhn announced the greatest player, Babe Ruth, and the greatest living player, Joe DiMaggio.

Writers selected Williams as the left fielder for the team of greatest living players. Two weeks earlier, at Fenway Park, he received the honor of Greatest Red Sox Player. He delighted the Boston crowd by tipping his cap to acknowledge their affectionate standing ovation. Williams decided to skip the event in Washington, however. He sent his wife Dolores to accept his awards.

Some speculated a piqued Williams decided to snub the posh affair when he learned the news about DiMaggio. Others surmised he preferred to avoid the crowds, the attention and, most of all, the press. His wife offered, "He just doesn't go to these functions. He hasn't changed. It's part of his image." A nattily dressed Williams did attend Nixon's White House reception.

The next afternoon, as workers prepared RFK Stadium for a crowd of more than 45,000, including President Nixon, a massive thunderstorm, fueled by days of oppressive heat and humidity, unleashed a deluge. Rain poured in buckets for hours, swamping the field and flooding both dugouts. Waterfalls gushed down the stadium's concrete steps.

Glum baseball officials postponed the contest, a first in All-Star game history, hoping for enough dry weather to play the game the next afternoon. Players from both teams scrambled to alter travel plans. Fans raced to rearrange work schedules or sell their non-refundable tickets to optimists who felt certain the weather would break.

The storm raged through the night. At daybreak, threatening clouds hovered overhead as Head Groundskeeper Joe Mooney and crew worked to dry the infield and drain the outfield. The D.C. Fire Department pumped water from the dugouts and the stands. Laborers cleaned debris and frantically dried off seats and shook out soaked bunting. In the late morning, as Mooney declared the field playable, the sun broke through.

The energetic crowd cheered most of the all-stars during player introductions, but booed Boston's Rico Petrocelli, who fans felt usurped Brinkman's rightful place as the American League starting shortstop. Knowles heard loud cheers and whistles. Willie Mays, appearing in his 20th All-Star game, received a standing ovation. When Howard stepped forward, the gathering stood and cheered for 27 seconds, the day's longest ovation. The roar enveloped the city, united in joy for the first time in years.

Opera star Robert Merrill, known as "America's Baritone," sang the "Star Spangled Banner." Vice-President Spiro Agnew threw two ceremonial first pitches, one to each league's starting catcher. Agnew stood in for Nixon, who was en route to Romania for a state visit and to welcome Apollo 11's astronauts back to earth after the lunar module's safe splashdown and recovery.

In the 1st inning of the game, Howard dropped Aaron's fly ball and Matty Alou scored. The National League scored twice more in the 2nd inning and led 3-0.

In the bottom of the 2nd, with one out, Howard came to bat. Fans stood and hailed Washington's favorite son once again. National League pitcher Steve Carlton took the sign from Bench. Fastball. Carlton left the pitch high and just off the middle of the plate. Howard swung and hit a screaming, rising laser beam of a line drive. Fans gaped in wonder as the ball rose in an ever-increasing arc, sailed over the fence, cleared the big black Longines clock in right centerfield and crashed off of the upper deck's mezzanine. The giant slugger's tape measure home run brought the crowd to its feet again in joy. For perhaps the first time, RFK Stadium shook on its foundation. Recalling his historic blast, Howard said, "Anytime you get a chance to perform in a premiere event like that in front of your people, Washingtonians, your fans, it's one of the highlights of my career."

The next inning, the National League, led by the first of Willie McCovey's two home runs, scored five runs against Odom. Knowles replaced the ineffective Oakland A's pitcher and stopped the rally. He retired Alou and Cubs' shortstop Don Kessinger on routine ground outs. Knowles enjoyed his cameo appearance. "I was elated," he said. "It was one of the biggest thrills I ever had in baseball. That it was in Washington was a big plus. This sounds corny, but as a child, you grow up thinking about All-Star games and the World Series and I was no exception. Getting chosen was totally unexpected."

As Washingtonians filed out of RFK after the National League's 9-3 win, thoughts turned to the Senators upcoming 61 games. With 101 contests in the books, Williams and his scrappy team proved themselves competitive to Washington and a doubting baseball world. Yet, they limped into the All-Star break with six losses in seven games. Did the Senators have the talent and moxie to win more than 81 games?

The first major test put a crucial game in the hands of the Senators oldest, craftiest and most obscure relief pitcher.

13: Victory in Simplicity

"Ted always told us to be ready to hit. I thought I already knew how, but Ted showed me."
-Ed "The Streak" Stroud, Outfielder, Washington Senators

On a cool evening, August 2, 1969, in Anaheim, California, Senators' relief pitcher Bob Humphreys stood serene on the pitcher's mound, even though three California Angles filled the bases and the game hung in the balance. In the ninth contest of a 12-game road swing west, the Senators led 8-7, with two outs in the bottom of the 10th inning. Ted Williams' team rebounded from its pre-All-Star break slump and split the trip's first eight games. Washington's record stood one game above the .500 mark at 55-54.

Williams depended on Humphreys to prevent a spirit-crushing defeat. The Senators shaky pitching staff turned a 5-0 lead into a 7-7 tie. Both teams squandered chances to win the game in the 9th, forcing extra innings. Williams paced the dugout floor, muttering curses about stupid pitchers.

The Senators took the lead, 8-7, in the top of the 10th inning thanks to Ken McMullen's pinch-hit sacrifice fly. Williams, who had already used five pitchers, turned to Humphreys to save the day. In a game for the first time in 13 days, Humphreys struggled to throw strikes to the California hitters. He walked three of the first five batters he faced, leaving the bases loaded with two outs. Nervous teammates fidgeted in their positions, kicking at the infield dirt and outfield grass. Humphreys looked so calm and confident he could have yawned. Little about baseball surprised or frightened the slight relief pitcher, 5'11" and 165 pounds with wide, intense blue eyes. Two weeks shy of his 34th birthday and an eight-year major league veteran, he had faced plenty of jams before. The intelligent, but plain-spoken man from Covington, a small town in west central Virginia, strolled off the mound, squeezed the rosin bag and rubbed the baseball in his hands, considering his next pitch to catcher Jim French.

The wily veteran threw almost every pitch imaginable, all at varying speeds and with Humphreys' self-described "funky wind-up." He said, "By that time in my career, I was relying mainly on the breaking cutter, I called it my slider, and a four-seam fastball. I'd mix in the knuckleball." Humphreys, who also threw a change-up and a curve, outsmarted hitters he could no longer overpower. He offered to pitch in any situation; one inning, four innings, one batter, it made no difference to him. Whenever Williams gave him the ball, he took it.

Humphreys needed one more out to seal a Washington victory. A young pitcher, knowing his team stood one bad pitch from defeat, might panic. Humphreys remained cool. He said, "I felt like the players on my club knew they didn't have to worry about me. When I went to the mound, I guarantee you the guys I played with felt like we had a chance to win."

The Angels' third baseman, Aurelio Rodriguez, stepped to the plate. Humphreys peered in for the sign from French. Humphreys threw a tantalizing pitch too tempting for Rodriguez to let pass. He swung, but, at the last moment, the ball broke beneath the bat's barrel. Rodriguez topped the ball, sending a routine grounder to Ed Brinkman. The Senators' shortstop fielded the ball and flipped it to second baseman Tim Cullen for the game's final out. Humphreys notched his second save of the year. His teammates worked three-and-a-half hours to earn the victory, their 56th in 110 games.

When the Senators traded Camilo Pascual to the Reds in July, Humphreys became the oldest pitcher on the Senators roster. He gave the staff a veteran's steady, patient hand. In August, Humphreys contributed 21 innings in 17 appearances, with three saves and a win. Rival managers noticed the excellent work he and his mates in the Senators' bullpen performed in 1969. Baltimore skipper Earl Weaver told Humphreys, "Your D.C. club has one of the best bullpens in the league."

The 1969 season marked Humphreys fourth in Washington. He became a fixture in the Senators bullpen the moment the team acquired him from the Chicago Cubs days before the 1966 season. Humphreys played the best season of his career in 1966 with a 7-3 record and 2.82 ERA. He said, "I pitched 112 innings in 58 games. Teams didn't use pitchers then like they do today. If you came in for the 5th inning, you were expected to pitch the sixth, seventh, and eighth, at least, and the ninth too, if you could. If you got in trouble you were expected to get out of it yourself."

From 1966-70, the Senators enjoyed the crafty little pitcher and his underwhelming menagerie of junk balls. When Williams arrived in 1969, he loved to taunt Humphreys and his fellow pitchers with insults about their weak physical condition and inadequate brains. The barbs bothered some, but Humphreys found his mouthy manager amusing. Humphreys said, "I would tell him, 'You hit .400, right?'

128

"He would say, 'Yeah,' like he's proud of it and I would say, 'I'd like to have a job where I could fail six times out of ten and be a star. You hitters make seven outs out of ten times and think you're good.'

He'd reply, 'With the crap you got I might have hit .600!'

"With Ted, you had to believe in yourself, that you could play. I think he liked it if he knew you wouldn't take too much static. We had a good relationship."

Years before he met Williams, Humphreys learned tactful ways to speak the truth to powerful men. In the off-season, he worked on the staff of Republican Congressman Richard Harding Poff, who represented Virginia's 6th District, the Bedford/Lynchburg area where Humphreys grew up. He toiled seven years on Capitol Hill for Poff.

Humphreys said, "Working for Rep. Poff was a neat off-season job. A friend of mine was a neighbor to Poff's administrative assistant. One Sunday, they came to a game and met some of the guys afterwards. He called me back later and suggested I come down to Congress for lunch. I told him I was looking for a job, but the thought of working for Congress hadn't crossed my mind."

With his job downtown, Humphreys lived in Washington during the off-season. He became close friends with other Senators who lived in the area year-round, including Dick Bosman, Casey Cox, Cullen and Brinkman. "They were a good bunch of guys. We had some good times together," Humphreys said.

Humphreys knew better than anyone else on the Senators how much ballplayers in the 1960s depended on off-season income to make ends meet. In 1967-68, he served as one of the Senators' representatives to the players' union. Humphreys worked hard at the role. He and the Senators' general manager George Selkirk often locked horns over player salaries and working conditions.

Humphreys said, "I never got paid much. It was really difficult to make money with Selkirk. He was cheap. I held out every year with Selkirk. One of my worst memories of playing baseball in Washington is dealing with Selkirk. I didn't miss him at all when Bob Short fired him."

Humphreys' tenure as a player representative coincided with the beginning of Marvin Miller's reign as head of the players' union. In one of his first acts, Miller directed each team representative to take an anonymous salary survey. Humphreys explains, "I put a hat on the table and gave everyone a slip of paper and asked them to write down their salary, but not their name. At the time, I was making $18,000. I knew Frank Howard and Pascual were the highest paid team members.

"I took the pieces of paper out of the hat and found that the highest salary was $50,000. I figured that was Hondo. The next was

$42,500. That had to have been Pascual. The next highest salary was $18,000. Mine. I was the third highest-paid member of the club. I was not the only Senator having trouble earning a living playing baseball."

By the end of the 1969 season, Humphreys appeared in 47 games. In 79 $2/3$ innings, he earned a 3-3 record, five saves and a 3.05 ERA. He pitched equally well against right and left-handed batters, holding both to a .233 batting average. His versatility and cunning on the mound helped the Senators win.

During the 1970 season, age started to wear on Humphreys. Injuries sidelined him until May 23. When he tried to pitch, his pinpoint control abandoned him and he walked more than one batter an inning. The Senators judged Humphreys washed up. The club gave him his release in June. He spent two days out of work until the Milwaukee Brewers, desperate for pitching, signed him.

With the Brewers, Humphreys decided to rely on his knuckleball alone. He performed well enough to remain on the Brewers' pitching staff for the entire season. Humphreys attributed his successful season in Milwaukee to his catcher, Jerry McNertney. "He was the best knuckleball catcher in baseball," Humphreys said.

The aging pitcher ended his nine-year tenure in the big leagues on September 25, 1970. Humphreys agreed to start the second game of a doubleheader in Chicago, just the fourth starting appearance of his career. He pitched five solid innings, giving up a single run, and earned the last of his 27 career wins.

Humphreys took great pride in his major league career. He said, "I only had two losing seasons, 5-7 in 1968 and 2-4 in D.C. and Milwaukee in 1970. I had winning records even though I played for losing clubs. Winning is what drove me."

Out of baseball, Humphreys needed a steady income. He returned to Washington and joined Rep. Poff's staff full-time. After Poff retired from Congress in 1972, Humphreys worked for the congressional liaison offices of the Patent and Trademark Office and the Department of the Interior.

Government desk jobs suited Humphreys like a small boy wearing a suit and tie on Easter Sunday. He sat at his desk, made a few phone calls, shuffled papers, and daydreamed about baseball. "I was about to go crazy," Humphreys said.

He found an opening for a baseball coach at a university near his boyhood home of Covington – the Virginia Tech Hokies. Humphreys coached at Virginia Tech from 1975-78. The club played in two NCAA Regional tournaments under his leadership. Humphreys experience at Virginia Tech made him an attractive candidate for minor league coaching opportunities. He said, "For me as a coach, Virginia Tech helped more than anything. I had no assistants. I had to know everything, pitching, infield and outfield. I had to teach it all."

The Toronto Blue Jays hired Humphreys to serve as the club's minor league pitching coordinator. He remained with the Toronto organization until 1984, working year-round. During winter, Humphreys traveled to Venezuela to coach pitchers there. He fell in love with South America.

Humphreys worked hard to brush up on his long forgotten Spanish. He said, "I had Spanish in college and could communicate pretty well. At night, I would take cab rides and talk to the drivers to help me learn Spanish. Eventually, I learned it pretty well." He coached and scouted Latin American players for 11 seasons, primarily in Venezuela, for the Blue Jays and Brewers.

When he broke ties with the Toronto organization, Humphreys teamed up with friend Bruce Manno, the Brewers' Farm Director. He became Milwaukee's coordinator of minor league instruction. He spent 14 enjoyable and productive years with Manno, yet he grew weary of the constant travel.

He returned to schoolboy coaching at his alma mater, Hampden-Sydney, a small college in Salem, Virginia. Humphreys found no honor at his former home. He coached at Hampden-Sydney in 1997-98, but said, "I hated it. It wasn't the same as Virginia Tech."

After leaving his alma mater, Humphreys felt old and tired. He endured double knee replacement surgery. After three years, the yearning to return to baseball grew too strong to ignore. In 2001, Humphreys contacted Manno and landed a job with his old friend's new organization, the St. Louis Cardinals. After three years working with the Cardinals pitching prospects, Humphreys resigned.

The energy and passion he brought to coaching disappeared until an unexpected coaching opportunity cropped up in Venezuela. Humphreys explained, "One club didn't have a pitching coach because, back a couple of weeks before, the other man died."

Fate beckoned Humphreys back to South America. Hired to fill in for one month in December 2004, he did such impressive work that the Araqua Tigers hired him for the 2005-06 seasons. With Humphreys help, the Tigers won the league championship twice in three seasons.

He said, "We had a lot of major leaguers on the team – Miguel Cabrera, Alex Gonzalez, Henry Blanco, Bobby Abreu in right field, and Endy Chavez in center field. We had everything."

Hip replacement surgery prevented Humphreys from returning for the 2007 winter season, but he vowed to go to Venezuela, if his aging

131

body permitted, to stay connected to the game. He said, "It's all I ever wanted to do from the time I was 12 years-old."

Sadly, that opportunity never game. Humphreys, now retired, lives in Bedford, Virginia, enjoying the lovely mountain views and savoring his rich, international contributions to the game he loves.

While Williams celebrated Humphrey's save of Washington's victory over the Angels, traveling secretary Burt Hawkins burst into his office in the visitors' clubhouse. He carried distressing news. Back east, the Washington Redskins and Chicago Bears played an exhibition game, Vince Lombardi's first as Washington's head coach. Rain soaked the field before, during and after the game, enough to flood the visitors' dugout with two feet of water.

For three hours, the Redskins and Bears turned RFK Stadium's carefully manicured field into a sea of mud, leaving divots everywhere. The site of the team benches, where the football behemoths sat, sank two feet into the ground. The next morning, Head Groundskeeper Joe Mooney inspected the remains of his barely recognizable baseball diamond.

His face fell. To bring RFK back to even minor league quality required a Herculean effort – and hot, dry weather. In the midst of one of the most humid summers in Washington memory, Mooney had six days to restore the devastation before the Senators returned. If he failed, multiple postponements or the outright transfer of games to other cities looked likely. Facing long odds, Mooney and his crew slogged into the mud and went to work. They first graded the dirt around home plate to coax the running water toward a drain in the home dugout. Other workers patched dead grass and repaired divots.

A livid Bob Short called a press conference. He made threats of retribution against the Redskins, the Stadium-Armory Board and anyone else who came near. He had spent $200,000 to upgrade RFK's substandard turf only to have it destroyed on one rainy night.

He vowed to sue the Armory Board if it failed to have the field in an acceptable condition. Next year, Short raged, he would get a court order to stop any Redskins' home exhibition games on rainy nights during baseball season. Short's grievances fell on deaf ears at the Armory Board. They dismissed the situation as inevitable in a multi-purpose municipal facility. Mooney and crew could repair the field on Short's tab. In the end, Short sued no one. He instead spent an additional $100,000 in repairs, including hiring a helicopter to hover over the infield in a desperate attempt to dry it out.

Out west, the Senators lost their final game with the Angels and split two against the Chicago White Sox. Williams' team finished the

12-game road trip with a 6-6 mark, 57-56 for the season. Before returning to Washington for 11 games, the Senators had a day off. The Baltimore Orioles, originally scheduled to play International League All-Stars in Louisville, decided to stay home. Short, savoring the chance to scout another market clamoring for major league baseball and offset a portion of his $100,000 field repair bill, agreed to have his team play instead.

Back in Washington, Mooney and crew worked overtime and the weather cooperated. On August 8, the Senators began their 11-game home stand on schedule. The field, however, remained in poor condition. More dirt than grass, it still contained numerous divots and uneven terrain. One visiting player, Seattle's shortstop Ray Oyler, turned an ankle when he stepped in a hole on the field.

In their first seven games at home, the Senators won three and lost four. With two-thirds of the season in the books, the Senators record stood at an astounding 60-60. Williams kept his team sharp and enthusiastic and avoided long losing streaks. Atlantic salmon running in large schools in Canadian rivers and streams beckoned, but Williams remained at the Senators' helm, working hard to give a winning team to Washington.

On August 16, in the bottom of the 8th inning of the eighth game of the home stand, Billy Martin's first-place Minnesota Twins led the Senators, 5-3. Martin sat smug and comfortable in the Twins' dugout, waiting for his pitcher, Jim Kaat, to close out the victory.

The Senators made Martin sweat a little. With one out, Brant Alyea and Tim Cullen hit consecutive infield singles. Right fielder Ed Stroud strolled to the plate. Nicknamed "The Creeper," Stroud walked with an irregular, ambling gait. A shy, reserved person, the title also fit his ill-at-ease manner in public gatherings. He kept to the room's corners, trying to blend into the walls and the scenery.

When he ran, though, it appeared as if a different person inhabited his body. The 5' 11", 180-pound ballplayer, born October 31, 1939 in Lapine, Alabama, seemed to fly over the ground, a combination of speed and grace. His ability to blaze around the bases earned him a second moniker, "The Streak."

Martin felt Kaat overpowered Stroud during his first three at-bats – walk, strike out and ground out. He motioned for his outfield to move in closer, especially left fielder Rick Renick, who took an extremely shallow position, not far from his shortstop. Kaat checked the two Washington runners, and threw a high fastball over the outside corner. Stroud took a quick, inside-out swing, guiding the pitch to left field.

133

As soon as the ball met Stroud's bat, Renick regretted his close-in position. The high arching fly ball carried into deep left centerfield. Renick gave chase, but the ball fell just beyond his reach and rolled to the wall. Alyea and Cullen scored to tie the game.

Stroud dashed around the bases, thinking triple. Rounding second, the normally agile outfielder stumbled and started to fall. He regained his balance just as Renick corralled the ball and made a strong throw to his cutoff man, shortstop Leo Cardenas. Stroud sprinted for third base. Cardenas looked at Stroud fly and double-clutched on his throw. The delay gave Stroud just enough time to slide toward the outside part of the base, his foot slamming into the bag a millisecond before Minnesota third baseman Harmon Killebrew made the tag. The Senators' next batter, Paul Casanova, hit a fly ball to left field, plenty deep enough for Stroud to race home with the go-ahead run.

In the 9th inning, Darold Knowles, thanks to Ken McMullen's spectacular diving stop to start a double play, preserved the Senators' 61st victory. After the last out, Stroud's teammates shook his hand and slapped him on the back in gratitude for his leading role in the win.

Since the Senators return home, Stroud enjoyed a week-long run of fine hitting. He stroked six hits in seven at-bats, including four consecutive pinch-hits. The hot streak resurrected Stroud's season, raising his batting average by 30 points (.225 to .255). Stroud felt his success stemmed from, at last, understanding Williams' hitting philosophy. Stroud said, "Ted always told us to be ready to hit. At first, I didn't know what he was talking about. I thought I already knew."

Williams' lengthy sermons on hitting, with intricate technical details about strike zone areas and bat plane angles at first confused Stroud, who liked to keep baseball and life simple. Once he boiled down Williams' advice to two words, "Be ready," he began to experience success.

Stroud scorched the ball throughout August. In 34 plate appearances, he hit .429 with a .529 on-base percentage. He scored eight runs, drove in 10 and stole two bases. He overcame his early season struggles to finish 1969 with a respectable .252 batting average (.746 OPS) in 123 games. Stroud also became Washington's most reliable pinch-hitter. He hit .318, scored nine runs and drove in 11 in the role.

Stroud also disrupted other teams with his speed. He stole 12 bases in 14 attempts. He excelled at reading pitchers and getting good jumps. He implored the Senators' organization to let him run on his own, but 58 stolen bases and a 73 percent success rate over four seasons failed to convince the club to turn The Streak lose. Stroud said, "The

American League wasn't ready for that. They were still into the home run thing."

In 1970, Stroud manned centerfield for the injured Unser and, for half a season, performed like an all-star. In mid-June, he enjoyed a .313 batting average and reached base at a near forty percent rate until an injury ruined his season and, perhaps, his career.

On July 9, 1970 in Cleveland, pitcher Fred Lasher's fastball hit Stroud in the face. He crumpled to the ground, his jaw broken. He spent the next 21 days on the disabled list. Stroud recalled, "I had a good year in 1970. If I didn't get hurt, I would have done better." Still, Stroud gave the Senators the best season of his career, hitting .266 (.680 OPS), with 29 stolen bases. He also played superb defense in the outfield.

Six days before the start of the 1971 season, Washington traded their fleet outfielder to the Chicago White Sox for first baseman and outfielder Tom McCraw. Stroud experienced a sad, short tenure in Chicago. He hit .177 in limited playing time. He played his final game in the major leagues on June 29, 1971. In the aftermath of his beaning by Lasher, Stroud never recaptured the confidence and fearlessness a major league hitter needed to be successful.

Despite the frightening experience of being hit in the face with a baseball, Stroud harbored no regrets or ill feelings about his six seasons in the big leagues. He felt thankful, especially for the four seasons in Washington. With a smile in his voice, Stroud said, "I have good memories of Washington. The ballpark was beautiful. I loved the city, the people, and the surrounding suburbs. We were a very close team. Everybody got along. Frank Howard wouldn't have it any other way."

After baseball, Stroud settled into his adopted hometown of Warren, Ohio. He worked in the local government and rose to the position of Equal Employment Opportunity Commissioner. In 1989, Stroud was a charter inductee into the Warren Sports Hall of Fame. He retired in 1998, living on his government and baseball pensions.

Stroud stayed fit by working out and playing in as many local softball leagues as his schedule allowed. Stroud looked like he leapt out of his baseball card and onto the Warren Parks and Recreation Department fields. Stroud played in the open men's division – serious softball, not the glove in one hand, beer mug in the other variety. He hit better than men half his age and outran all of them.

Stroud never considered baseball his lifelong career. He viewed the game as a chance to do something he loved. He never sought a job coaching or scouting in the minor leagues. Stroud rode enough buses from one small town to another to satisfy him for a lifetime.

He preferred life in a small mid-west town like Warren. No crowds. No autograph shows. Just a few softball games and a slow, simple life where, Stroud said, "I can do what I want to do." Stroud enjoyed that placid, fulfilling lifestyle daily, until his death on July 2, 2012.

The victory over the Twins that Stroud made possible gave the Senators a boost. The team won five of the next seven games, with both losses by a single run. The week of fine baseball lifted the Senators' record to 66-62, but the club lost its next three games to quash any thoughts of a long winning streak.

The next day, August 30, marked Williams' 51st birthday. Frank Howard, the Senators' marquee player and team leader, resolved to give his manager the present he wanted most – a victory.

Ed Stroud
(National Baseball Hall of Fame Library, Cooperstown, NY)

Bob Humphreys, Autograph Day, July 12, 1969
Private Collection of Mark Hornbaker (Used with Permission)

14: Frank Howard: Washington's Hondo

"From centerfield, it's safer there."

-Ron Law, Cleveland Indians' rookie pitcher on the best way to pitch to Frank Howard

A large crowd filed into RFK Stadium on August 30, 1969 to watch the Senators play the Oakland Athletics and to wish Ted Williams a happy birthday. Frank Howard, enjoying the best season of his career, vowed to play a great game for the man who revolutionized the giant slugger's approach to hitting. The metamorphosis began in spring training. Once the perennial holdout signed his contract, Howard worked like a fanatic to get in game shape. He hit until calluses filled his massive hands. He jogged for hours, wearing a warm-up jacket to sweat off pounds and lead weights on his ankles to build strength in his legs.

Exhausted and sore after his workouts, Howard sat in a whirlpool to salve his burning muscles. He then lumbered to the sauna to sweat off a few more pounds. Sometimes, he would sneak in a few cans of his favorite beverage. Ed Brinkman remembered, "He'd take a six-pack of beer with him into the sauna, so what good was he doing sitting in there?"

Williams tolerated Howard's excesses and late night bar runs with his best friend Brinkman when he watched Howard play baseball. He loved Howard's work ethic. Howard said, "He probably paid me the highest compliment I've ever received. Ted Williams walked up to me one day and said, 'I'll say one thing for you, you enjoy playing this game don't you?'"

"I said, 'I certainly do.'"

"He said, 'It shows and I respect that.'"

While Teddy Ballgame loved Howard's hard work and affection for baseball, he loathed his hitting strategy. Howard approached each at-bat the same way he approached life – all or nothing. He took a full-powered, looping swing at the first fastball anywhere near the strike zone.

Studying his team's 1968 statistics, Williams examined Howard's numbers and cringed. For all his fearsome power, Howard drew few walks and struck out too often. The importance of taking pitches, getting on base and putting balls in play seemed lost on Howard. The 1968 American League home run champion failed to reach a .360 on-base percentage in any of his first nine seasons in the major leagues. The enormous number of outs Howard made more than counteracted his home runs. Fans loved him, but his impatience reduced his value to the club, especially with his pedestrian defense at first base and left field.

Howard's dunce-like approach to hitting puzzled Williams. How could a hitter with such power swing at everything in sight like a light hitting shortstop? Why did the Senators let him get away with it? With patience, Howard had the talent to become one of baseball's most feared hitters. Williams wondered if Howard would be willing to change.

The moment Howard arrived in Pompano Beach, Williams summoned him to his office. He said to Howard, "Hey Bush, get in here. How can a guy hit 44 home runs and only get 48 walks?"

Howard replied, "Well, I try to be aggressive with the bat."

Williams asked, "Did you ever take two strikes?"

"Oh God, Ted," Howard said, "I don't make that much contact. If I took two strikes, I'd be walking back to the dugout 300 times a year instead of 125."

Williams laughed at Howard's candor and replied, "But can you take a strike? I'm talking about if it's a tough first pitch fastball in a tough zone, or a breaking ball and you're sitting on the fastball." Williams paused, looked straight at Howard and asked, "Can you do that?"

Howard sat in silence for a few moments. His manager just asked him to turn his hitting philosophy upside down. Howard pondered the radical change. Why bother? He was already an all-star. Fans adored him.

On the other hand, across the table patiently waiting for his answer sat the greatest hitter of all-time. Years later, Howard said of this man, "I've met a lot of great individuals in my lifetime, but Ted Williams, he's charismatic. He's electric. Whether it's at a ballpark or a banquet hall or wherever it is, he's going to light that room up. Ted Williams was a great, great man."

Howard made his decision. He resolved to do it Williams' way. He said, "Certainly, Ted, anybody can take a strike."

The change in Howard unfolded gradually. Once the season started, he hit plenty of home runs, but kept jumping out of his cleats to hack those first pitch fastballs. Williams continued to preach patience, using profanity when necessary. By the time Williams' birthday rolled around, the Splendid Splinter's philosophy permeated Howard's baseball DNA. Howard said, "By being more selective at the plate I started getting more hitters counts, 2 and 0, 3 and 1 in my favor. I started laying off some of those breaking balls in the dirt that I used to chase. I started laying off that live high fastball out of the strike zone. I scored runs. I drove in runs. I was on base. My value to the ball club went up."

Howard's statistics confirmed Williams' ways. He entered the August 30 game against Oakland with a .302 batting average, .406 on-base percentage, .592 slugging percentage, 40 home runs, 81 walks and 74 strikeouts (one of the lowest strikeout totals of his career). He battled Oakland's young slugger Reggie Jackson and Harmon Killebrew for the home run crown. Dear to Williams' heart, he challenged for the league lead in on-base percentage.

With the August 30 game against the Oakland A's ready to begin, Howard prepared to add to his gaudy numbers and give Senators' fans another glorious day to enjoy in a season full of happy moments. The late summer sky shone bright and clear, a perfect day for baseball. More than 10,000 fans turned out to bask in the summer sun before school and jobs beckoned. They came to enjoy one more day at the ballpark before the summer of '69 faded into memory.

At 66-65, Washington needed a win to stay on the good side of .500 and send the birthday boy, Williams, home happy. The players learned their manager planned to celebrate the occasion with family and friends at his apartment after the game. The Senators intended to spare the guests from a crabby host.

Once the game started, Howard made his skipper smile right away. In the 1st inning, he singled. Then, the prodigious slugger did the unfathomable. On the next pitch, with Mike Epstein batting, Howard took off. The shocked Oakland catcher Phil Roof stood transfixed as he watched Howard lumber toward second base. His hurried throw arrived a split-second late.

Howard stood up and grinned, the infield's dirt caked on his red and white jersey and trousers. He brushed the dirt from his uniform and savored his first stolen base since 1966. His teammates howled with laughter. Though Epstein, perhaps as dumbfounded as Roof, struck out, McMullen and Bernie Allen each belted RBI singles to give the Senators a 3-0 lead.

The next three frames, the Senators piled on runs. Howard led the charge. In the 4th inning, he hit his 41st home run of the season to give the Senators a 9-0 lead. With pitching ace Dick Bosman on the mound, victory was certain. A relaxed Williams laughed and cheered, enjoying his day.

In the 7th, Howard clubbed a double to drive in two more runs. He finished a stellar game with four hits in five at-bats, a home run, the stolen base and four RBI. He and his teammates' fine play gave

141

Williams an 11-3 victory and sent fans home to face September with smiles on their faces.

Before the game ended, though, Washington added low comedy to the most joyful Saturday afternoon of the season. To start the 8th inning, second baseman Tim Cullen, a sure-handed fielder, deftly handled a ground ball for the first out of the inning. Senators' pitcher Bob Humphreys induced the next batter to hit a ground ball to Cullen. He bobbled it for an error. The following batter hit the ball to Cullen as well. He threw it away for a second miscue. The A's third baseman Sal Bando came to bat and hit a grounder right at Cullen. He positioned himself to field a hop that never came. The ball skidded along the dirt, right between Cullen's legs for a record-tying third consecutive error.

Everyone in RFK Stadium howled with laughter. The Senators 11-run cushion made Cullen's bumbling hilarious instead of infuriating. It led to three meaningless Oakland runs and gave Williams and the crowd more time to celebrate together.

When Cullen led off the Senators' 8th, he chuckled at the crowd's mock boos to honor his unique feat. In his turn at bat, Cullen hit a ground ball toward Oakland first baseman Tito Francona. In a perfect display of unintended sportsmanship, the ball squirted between Francona's legs for yet another error.

The crowd capped the splendid day by singing "Happy Birthday" to their beloved manager. Ted Williams, the man who transformed hopeless losers into tough-minded winners and good hitters, like Howard, into great ones. When the Senators made the last out, Howard, Jim French, Brinkman, and the rest of the gang raced to the locker room for another raucous victory celebration. The Nasty Nats cheer rang out loud and clear, with special earthy lyrics for the birthday boy.

Howard rejoiced until French and Brinkman chased him around the clubhouse, swatting him in the shins with fungo bats. The two Lilliputians teased their giant friend until he said, "Knock it off guys, someone's going to get hurt." Both agitators immediately complied.

Brinkman said, "I never got too close to him. You don't mess with no 300 pounders, not when you weigh a buck fifty."

Dave Baldwin remembered, "They'd just wear Hondo out. What was really funny was Hondo could have squished both of them at the same time with one hand."

Howard enjoyed the friendship and horse play as long as his shins held out. He said, "Washington ball clubs always had a great sense of camaraderie. Even in the bad years we hung tough together. For a lot

142

of us who had struggled and maybe not had the success in the game that we would have liked, [1969] was a phenomenal year."

The August 30 frolic added another fine moment in a season full of outstanding games for Howard. A late season tailspin left him just short of 50 home runs and a .300 batting average. He hit 48 homers, one behind league leader Killebrew. His .296 average tied the career best mark he set in 1962 with the Dodgers. He achieved one personal milestone when he completed the year with 96 strikeouts, his first full season below 100.

At 33, when most players begin to fade, he increased his on base percentage by 64 points over the previous season (from .338 to .402), while still hitting more than 40 home runs. By accepting walks when teams pitched around him, teammates Epstein and McMullen saw more good pitches to hit. Both had career highs in RBI in 1969. They often drove in Howard, who scored 111 runs, a career best, to complement his 111 RBI. He remained the Senators' number one star, but became one of the most valuable players in baseball as well, the heart and soul of his team.

Howard followed his fine 1969 season with an equally strong 1970. He hit 44 home runs, drove in 126 and earned 132 walks. By then, Washington had given its heart completely to the man they called the Capital Punisher and the Gentle Giant. Howard became their favorite adopted son. He hit hundreds of homers, signed thousands of autographs, and showed infinite kindness.

His relationship with Washingtonians grew from awe to deep affection. Across the metro area, kids clipped Frank Howard baseball cards to the spokes on their bike wheels. Children clamored for their hero to hit one just for them. Around town at autograph shows or in the throng pleading for his signature on Autograph Day, child after child beamed when Howard stooped down, looked them in the eye, and, as he signed their bats, balls, caps, programs, notebooks, and scorecards, thanked them for coming to the game and making his day. Childhood dreams became lifetime memories.

When Howard appeared on the field, fans followed every move, every mannerism. One fan recalled, "I remember he used to get down on one knee in the on deck circle and he had this towel he would use to wipe off the bat as he got ready to hit. Even there, down on one knee, he looked huge, just really impressive."

Another fan commented, "We never had good teams, but we had Frank Howard. He was ours, our gentle giant."

Fan Carol Allen said, "My Dad took me and my brother to a game at RFK Stadium. That's [the first time] I saw Frank Howard. I've been hooked on baseball ever since. When Frank came up to bat, he was our hope for scoring. Once he said, 'To be a major leaguer, it's not just the talent you have, but how you treat other people.' He's a prime example of that; a wonderful human being."

Charlie Morgan, former public address announcer for the Prince William Cannons said, "He's a gentleman, that's what he is. Frank Howard is a gentleman."

As the people of Washington opened their hearts to Howard, he fell in love with them. He said, "I had seven great years in Los Angeles with the Dodgers (1958-64). They're an outstanding organization. But the seven years I had in Washington, they're unparalleled. Nothing will top it."

Frank Howard witnessed the passion of Washington baseball fans first-hand. Disparaging comments about his town and his people raised his ire. "Many people say Washington's not a baseball city," Howard said. "That's a bunch of baloney. Washington's a great sports town. All you have to do is produce. All you have to do is play with your heart. All you have to do is play hard-nosed, hustling sports and these fans will love you for it."

As Howard's renown grew, so did local folklore surrounding the 6'7" Hondo. Everything, from his giant frame to his massive appetite, seemed larger than life. Howard hit tape measure home runs, peppering RFK's upper deck with baseballs. The Senators adorned the seats he dented with bright white paint. In the three seasons (2005 – 2007) the Washington Nationals played at the old stadium, current major league players stood at home plate and stared in awe at those seats, stunned that Howard, abusing no substance except beer, could hit a baseball that far.

Even Howard, though, never managed to crush a ball out of RFK and into the Anacostia River, a fable fathers and kindly old uncles told wide-eyed children on their first visit to RFK Stadium. When the little ones first glimpsed Howard towering over the other players on the field below, they believed.

Other tales that seem legend are true. Howard's teammates insist they could smell wood burning when he took a mighty swing and fouled the ball straight backwards, missing a home run by millimeters. When he did connect, infielders sometimes leapt in vain to catch line drives that soared over fences in ballparks across the American League. Brinkman said, "I've heard players say that they reacted to a ball off of his bat like maybe they had a shot at catching it and it would go out of the ballpark. Hondo hit level or swung down a little bit and the ball would just rise like a two iron shot. It was like watching a golf ball take off. If they would have let those balls travel without hitting the stands, there's no telling how far some of them would have gone."

The speed at which Howard's homers left ballparks and the long distances they traveled impressed even Williams. He insisted that Howard hit the ball harder than anyone he ever saw – including himself. Other Senators' coaches resorted to hyperbole. Wayne Terwilliger said, "My God, those were monster drives!"

Howard's hitting drove one team and their manager to distraction. The Cleveland Indians' manager, Al Dark, so feared Howard he gave him an intentional walk with two outs and the bases empty on two occasions in 1969. Dark grew weary of Howard pounding his pitchers. In 18 games against Cleveland in 1969, Howard hit seven home runs and drove in 16.

He hit Cleveland star Sam McDowell especially hard. In his career, Howard pounded the flame throwing southpaw with five homers and a .368 batting average. McDowell walked his nemesis 25 times in 95 plate appearances. With characteristic graciousness, Howard denied he owned McDowell. He said, "That's a fallacy. I hit most left-handers better than I did right-handers. But to say you own a guy, no, you don't own anybody in the major leagues. When a major league pitcher's got command of his quality stuff that particular day he's a tough piece of work."

After 1970, the toll of 14 seasons and 1,701 baseball games started to show in Howard's play. He hit just 26 home runs for the dreadful 1971 Senators. His RBIs and walks fell. His bat slowed just enough to make him vulnerable to solid pitching. His body rebelled against playing every day.

With the end of his career and his stay in Washington in sight, he gave the fans he loved one final, unforgettable moment. Howard's home run in the final game at RFK Stadium, September 30, 1971, endures as one of the most poignant moments in Washington sports history. It was a moment so vivid, those who witnessed it, or heard Ron Menchine describe it on the radio, can still close their eyes and relive it in an instant.

Fans cheered and wept at the same time, while, Howard stood in front of the Senators' dugout, drinking in the adulation, burning it into his memory. The ovation went on and on and on as if fans could keep baseball, and Howard, in Washington if only they kept cheering. Overcome with sadness and gratitude, Howard hurled his batting helmet, batting gloves, and cap into the stands as cheers swelled again in a final outpouring of passionate tenderness for Washington's giant hero.

With a heavy heart, Howard packed up with Williams and the remnant of the 1969 club and headed to Texas for the 1972 season. In September, the Rangers shipped him to Detroit, reuniting Howard with his old chum Brinkman. Howard's homer and four RBI on September 13 helped the Tigers win a key game in their close pennant race against the Boston Red Sox for the American League East Division crown.

The advent of the designated hitter rule in 1973 enabled Howard to play one more season in the major leagues. He hit 12 home runs for Detroit to finish his career with 382. He played his final game on September 30, 1973 in Yankee Stadium. In October 1973, the Tigers released Howard.

He refused to believe the end had come. Washington's Gentle Giant signed a contract to play baseball in Japan for the Taiheiyo Club Lions in 1974. Fans speculated that Howard might hit 75 home runs in Japan's small ballparks against pitching well short of major league quality. Such predictions became moot after Howard's first at-bat. Always hustling, he tore his hamstring trying to run out a grounder to earn an infield hit. He tore the muscle so severely he never played for Taiheiyo or any other baseball team again.

To remain in the game, Howard turned to coaching. He joined the Milwaukee Brewers organization as a minor league coach. In 1976, he managed the Spokane Indians of the Pacific Coast League, the Brewers' AA affiliate. Howard impressed the Brewers brass so much they promoted him to hitting coach in 1977 and to first base coach in 1978. With the Brewers, he helped form two future Hall of Fame members, Robin Yount and Paul Molitor, into fine hitters and men who played baseball the same clean, hustling, hard-nosed way Howard displayed with the Senators. Howard coached for the Brewers through the 1980 season.

In 1981, the San Diego Padres hired Howard to manage their woeful club. His team struggled to a 41-69 record in the strike-riddled season. With the Padres he helped teach a young, slick-fielding shortstop named Ozzie Smith how to hit. Unhappy with Howard's performance and his supposed inability to discipline wayward players, the Padres fired him at the end of the season.

Howard coached for the New York Mets in 1982. In 1983, he took over as manager 47 games into the season when New York fired George Bamberger, the former Baltimore Orioles' pitching coach from 1968-77 and Brewers' manager (1978-80), who Howard befriended during his coaching stint in Milwaukee. It hurt Howard to replace his friend, but he dutifully performed the task of managing a Mets team in transition from a poor club to, in 1986, a World Series winner.

146

Howard helped future Mets' stars Ron Darling and Darryl Strawberry become solid major league players, but his team still lacked the talent to compete with the National League's best. Howard's assessment of the Washington Senators teams he played for applied to the two clubs he managed. He said, "What we lacked was overall depth in personnel. We just didn't have enough good quality players."

While Howard helped form the foundation of a future champion, in 1984 the Mets decided he was not the right man to lead them. Howard remained with the Mets, but as a member of Davey Johnson's coaching staff.

In 1985, Hondo returned to the Brewers' organization. Through 1999, he served as a major league coach for Milwaukee (1985-86), Seattle (1987-88), the Yankees (1989, 1991-93), the Mets (1994-96) and Tampa Bay (1998-99). Hundreds of former and current major league players benefited from Howard's enthusiasm for and knowledge of baseball. He also taught players the right way to treat fans, especially children.

Howard said, "At the end of batting practice, sign one of those balls and take it over to the stands and give it to some kid. On your way out of the ballpark, take five minutes, just five minutes that's all, and sign ten autographs. And on your way in, pat some kid on the head and say, 'Hey, [I'm] going to try to hit [a homer] for you today.' If you can do those things, you've done a great job of giving something back to the game."

Since retiring from coaching, Howard has worked as a major league scout and player development consultant for the Tampa Bay Rays and New York Yankees. In 2008, he and the Yankees mutually agreed to part ways and Howard retired from baseball.

In Washington, nearly 40 years removed from his final appearance in a Senators' uniform, Howard's place in fans' hearts remains. When fans notice him at any baseball venue, from the Bethesda Big Train's tiny stadium in Bethesda, Maryland to the minor league Potomac Nationals ballpark in Woodbridge, Virginia to the Nationals' new stadium in Southeast, Washington, D.C., they greet Howard with a standing ovation.

The adulation makes Howard feel conflicted. He said, "I'm not a guy who lives in the past. Today's the most important day of our lives. But, it is still nice – and probably because we're older and more accessible to the public – when somebody walks up to you and says, 'Hey Big Frank, I saw you hit one here, I saw you play here.' That's a nice feeling."

147

The night baseball returned to Washington in April 2005, Howard led a contingent of former Senators onto the field to await the arrival of the Nationals' starting nine. He jogged out to left field, head bent, looking a little stooped over and thinner than in his halcyon days. Spotting him, the sell-out crowd's cheers grew ever louder and magic happened. He grew taller, younger, heavier and stronger.

A blink of an eye later, Howard shook hands with the Nationals' left fielder, Brad Wilkerson. The Gentle Giant handed the young man his glove. With that, the vision faded. Howard – the gentle, powerful, unforgettable Hondo –became an old man again, aged, but ever cherished in Washington.

On April 8, 2009, the Washington Nationals erected a statue to honor Howard's iconic status in D.C. baseball. His bronze figure stands alongside Hall of Fame members Josh Gibson and Walter Johnson. Seven years later, the new Washington baseball club added D.C.'s Gentle Giant to its Ring of Honor. His name appears on the right field façade, near the foul pole, beside two of baseball's all-time best, Jackie Robinson and Frank Robinson. Howard's place among baseball royalty reflects the esteem he will forever hold in the hearts of Washington area fans.

The day after Williams' birthday bash, August 31, 1969, Howard continued to shine. He belted a home run and contributed two RBI in the Senators 8-3 rout of Oakland. The win gave the Senators a 14-11 record in August, the club's third winning month in a row. Howard and his mates entered September with a 68-65 record.

Washington needed to win 14 of its final 29 games to reach that Promised Land of a winning season, uncharted territory for the expansion franchise. The club began its September sojourn with back-to-back doubleheaders against the California Angels. The clubs split the first twin bill.

The next afternoon, in Game 1, the Washington Senators placed their fortunes in the hands of young Jim Hannan, a temperamental, inconsistent pitcher and the team's most intelligent player. The Angels countered with ace Andy Messersmith, one of baseball's best. The outcome surprised everyone.

Frank Howard
(National Baseball Hall of Fame Library, Cooperstown, NY)

Tim Cullen, Autograph Day, July 12, 1969
Private Collection of Mark Hornbaker (Used with Permission)

15: The Passion and the Sarcasm of Leadership

"If you can't laugh, if you're too uptight, you can't perform in the major leagues. You stay loose off the field so you can play with the right focus."

-Ken McMullen

John James Hannan, the 29-year-old man from Jersey City, New Jersey stood on the pitcher's mound three outs away from a complete game. He let the cheers of the tiny crowd, all 6,042 of them, serenade him. On September 2, the day after Labor Day, in the cloudy Tuesday twilight that threatened rain, most of Washington concerned itself with returning to work and enduring the melancholy first day of school. Hannan focused on finishing the masterpiece that would become his fifth win of 1969.

With a thin 2-0 lead against the California Angels, the Notre Dame graduate knew he needed to snap back to game-level intensity. Still, he intended to enjoy a brief moment of stardom after a year full of inconsistent play. Earlier in the season, Hannan felt the sting of banishment from the starting rotation to the bullpen. Williams burned his ears with angry reactions to his failures, including the inability to finish any of his 22 starting assignments.

Hannan refocused, determined to get a shutout. He had retired 20 of the last 22 batters he faced. Only one runner managed to reach second base. Hannan, throwing the ball with all his might, struck out the first two batters. He next faced Jay Johnstone, California's smooth swinging young outfielder and the Angels last hope. Hannan pumped in two strikes to Johnstone with the same pinpoint control he displayed the entire game. On the next pitch, the Angels' outfielder swung at a knee-high fastball and lofted a lazy pop fly to right field. Ed Stroud jogged in and made the easy, game-ending catch.

Hannan's three-hit shutout gave the Senators victory number 70. Washington also won the nightcap, 3-2 in six innings as a driving rain made further play impossible. In the damp, humid, but happy Senators' clubhouse, Hannan reveled in his triumph. A Senator since 1962, Hannan savored every victory.

Until his September gem against the Angels, the 1969 season frustrated the analytical pitcher. With the mound moved five inches lower than the previous season, Hannan struggled with his control. He gutted out a winning record (7-6) and a 3.64 ERA in 28 starts and 140

151

innings, but the uneven season erased the promise of 1968 when Hannan won 10 games for the last-place Senators.

Hannan played baseball with toughness and determination. In one 1969 contest, a line drive knocked him to the ground. He crumpled and remained prone until Williams and trainer Tom McKenna reached the mound. Once Hannan realized the two men hovering over him planned to remove him from the game, he bounced to his feet, grabbed the ball, and raced to the pitcher's mound, determined to continue. He shooed a dumfounded Williams and McKenna away. Tall (6'3") and well-built (205 pounds), the freckle-faced right-hander's innocent appearance belied a bulldog intensity. He displayed equal fervor while on the pitcher's mound or as the Washington Senators' representative to the players' union. He fought for victory on the field and justice for his fellow players in salaries and pensions.

He became a passionate advocate for players' rights. He served on the Major League Pension Committee and as the assistant players' union representative for the Senators in 1969. During the spring training work stoppage for improved pensions, Hannan convinced all but three Senators to stay away from camp until the union and baseball owners reached an agreement. The brainy, ardent right-hander forged an impressive show of solidarity in an era when owners held the upper hand in labor issues and players' job security wavered at their employers' whims.

Hannan won nine games for the 1970 Senators, and then left for Detroit in the Denny McLain trade. By then, the young man from New Jersey pitched with more moxie than talent. In May, the Tigers traded Hannan to Milwaukee, the last stop on his 10-year major league career. As a player, Hannan won 41 games and lost 48, with a 3.88 ERA.

He earned many more victories for baseball players after he retired from the game. Hannan put his Masters' degree in Finance from New York University (NYU) to work and became a successful businessman. He brought zeal for fairness and a commitment to serve others to his work, forged in his Catholic upbringing and the influence of the Congregation of Holy Cross (C.S.C.) priests at the University of Notre Dame.

Hannan fought for pensions for former major league baseball players. At NYU, he wrote his Masters' Thesis on the subject. Players' Union president Marvin Miller used the thesis to help forge the union's demands during the 1969 work stoppage. In 1981, with former Washington Senators Don Loun, Chuck Hinton and Fred Valentine, Hannan pursued the goal of creating a Major League Baseball Players Alumni Association (MLBPAA). Soon, 10 additional former players, including Dick Bosman, Rex Barney and Brooks Robinson joined as founding members.

In 1982, Hannan's vision became reality. The MLBPAA began operations, with Hannan as its founding director and Chairman of the Board of Directors. He remains in that role today. Under his leadership and foresight, the association has grown in membership and exposure. The MLBPAA's non-profit arm raises millions for charitable causes such as Special Olympics, the Leukemia Society of America and Little League Baseball through baseball clinics and golf tournaments. The for-profit organizations, Major League Alumni Marketing and Major League Alumni Services, help former players gain the benefits they deserve as well as endorsement and speaking opportunities. Hannan still labors to protect retired players' rights and dignity. With the same tenacity he displayed when he pitched for the Senators, Hannan fights to assure no former major league baseball player is ignored or lives in unnecessary financial hardship.

The rain-shortened second game of the Senators' September 2 doubleheader sweep fronted two consecutive off days for Williams' club, 48 precious hours to reconnect with family and friends and heal five months of aches and pains. Once they returned to baseball, the break seemed to blunt Washington's edge, sap the team's ability.

The Senators dropped four of five road games in Boston and Baltimore. On September 10, Williams' humbled club returned home and righted themselves. The swept a two-game series with the Yankees and beat the Tigers, 4-3, in the opening match of a three-game series. The Senators record improved to 75-70.

The impossible dream of April – a winning season – now became a quite reasonable expectation. Though out of the play-off race, the Senators next game had post-season implications for Detroit. A Washington victory over the Tigers would wrap up the American League East Division title for the Baltimore Orioles.

Ken McMullen, the Senators' regular third baseman, thought beating the Tigers the neighborly thing to do. Born June 1, 1942 in Oxnard, California, McMullen grew from a child collecting baseball cards to a man who played at baseball's highest level for 16 seasons. Kindness came as naturally to him as scooping hard hit ground balls from RFK Stadium's dirt. A friendly, affable sort, in retirement he co-owned a minor league baseball team, ran several baseball camps, created a youth benefit golf tournament, and visited Little League baseball teams in California as part of the Los Angeles Dodgers' speaker's bureau. With a big smile, he told the youngsters, "I loved it so much I would have played for free, but those fools paid me to play."

While with the 1969 Senators, McMullen enjoyed his best streak of hitting in September. He roped 24 hits in his last 56 at bats, with five home runs and 16 RBI. He looked forward to playing the Tigers again on this Saturday night in Washington, September 13 and adding to his gaudy numbers.

More than 14,000 fans, including 5,000 children let in for free to honor their service as safety patrols, filed into RFK Stadium, eager to see if the Senators could improve to a season-best six games over .500. The late summer sunset made the field glow a little brighter even as an occasional chill filled the air, a harbinger of autumn. The cool breezes reminded everyone that precious few games remained in the Senators' uplifting season.

After four scoreless innings, McMullen jolted fans from their seats. With two outs in the 5th, he lined a three-run homer over the left field fence to cap a five-run rally. His 17th home run of the season gave the Senators a 5-2 lead and knocked Tigers' starter Mike Kilkenny out of the game.

In the 6th inning, Detroit's top power hitter, Willie Horton, hit reliever Dennis Higgins' first pitch over the left field wall for a grand slam. The Tigers led, 6-5, but Jim French's sacrifice fly in the Senators' half of the 6th tied the score.

In the 7th inning, McMullen came up with the bases loaded and no one out against Detroit's top relief pitcher, Tom Timmerman. A hot, confident hitter, McMullen decided to swing at the first strike Timmerman threw. He knew his manager expected patient hitters willing to take a few pitches, but McMullen questioned that approach. Of Williams' mantra "get a good pitch to hit," McMullen said, "That's fine for Ted. Not many umpires called strikes on pitches he didn't swing at, but that approach might not work for mere mortals."

He knew a base hit against Timmerman might decide the game. The Detroit pitcher, wanting to get ahead in the count, threw a first pitch fastball over the middle of the plate, slightly above McMullen's belt. The veteran third baseman swung, but at the last moment the ball broke inside, toward McMullen's wrists. The ball splayed off the thin wood of the bat handle, inches above his hands. As he ran out the pop fly he felt sure he had just hit, McMullen expected to hear a groan from the crowd and Williams' curses from the dugout.

He forgot that hitters get lucky breaks during hot streaks. On his way to first base, McMullen spied the ball drifting toward right centerfield, far enough to elude Detroit second baseman Ike Brown's reach and shallow enough to escape centerfielder Mickey Stanley's grasp. The ball bounced into the outfield for a textbook Texas League single. Ed Brinkman scored to give the Senators the lead. McMullen's teammates rallied for three more runs.

In the 8th inning, McMullen smacked an RBI single off the leg of rookie pitcher Norm McRae, a painful major league debut for the Tigers' pitcher. The hit gave McMullen four in five at-bats and five RBI for the game. Darold Knowles threw three shutout innings to seal the Senators' 11-6 win and eliminate Detroit from the pennant race. Thrilled Washington fans spent the entire game marching around RFK Stadium's upper deck with bed sheet banners that displayed messages in praise of their heroes.

McMullen enjoyed the victory, but he needed no banners to sing his praises. He sought quiet acknowledgement from his teammates for his central role in another Senators' triumph. Small gestures, without fanfare, from one professional to another, satisfied McMullen.

While in Washington, McMullen worked hard to mold himself into a complete player, a man able to win games with his glove and bat. He arrived in Washington in December 1964, part of the blockbuster deal with the Dodgers that sent Howard, Dick Nen and pitchers Phil Ortega and Pete Richert to the Senators in exchange for star southpaw Claude Osteen and utility infielder John Kennedy. The Senators received an unpolished gem in McMullen, then 22 with a scant 109 games of major league experience. He blossomed in Washington and claimed the third base job in 1965 when he played 150 games and hit 18 home runs.

He remained the Senators' regular third baseman until his final game for Washington, April 26, 1970, the day before his trade to the California Angels. In his five seasons with the Senators, he played in at least 146 games every year. By 1969, teammates and fans considered McMullen one of the top third baseman in the American League.

In 1969, McMullen shined on offense and defense. In the field, he led third baseman in putouts and made only 13 errors in 154 games. At bat, he hit 19 home runs and set career highs in RBI (87), topping his previous best by 20, and batting average (.272). McMullen's consistent hitting made teams pay for pitching around Howard and fellow slugger Mike Epstein.

McMullen credited Williams for his 1969 performance. He said, "He wouldn't let you get down. When a team hits better you have more opportunities to drive in runs. It makes you bear down a little more when you hit, to be more focused."

Few outside Washington noticed or appreciated McMullen's play. He rarely called attention to himself. He loathed making routine plays look flashy. In addition, playing for the Senators limited his exposure. Washington teams played losing baseball for so long that, except for the

155

Presidential Opener, Howard's home runs and the occasional visit from the President, the team received minimal attention from the national media.

McMullen said, "I regretted not making the All-Star team in 1969, but Tigers manager Mayo Smith decided to choose other guys (Brooks Robinson and Sal Bando). I was with the Senators and people just did not hold us in high regard then."

His Senators' teammates noticed and appreciated his value to the club. McMullen's tenure with the Dodgers helped him to bring the experience and attitude of a winner to Washington. Frank Howard said, "Kenny had played for a world championship team in Los Angeles. He knew the difference."

With typical modesty, McMullen deflected such praise saying, "If I led at all it was by example, by the way I approached the game and prepared for it. When you're losing, you're worried too much about yourself. But when you're winning it feels like a team effort. Everyone's happy to do their jobs. Winning brings people together."

He credited former Senators' manager Gil Hodges and his staff with doing more than he did to teach the club the characteristics of winners. "Gil Hodges and his coaches instilled discipline. I learned an important lesson from them – if you're going to play, give 100 percent effort to win. It took some time for me to understand what that meant – that if you gave 100 percent you were a winner regardless of the score. It takes being on a losing team to understand that. Without that attitude, losing games can get frustrating and affect your effort," McMullen said.

When Ted Williams arrived in 1969, McMullen felt his manager willed the club to victory. He said, "Compared to someone like Gil Hodges, Ted Williams was not a good manager, but that first year, we were in such awe of him. We had a lot of veterans on that team, but that might have been part of the problem. With us losing, they started playing loose, just playing out their careers. Ted changed that with his attitude and his enthusiasm. His energy was contagious."

McMullen inspired his teammates with daily work on baseball fundamentals. He asked Sid Hudson to throw extra batting practice to him, swinging at pitch after pitch until he could wait on a curve ball or recognize a slider. He cornered Wayne Terwilliger and asked the Senators' third base coach to hit hundreds of ground balls, especially slow dribblers up the third base line, until the 6' 3", 195-pound third baseman could reach down, pick up the ball with his bare hand and snap a throw to first base in time to beat the league's fastest runners. He practiced the maneuver so often it looked routine.

156

Del Unser said, "He couldn't run, but he was quick. He had a quick first step at third base. He was one of the best – better than Brooksie in my opinion – at coming in on the ball, making that slow roller play on a bunt. He had real long fingers, so he could just come in and catch the ball even on a bad hop and make the play. He never broke stride. Just boom! He got there."

Players, coaches and scouts throughout baseball shared Unser's opinion of McMullen's magic glove. McMullen said, "I was a good defensive player. Unfortunately, a guy named Brooks Robinson played in Baltimore and he won all the gold gloves. Not to take anything away from him – he was a great player – but I would have won a few without Brooks."

After games and practices, McMullen's demeanor changed. He joked and teased and made a good-natured nuisance of himself. He said, "I tried to keep the guys loose with what I'll call sarcastic humor. If you can't laugh, if you're too uptight, you can't perform in the major leagues. When you're on the field, practicing or playing, it's all business. But in the locker room you can do a lot of kidding around. You stay loose off the field so you can play with the right focus."

Unser described McMullen's unique off-the-field personality. Unser said, "[Ken] had a very quiet, sarcastic, but professional personality. He was the type of guy who would always have a toothpick in his mouth, poking you. He'd sting you with it. We stayed up and played cards on flights back to Washington. He mixed in well."

With Brinkman as his co-conspirator, McMullen enjoyed pulling pranks on Howard. Senators' bat boy Paul Oppermann recalled the night McMullen and Brinkman, tired of seeing Howard's unfashionable duds, decided to hide them. Oppermann said, "Eddie and Ken McMullen's lockers were right next to each other, so they were always instigating things."

After the game, Howard took a shower, returned to his locker and found his clothes had disappeared. Oppermann recalled, "That night he went home in his underwear and a t-shirt and his shower shoes. We had to go up and get his car and bring it down underneath the stadium so he could drive it out and not be seen."

On April 27, 1970 the Senators traded McMullen to the Angels for slick fielding Aurelio Rodriguez and former bonus baby outfielder Rick Reichardt. Many of the 1969 Senators point to the trade as the beginning of the club's downfall. McMullen disagreed. "The guys the Senators traded me for had good years in 1970."

Reflecting on his time in Washington, McMullen said, "I enjoyed my years in Washington. I developed personally and as a player. I was

157

young and proving to myself that I could play day in and day out in the major leagues. Being from the west coast, I was disappointed at being traded [from the Dodgers]. When I first started playing there, I did not feel I belonged. But I earned my spot there as the regular third baseman. I may not have had that same opportunity in Los Angeles. The trade gave me a chance to prove myself. I eventually looked at the trade as the best thing that could have happened to me."

After he left Washington, McMullen continued his consistent play on defense, but struggled with his hitting. In 1970, his batting average fell to .229 (.672 OPS). McMullen's peak years with the Senators soon became a distant memory.

After the 1972 season, he left the Angels and played for two other west coast teams – the Dodgers and Athletics. By then, McMullen was a part-time player, a veteran presence on the bench. He spent 1977, the final season of his 16-year career, with the Milwaukee Brewers. There, McMullen ended a baseball career full of grace and class with a distinction only he, Ted Williams and 39 others share. On September 17, 1977, in the brand new Seattle Kingdome, McMullen hit a pinch-hit home run in his final major league at-bat.

He finished his major league career with modest batting statistics, 1,273 hits and 156 home runs. "I tell current players that I played during the dead ball era when Carl Yastrzemski could win the battle title with a .301 average. For me, hitting never came easy. I believe my defense is what kept me in the league for so long," McMullen said.

For McMullen, the opportunity to play even one big league game thrilled him. He recalled the first time he played in New York against Mantle. "I was in Yankee Stadium seeing guys that I had baseball cards of just a few years before," he said. "The history. The monuments. I was in awe. Then you quickly come to realize that this is your job now. You have to get ready to play."

Ken McMullen appears to be a satisfied, content man. He said, "I loved the game. It's still hard to believe I was a kid collecting baseball cards and then I made it there myself, got to hold one of my own cards. I didn't set any records, but I can say I was part of baseball history. I had my day in the sun."

The day after McMullen's star performance, September 14, 1969, the Senators appeared to have another victory over the Tigers in hand. In the 8th inning, Mike Epstein smashed a Mickey Lolich pitch far over the right field wall for a grand slam and a 4-2 lead. Knowles entered to close out the win, but failed. He surrendered back-to-back 9th inning home runs to Jim Northrup and Al Kaline that tied the game. The Tigers eventually prevailed in 12 innings, 7-4. The Senators' record fell to 76-

71. With two home games against the Baltimore Orioles next on Washington's schedule, Brinkman looked forward to getting back on the field to put the meltdown against Detroit behind him. Ed Brinkman despised losing.

Ken McMullen
Art by Ronnie Joyner (Used with Permission)

Ed Brinkman, Autograph Day, July 12, 1969
Private Collection of Mark Hornbaker (Used with Permission)

1969 WASHINGTON SENATORS BASEBALL TEAM

First Row: Trainer Tom McKenna, Coach Sid Hudson, Coach George Susce, Traveling Secretary Burton Hawkins, Public Relations Director Ed Doherty, President Robert E. Short, Manager-Vice President Ted Williams, Vice President Joe Burke, Coach Joe Comacho, Coach Wayne Terwilliger, Coach Nellie Fox, Coach Doug Camilli.

Second Row: Frank Howard, Barry Moore, Mike Epstein, Bernie Allen, Jim Miles, Darold Knowles, Del Unser, Bob Humphreys, Dave Baldwin, Ken McMullen, Joe Coleman, Equipment Manager Fred Baxter.

Third Row: Jim Shellenback, Ed Brinkman, Ed Stroud, Sam Bowens, Dick Bosman, Lee Maye, Brant Alyea, Dennis Higgins, Jim French, Casey Cox, Hank Allen, Paul Casanova, Tim Cullen, Jim Hannan.

162

16: Ed Brinkman: It's Funny When We Win

"Nobody wants to go out there and get their butt beat every day. I don't care who you are."

-Ed Brinkman, Shortstop, Washington Senators

If the 7-4 loss to Detroit on September 14 angered Darold Knowles and frustrated Ted Williams, it made Ed Brinkman furious. A clubhouse clown, hilarious story-teller, mod fashion maven, and the only man on earth able to drink Frank Howard under the table, Washington sportswriters and fans placed Brinkman at the head of the Senators merry band of lovable losers.

Yet, Edwin Albert Brinkman, born December 8, 1941, in Cincinnati, Ohio, ached to win at everything he did – from backyard ball games with his brothers to Howard's challenges in Washington, D.C. bars, to every one of the 1,845 games he played in the major leagues. Brinkman hated to lose.

True, the engaging and funny man often made his teammates double over with laughter. Young and impetuous during the decade he spent with the Senators (1961-70), he admitted he did crazy things sometimes. He reluctantly acknowledged wearing a few wild, Austin Powers-type outfits in the psychedelic 60's. He shared a drink or ten with Howard the man Brinkman called, "The big boy, one of my best friends in baseball."

Teammate Bernie Allen recalled Howard and Brinkman's close friendship, the classic case of the prickly little guy and his giant protector. Allen said of their relationship, "If you did anything to Brinkman, Frank would be right there, bashing your head in."

Howard and Brinkman enjoyed their share of escapades. Brinkman recalled, "Me and Hondo used to have a lot of fun out there. When a ball went up in the air he never said, 'I got it.' He'd say, 'You're all right.' That's all I ever heard. A pop up goes out to left and I'm running back and he's saying 'You're all right. You're all right.'

"He had a little bald spot out there, ten foot on either side. He caught everything that came in there, but his range was a little shaky. I used to get on him about it all the time. He would say, 'Just catch it. You're getting paid to catch it and I'm getting paid to hit it so just get the hell back in there.' He was terrific."

Brinkman's whimsical side, what one teammate called his "goofiness," hid his true motivation. He took refuge in his shenanigans, wardrobe, and beer to dull the pain of losing, not because he grew comfortable with defeat. The quest to win drove him. He said, "You always want to win. Nobody wants to go out there and get their butt beat every day. I don't care who you are. You may not have the best club in the world, but nobody goes out there with the intention of losing. Ever. No way."

When Brinkman stepped onto a baseball field, his daft ways disappeared. He zeroed in on the game alone. At shortstop and in the batter's box, Brinkman strove to perform with single-minded intelligence and precision. He said, "Once the season starts, your concentration level is such that you don't think about anything but that ball game. Everything else leaves."

A slight, awkward-looking man with a long, thin neck, Brinkman stood six feet tall and, if one believed the Senators' media guide, weighed 170 pounds ("I weighed a buck fifty wringing wet," Brinkman confided). Since high school, when he starred for Cincinnati's prep baseball powerhouse Western Hills High School, Brinkman prevailed over those who doubted his ability and zeal to succeed. At Western Hills, a school that boasted many major league ballplayers including Russ Nixon, Don Zimmer, Art Mahaffey and Herm Wehmeier, Brinkman shined. He outplayed another schoolboy named Pete Rose. Brinkman hit better than Rose and starred as the team's top pitcher.

The Senators signed Brinkman in 1961, complete with a $65,000 bonus. After 60 minor league games, Brinkman debuted for the Senators at third base on September 6, 1961. By 1963, he manned Washington's shortstop position for 145 games. Once Brinkman earned the job, nothing could wrest it from his grasp. He became the Senators' great fielding, poor hitting, fast-living shortstop. He loved playing in the major leagues, but season after season of losing grated on him.

In 1967, unrest during the Washington summer made the Senators' troubles seem trivial. That summer, the city called Brinkman's D.C. National Guard unit into active duty. He managed to play in 109 games, splitting time between guard duty and baseball. The next April, riots and violence rocked the nation's capital and cities throughout the U.S. when people learned Martin Luther King, Jr. had been shot and killed. Brinkman spent nearly the entire summer of 1968 patrolling the city with his unit to help restore Washington, D.C. to some semblance of calm. Often, he guarded the area inside and around what was then called D.C. Stadium.

In a bitter irony, while Brinkman patrolled stadium parking lots, his teammates entered to play baseball. Brinkman seethed inside, but obediently performed his duty. He appeared in only 77 games in 1968.

He said, "Most of my time was spent in a National Guard uniform as opposed to a baseball uniform during those two years."

For Brinkman, 1969 dawned like a breath of fresh, spring air. He said, "They made some changes in my military obligation, so I was able to be with the club full time." Brinkman looked forward to improving his hitting under Ted Williams' guidance. Always a weak hitter, with a career best batting average of .229 in 1966, the sporadic playing time he received in 1967-68 destroyed his rhythm and timing. His batting average plummeted below .200.

Williams urged Brinkman to alter his mental picture of himself. Despite his slight build, he often took huge, looping swings like a power hitter. Williams told him those days were over. Brinkman explained, "I was a little guy. If I hit a home run it was an accident. So Ted tried to get me to hit the ball line drive down all the time. No fly balls, because I wasn't big enough to hit the ball out of the ballpark."

During batting practice, Brinkman said Williams "would be all over me, saying 'hit the ball line drive down, line drive down.' I mean, it was constant. He helped me with my concentration level at the plate. That was the number one thing. I think it carried over into the games."

Williams also worked to restore Brinkman's fragile confidence. "Ted told me, 'you're better than what you've done in the past.' I got off to a good start and my confidence went up. He was responsible for it, because he was constantly on my tail."

To encourage a level, line-drive producing swing, Nellie Fox gave Brinkman a new set of bats. "Nellie ordered my bats for me," Brinkman said. "He wanted me to go with that big bottle bat that he used and choke way up. Try to get a little more bat control and hit behind runners. I think I became a better hitter because of that, too."

A renewed, self-assured man at bat, Brinkman took the American League by storm with his hitting. He appeared among the league leaders in hits the entire season. He was Exhibit A in Williams' magic ability to transform poor hitters into tough outs. A late August knee injury failed to cool Brinkman's hot bat. He stroked hits in 11 of 13 games after the injury. Entering the September 15 game with Baltimore, Brinkman's batting average stood at .275, a quantum leap from any previous season.

The upcoming game with the first-place Orioles mattered to both teams. The pitching match-up featured Dick Bosman against Jim Palmer, two red-hot players running neck and neck for the ERA title. Bosman sported a 2.21 ERA with victories in his last six decisions. Palmer, on an 11-game winning streak, had a 2.33 mark. Bosman loved to pitch with Brinkman manning shortstop. He said, "Ed caught everything hit his way and more. He saved me an awful lot of runs."

Bosman and Palmer settled into a heavyweight pitcher's duel, but Baltimore's pitcher was winning. After seven innings, Palmer seemed invincible. He permitted a pair of hits and walks, but no runs. Baltimore managed five hits and two runs against Bosman. Six outs remained for the Senators to end Palmer's shut out and prevent him from wresting first place in the ERA race away from Bosman.

In the bottom of the 8th inning, with two men on base and two out, Mike Epstein faced Palmer. He knew his ex-teammate well. The two played together as budding stars in the Baltimore farm system. Epstein expected and got an outside fastball from Palmer. The Senators' first baseman drove the pitch to the left-center field gap for a game tying triple. Epstein's clutch hit secured Bosman's lead in the ERA race, but Brinkman wanted the win.

In the 9th, Bob Humphreys replaced Bosman, removed for a pinch hitter during the Senators' rally, and retired Baltimore in order. Leading off the Washington 9th, Bernie Allen doubled. Young speedster Colbert Dale "Toby" Harrah, a September call-up, ran for Allen. The wide-eyed 20-year old debuted on September 5 and appeared seven times as a pinch-runner. He played his final major league game on October 4, 1986 for the Texas Rangers, the last man in baseball to don the Washington Senators' uniform.

Brinkman followed Allen. The Washington shortstop took a final swing of his bottle bat and pounded it on the ground to shake loose the lead weight donut around its barrel. On his way to the batter's box, he paused, remembering all the situations over the years when his manager would holler, "Brink, take a seat, I'm sending in a pinch-hitter."

By September 1969, Brinkman had put those days far behind him. He heard only encouragement from the Senators' dugout. Brinkman remembered the moment. "With Ted, I swung the bat well for him, better than I ever had, and he let me hit."

Expecting a sacrifice bunt, the Orioles' first and third basemen crept in as Palmer prepared to throw his next pitch. Brinkman looked toward third base, watching Terwilliger's fake signs that said, in pantomime, "Forget the bunt, Brink, the game's in your hands."

Palmer delayed, staring down Harrah to hold him close to second base. Brinkman held his bat high, choked-up a quarter of the way up the handle. As Palmer began to throw, Brinkman slid his left hand down the bat handle, feigning a bunt. Palmer threw a high fastball, tough to bunt, but perfect to hit line drive down. At the last moment, Brinkman pulled his bat back and took a full swing. He chopped the ball hard off the dirt in front of home plate.

As Baltimore first baseman Boog Powell raced forward, the ball bounced high in the air, down the first base line. Powell, now less than 40 feet from home plate lunged in futility as the spinning sphere sailed over his head and trickled into the grass just beyond the infield. By the time any Oriole could reach the ball, Harrah had already stomped on home plate with the winning run.

The Senators streamed from the dugout to embrace Brinkman, who danced in joyful celebration near first base. The post-game beers, shared with Hondo and the rest of the happy Senators, tasted great, soothing Brinkman's parched, dusty throat. He looked forward to drinking three, maybe four more with Howard later. He said, "Hondo and I popped a few in our day. Ted got all over him about keeping me out. One day Williams called him into his office and said, 'Listen Frank, you're 6' 8", you weigh 300 pounds. You play left field. You're taking that skinny little shortstop out with you every single night. You're killing the little guy.'

"Hondo said, 'Gee, Skip, that little German son-of-a-gun's drinking me under the table. You ought to have him in here.'"

Even better than drinking with his friend Howard, Brinkman knew the Senators' 77th victory made a winning season likely. After seven losing seasons, Brinkman yearned to play on a winner. He said, "The biggest thing about 1969 was that we played 10 games over .500 for the first time. To do that for that town and the fans there after the way we struggled the previous nine years or so, it was terrific."

Howard understood the value Brinkman placed on each of those 86 wins. He said, "I'm sure it meant the world to him. You play year after year after year with ball clubs that can't compete for a championship it'll either make you tough or break you, one of the two. For guys like Eddie Brinkman, one of my dearest friends and one of the all-time great defensive shortstops, it was a great thing. Anytime you can sustain a winning record and be competitive it's a thrill. It's much easier to come to the ballpark when you know you've got a chance at winning."

When the 1969 season ended, Brinkman could look back and savor his best year in baseball. So much had gone so well. The Senators became winners. His military obligation no longer disrupted his baseball career. He played 151 games and finished with a .266 batting average, 37 points higher than his previous best.

Brinkman even earned renown for his wardrobe. Former Senator Ken "Hawk" Harrelson, who played for Boston and Cleveland in 1969, described the Senators as a club full of squares when it came to fashion. He mentioned Brinkman as one of the few "Mod" guys in Washington.

Brinkman remarked, "I was Mod? I can remember wearing plaid pants and yellow and bright blue and different sport coats, white shoes and white belts and all that stuff. That was the style, man. You had to be Mod. We were all Mod. Hawk just don't remember, that's all."

In 1970, Brinkman teamed with Aurelio Rodriguez to give Washington one of the slickest fielding infields in baseball. He hit .262 and topped American League shortstops in putouts, assists and double plays. At 27, Brinkman stood poised to enter the prime of his career.

Life was good in Washington. Brinkman lived near the city, in Oxon Hill, Maryland and saved enough money to buy a house. He said, "I had been there so long, I was hoping I could stay. If you're in one place for 10 years like I was you get to the point where you'd just like to play [there your] whole career."

Days before Brinkman and his wife closed on their new home, the Senators traded Brinkman to the Tigers, part of the infamous deal that brought Denny McLain to Washington. The day of the trade, the Tigers named Brinkman their starting shortstop. The trade disrupted his plans to settle down in Washington. He said, "I banged the closing on the house and moved back to Cincinnati and bought one."

For Brinkman, leaving Washington and a prospective new home behind hurt at first. When the shock faded, he realized the Senators had sent him to a team with a chance to win the World Series. Detroit manager Billy Martin discovered a kindred spirit when he saw Brinkman's tenacity and burning desire to win. Brinkman loved playing for Martin. "He and I got along terrific. We could have our screaming matches and stuff, but he played me every day. I had no complaints," he said.

Martin's Tigers won the American League East Division crown in 1972. Brinkman made record-setting contributions to the Tigers' success. He committed a mere seven errors the entire season and won the American League gold glove award. He played 72 straight games and handled 331 chances at shortstop without committing an error. His consecutive games mark stood until Mets' shortstop Kevin Elster broke it in 1989. The following season, Cal Ripken, Jr. broke Brinkman's record for chances fielded without error. An injury late in Game 1 of the American League Championship Series against Oakland ended his fine 1972 season. The loss of Brinkman played a major role in the Tigers' heartbreaking loss to the A's in five games. His replacement, Dick McAuliffe committed three errors at shortstop in the series.

In 1973, Brinkman played in all 162 games for Detroit and Martin selected him to the All-Star team as a reserve. He hit an astounding 14 homers in 1974, but, at 32, his hitting and fielding began to decline. The

Tigers felt Brinkman's best days were behind him. On December 10, 1974, they traded him to the St. Louis Cardinals.

The Tigers guessed right. Brinkman's hitting languished and his range at shortstop diminished. In 1975, he played 28 games for the Cardinals, one for the Texas Rangers, and 44 for the New York Yankees. Ironically, Martin managed the Rangers and the Yankees that season and acquired Brinkman for both teams. At the end of the 1975 season, Brinkman knew he had spent himself for baseball. After 15 seasons, he retired.

Brinkman continued his baseball career as a minor league manager and a coach for the 1979 Tigers. He reunited with Howard in 1981, when the big guy managed the San Diego Padres. From 1983-88, Brinkman coached for the Chicago White Sox and later became a scout and special assistant for the club. "I did a little bit of everything," said Brinkman, who retired in 2000, his 40th year in the game.

Brinkman provided scores of fond memories for Senators' fans. Anyone who attended a Senators' game at RFK from 1962–1970 brought home a vision of a diving stop or a perfect pivot to complete a double play. In 1969, he won games and made memories with his bat as well. He said, "[In 1969] we were finally playing some pretty good baseball and the people came out. The same ones that booed us before were cheering us now. It was the first time we had a ball club that put a good streak together and the fans treated us terrific."

In 1998, Brinkman crossed paths with his former Senators' coach Sid Hudson, then 83 years old. The hard-living, fun-loving old shortstop said, "Sid looked terrific. I know one thing. I have no chance at 83, not the way I've lived."

He paused, the thought of death jarring. After a short silence, Brinkman realized accepting death, though inevitable, felt like accepting defeat. He chuckled and said, a hint of determination in his voice, "Maybe I'll trick 'em." Sadly, death finally caught Ed Brinkman on September 30, 2008; but not before the determined little shortstop filled Washington – and everywhere he traveled – with joy.

The evening following Brinkman's game-winning hit to defeat the Orioles, Baltimore's Dave McNally shut out the Senators, 1-0. After the game, the Senators left Washington for their final road trip of the season. The club won four of the seven games, including a three-game sweep over Detroit on September 24-25 to run their record to 81-75.

With six home games remaining, the Senators needed one more win to guarantee the expansion club's first season on the good side of .500. It took an old veteran outfielder with a sweet voice and an even sweeter left-handed swing to lead Washington to that Promised Land.

169

17: Arthur Lee Maye & The Senators

"Everybody thought: 'This team is a loser.' But somehow those guys felt that they could win and we won."
                              -Arthur Lee Maye, Outfielder, Washington Senators

On Friday, September 26, the Washington Senators hosted the Cleveland Indians. A crowd of 6,727 settled in to watch Joe Coleman duel Cleveland's Stan Williams. Thus far in 1969, the Senators dominated the Indians, with victories in 12 of 15 games.

Coleman and Williams pitched brilliant baseball. Through 4 ½ innings, the game stood scoreless. In the Senators' half of the 5th, Cleveland's Williams started to labor. With two outs and Tim Cullen on second base Williams faced Coleman. A weak hitter, Coleman somehow began to make contact with every pitch Williams threw. With a full count, Coleman fouled off 13 consecutive pitches. An exasperated and exhausted Williams missed the strike zone with his next pitch and Coleman walked. The next batter, Del Unser, also walked on a 3-2 pitch to load the bases.

Arthur Lee Maye ambled to the plate to face his old teammate. In June, the Indians shipped Maye to Washington, thinking the 34-year old outfielder washed up. Maye said of the trade, "I thought I should have played every day over there, but it didn't work out that way."

The 6'2", 190-pound Maye, an African American, traveled a unique road to get to Washington. Born December 11, 1934 in Tuscaloosa, Alabama, his family relocated to California during his teen years as part of the Great Migration of African-Americans from the South. At Jefferson High School in Los Angeles, he found some friends who loved to sing. Together, they developed a unique style of doo-wop harmony called the "Jeff High Sound." It worked. Maye's high school buddies sang with famous 1950s groups like The Platters, The Coasters, The Flairs, The Medallions, and The Penguins.

In 2002, Maye told the Doo-Wop Society of California, "We were just kids and we didn't know much about harmony, so we'd rehearse in the dark to concentrate on our voices. Or we'd sing in hallways at school to get our harmonies to ring off the walls, because the echo would exaggerate our wrong notes." Maye recorded songs with the Platters and formed his own group, Arthur Lee Maye & The Crowns. The group recorded several tunes, including "Love Me Always," that became a west coast hit.

Maye gave up music to concentrate on baseball. He worked his way through the minor leagues and debuted on July 17, 1959 for the Milwaukee Braves. He spent his first six years in baseball (1959–64) with the Braves. Those teams, with superstars Hank Aaron, Eddie Mathews and Warren Spahn, knew how to win.

Aaron became Maye's mentor. Maye explained, "Hank helped me out with a lot of things. When you first go to the major leagues and hit the ball well, they go to school on you. I usually liked the ball away, but then they started coming inside. Hank was my roommate at the time and he told me, 'Lee, just forget about the pitch away from you. Look for the ball inside and jerk it a couple times and they'll come right back out there to you.' And that's the way it happened."

In Washington, fans clapped their hands in unison, pleading for Maye to drive in some runs for the Senators. Maye and Williams battled each other to a count of three balls and two strikes. Williams had thrown more than 40 pitches in the inning. Frank Howard waited in the on-deck circle, meticulously wiping his bat with a hand towel.

Williams wound up and threw a low fastball on the inside corner, the perfect pitch for Maye to drive. The old outfielder swung. His bat hit the ball with a crack that resounded all around RFK Stadium. The line drive to deep right field flew above Hawk Harrelson's head and over the right-field fence for a grand slam. Cullen, Coleman and Unser rounded the bases and waited for Maye to arrive at home plate. Happy teammates waited in the Senators' dugout to congratulate the team's latest hero. Williams walked over to Maye and shook his hand. The two baseball veterans, fellow students of hitting, became friends during Maye's four months with the Senators.

Maye's home run, one of three Washington hits the entire game, gave Coleman plenty of cushion. His late-breaking, explosive fastball and dancing forkball dominated Cleveland's hitters. The Indians managed one unearned run, courtesy of a McMullen error in the 7th inning. The Senators prevailed, 4-1 thanks to Maye's clutch grand slam and Coleman's complete game. The Senators 82nd victory thrilled Washington. Long-suffering fans at RFK Stadium and in homes and bars from Chevy Chase, Maryland to Falls Church, Virginia cheered as one, releasing 17 years of pent up frustration. At last, Washington's faithful rooters enjoyed a baseball season full of smiles and laughter. The Senators' victory meant now and forevermore that every man on the 1969 Washington Senators claimed the well-deserved title – winner.

Maye remembered the grand slam, but not its value to Senators' supporters. He said, "When you're playing as well as we were playing

171

all you think about is going out and winning. You never kept up with records."

Washington fans loved watching Maye pound the ball during the summer of 1969. From the first day he joined the Senators, Maye played a major supporting role in the team's success. In 71 games with Washington, he hit .290, (.811 OPS). Nine of his 10 home runs came with the Senators. He gave Williams another strong left-handed bat to complement power hitters' Epstein, Howard, and McMullen. With Maye on board, the Senators earned a 54-40 record.

Maye deflected credit for the team's stellar performance for those 94 games. He said, "I can't truthfully say I had that much to do with it. But I'll tell you one thing, these guys didn't play like losers. They played super baseball. I'll never forget that year. They weren't superstars, except for maybe Frank Howard, but they played together well. To end up 10 games over .500 was the greatest thing to happen in a long time in Washington.

"Everybody thought, 'This team is a loser.' But somehow those guys felt that they could win and we won. I really enjoyed playing with the Washington Senators in 1969. It felt good to be part of a winning team. I have fond memories of how a bad ball club became a good ball club."

During off days and before games, Maye whiled away the hours talking baseball with Bob Humphreys, Ed Brinkman and Cullen, veterans who lived and breathed the game. He conversed about hitting with Williams for hours on end. Like his manager, Maye yearned to think, talk, practice, even dream, hitting.

Maye said, "Ted Williams, he was a student of hitting. He studied the pitchers. He studied the ball. If you wanted to talk hitting with Ted, he'd talk all night long. I always wanted to talk to someone who had been successful. I don't care how long you're in the game, there's something you can learn every day."

Maye's dedication to hitting impressed Teddy Ballgame. Maye recalled Washington coach Joe Camacho tell him, "Ted really liked you as a ballplayer." Maye committed his conversations with Williams to memory. He knew he could use his mentor's teachings at bat and, after he retired from baseball, to coach other ballplayers.

Retirement arrived sooner than expected. In September, 1970, at the end of an inconsistent, injury-filled season, the Senators released Maye. The White Sox claimed him days later and he finished the season with Chicago. On July 7, 1971, Arthur Lee Maye played his final baseball game. Age and a bum ankle he first injured playing for Houston in 1965 caught up with him. Despite the sad ending, Maye appreciated his long, eventful career. He said, "I love baseball and will always love it. If it wasn't for baseball – I don't know what would have happened to me."

The man who sewed up the Senators' winning season enjoyed a fine 13-year run in the major leagues. He stroked 1,109 hits and had a .277 batting average. In 1964, he paced the National League with 44 doubles. As a left-handed hitter, Maye felt his platoon role held down his career statistics. He struggled to hit left-handed pitching (.217 average, .566 OPS). But in 1964, the one season he made more than 600 plate appearances, he hit .303 (.771 OPS) against southpaws compared to .301 (.788 OPS) against right-handers.

Maye said, "I always thought I was an everyday ballplayer. I hit .300 in the minors just about every year playing every day. As a left-hand hitter, they start platooning you. Then you start losing faith in yourself. I had a good career, [but] it could have been better and, if I had played more, it would have been better. If I had played every day, I would have put some numbers up on the board, believe me I would have. But I wasn't there to tell them how to play me. I did what I was told to do."

His playing days over, the desire to coach hitting burned within him. From his first minor league at-bat, Maye and baseball became inseparable and he longed to stay connected to the game he loved. He remembered his long conversations with Williams about hitting and how much Williams respected his knowledge. He recalled Aaron's tutorials after games in the locker room and at hotels in every city in the National League. When it came to hitting, he had an expert's insight. He knew deep within the marrow of his bones he could be a top-notch hitting coach. Major leagues, minor leagues, it made no difference, he wanted just one opportunity to prove himself.

Maye's chance never came. More than twenty-five years after he retired, he said, his speech halting, voice barely above a whisper, "I always wanted to be a part of baseball after I finished playing and I made it known. For 10 years – for 10 straight years – I wrote to every ball club in the major leagues after I retired, seeking employment. I never got one answer. All I got was, 'I'll put you in the files.'

"I played 20 years of professional baseball. You mean to tell me that there isn't a place for me where I could teach kids how to play baseball, helping them become major league ballplayers? I wasn't a bad guy. I just never got an opportunity. After 10 years I said, 'Hey, the hell with it.' I just gave up on asking for employment. It never happened and I just learned to live without it."

Maye found other work. He became a dedicated and valued employee for Amtrak, the passenger rail service, for more than 20 years. He lived a vibrant, full life as an accomplished singer, sweet-swinging baseball player, hard-working railroad man, and faithful friend. He delivered the wondrous clutch hit that made the dreams of long-suffering Senators' fans come true.

Still, the pain and frustration of being denied the chance to coach, despite his many qualifications, ached inside him. Everywhere but on the playing field, racial prejudice still infected baseball in the 1970s and early 1980s. Non-whites who applied for coaching and front office jobs, with few exceptions, did so in vain. The snub left a hole in Maye's spirit. When he died on July 17, 2002, exactly 43 years to the day of his major league debut, his dream to become a hitting coach died inside him, unfulfilled.

The Senators relished their new role as winners. The confident, relaxed club swept Cleveland aside with two more victories. The sweep gave Washington a six-game winning streak and an 84-75 record. Three home games with the Red Sox remained in the 1969 season. A sweep over Boston meant third place in the American League East.

Boston ended the Senators' hopes of finishing in the top half of the division in the first game. The Red Sox defeated Casey Cox, 8-5. Howard gave his teammates and the fans a thrill when he hit his 48th home run, tying Harmon Killebrew for the league lead, but the loss meant Washington would finish in fourth place in their division.

The next afternoon, September 30, Bosman clinched the American League ERA title in the Senators' 7-2 win over the Red Sox. He allowed two runs in 6 2/3 innings to finish 1969 with a glittering 2.19 mark. His 14 wins led the team. In the top of the 9th inning, Williams replaced Howard in left field with Hank Allen. The crowd saluted Howard with a lengthy standing ovation.

Joe Coleman faced Boston rookie Ken Brett in the final game of the season. Howard hit in the lead off position, but Big Frank went without a homer in four plate appearances. In Minnesota, Harmon Killebrew connected for his 49th homer in the first inning. The Twins' slugger won the title over Howard by a single home run. Oakland's Reggie Jackson finished with 47 for third place.

For the Senators, Mike Epstein's three-run homer in the first inning, his 30th of the season, provided Coleman with more than enough runs on the crisp October 1 afternoon. Carl Yastrzemski hit his 40th home run of the season in the first inning, but Coleman permitted only one more hit the rest of the game. He retired Boston's final 15 batters for a complete game victory.

174

Coleman's exceptional performance gave him a 12-13 record in 1969. He served as the Senators' workhorse, with 248 innings pitched, 12 complete games, four shutouts and one save. He started eight more games than any teammate and threw 55 more innings than his closest competitor (Bosman's 193). He finished the season with a solid 3.27 ERA. The third player chosen in the first round of the 1965 draft finally seemed to blossom, giving the Senators a return on his $72,000 signing bonus.

Williams failed to appreciate the talented young pitcher, a gritty workhorse ready to become one of the finest, most durable pitchers in baseball. Coleman's manager saw only a stubborn young man with a losing record who walked too many batters (100 in 1969). Williams felt Coleman, who pitched with a fluid, easy motion – a style that minimized arm strain – lacked drive and intensity. He wanted to hear Coleman grunt when he threw, like Sam McDowell did or Max Scherzer does today. Sid Hudson said, "I think Ted expected more out of him then he got."

For his part, Coleman, a short-tempered player who often clashed with his managers, took a dim view of Williams' managerial abilities. After he left Washington, Coleman called Williams impulsive, overmatched as a manager, and a poor communicator.

The two men knew each other before Williams arrived in Washington. Coleman, a star at Natick High School in Massachusetts, attended Williams' schoolboy baseball camp in Lakeville for three years. Williams knew Coleman's father, Joe senior, from their battles in the 1940s and 50s. The elder Coleman, a World War II veteran like Williams, pitched for the Philadelphia Athletics, Baltimore Orioles and Detroit Tigers from 1942–55.

With the Senators, the familiarity between Williams and the younger Coleman bred only conflict. They first clashed over Williams' affection for the slider. Coleman hated the pitch. It hurt his arm. Williams insisted he throw it anyway. After two attempts left him with an aching shoulder, Coleman stopped the experiment. Hudson mediated the many disputes. He said with gentle understatement, "He and Williams didn't get along too well. With us, Joe was just learning how to pitch."

Coleman pitched more than 200 innings again in 1970, but Williams felt his 8-12 record made him expendable. While he decried Short's failure to consult him before he traded Coleman, Brinkman, Hannan and Aurelio Rodriguez to the Tigers for Denny McLain and three other Tigers, Williams felt little remorse over losing the young, disobedient pitcher.

175

Coleman flourished once he escaped Williams' shadow and Washington. He displayed amazing resilience. At the end of 1971 spring training, a line drive struck Coleman in the head and fractured his skull. On the way to the hospital, he convinced the ambulance driver to stop and order him a hamburger and milkshake. In four weeks, he returned to the mound and began his first 20-win season.

Coleman won 19 games in 1972. In Game 3 of the American League Championship Series he shut out Oakland, 3-0 and struck out 14 batters, still one of the top pitching performances in post-season history. He won 23 games in 1973, logging 288 innings, but struggled in later seasons as he and his Tigers' teammates aged.

Coleman managed to last six more seasons in the major leagues, pitching for six different teams. He finished his career with 142 victories and 135 losses. Of all the 1969 Senators' pitchers, only Camilo Pascual, with 174, won more. After retiring as a player in 1979, Coleman remained in baseball, coaching for the California Angels and St. Louis Cardinals. In 2016, after nine seasons as a minor league pitching coach in the High Class A Florida State League (2007-2011, Lakeland Flying Tigers and 2012-2015, Jupiter Hammerheads), the Miami Marlins promoted him to senior advisor of pitching development.

Coleman spent his final two years in Washington locked in battle with Williams, but his season-ending win over Boston on October 1, 1969 filled the Washington-Metro area with joy. Within RFK Stadium, 17,482 souls became friends and turned the ballpark into a Sunday afternoon neighborhood block party to say farewell to their Washington Senators. Life-long Senators' fan Jim Hartley summed up the jubilant atmosphere in the stadium. "You identified with them," he said. "They were your extended family, your cousins that you went to see play their ball games. And they did so well."

The plucky, hard-working Senators finished the 1969 season with 86 wins and 76 losses, a 21-game upgrade over the previous season, to salute Williams' first year as their manager. Washington improved by more games than any other team in baseball except the eventual world champion Mets.

When Brinkman fielded Rico Petrocelli's ground ball and fired it to Epstein for the game and the season's final out, the crowd stood and cheered in a long, extended crescendo of joy to thank the Senators for their wonderful season. The din began in the box seats behind first base, near the Senators' dugout and grew to a full throated roar that rose to the topmost peaks of RFK, way up into the upper deck where Howard hit his most prodigious home run blasts.

Fans stomped, clapped, whistled and shouted as one. As the happy noise reached its peak and filled every corner of the ballpark, the 1969 Washington Senators departed. Some waved. A few tipped their caps. Others walked, heads bowed, into the clubhouse. Still the fans' loud adoration rang on. Williams, the last man to leave the field, stopped, peered into the crowd, smiled, waved his arms, slowly descended, step by step, into the dugout and disappeared.

Arthur Lee Maye
(National Baseball Hall of Fame Library, Cooperstown, NY)

Joe Coleman, Autograph Day, July 12, 1969
Private Collection of Mark Hornbaker (Used with Permission)

**1969 Senators Final Game Scorecard,
October 1, 1969 vs. Boston. Washington wins 3-2.**
(Scorecard provided courtesy of the private collection
of Rob Johnson.)

1969 Senators Final Game Scorecard,
Note Frank Howard leading off.
(Scorecard provided courtesy of the private collection of
Rob Johnson.)

Epilogue: Everything but the Memories

"Thanks for....remembering."

-Darold Knowles

Soon after Williams left the field, the last Senator to leave on the last day of the 1969 season, the cheers fell silent. Fans exited RFK Stadium with sweet memories. The following weeks brought more good news. Sportswriters voted Ted Williams the American League Manager of the Year. Dick Bosman won the ERA title. Del Unser led the league in triples. Frank Howard scored fourth in the league's most valuable player award voting. The Senators drew 918,106 fans, 6th best in the American League and 371,445 more than 1968 (a 68 percent increase).

Hope in a bright future for the Washington Senators faded all too soon. In 1970, the Senators struggled to recapture 1969's magic. Despite Ed Brinkman's great fielding at shortstop, third baseman Aurelio Rodriguez's acrobatics, Howard's slugging and a 16-win season from Bosman, the team limped to a 70-78 record. With 14 games left to play, a strong finish like 1969 meant another .500 season.

Instead, Williams' men lost every game. The absurd streak of futility sucked the spirit and vigor from fans and team alike. It marked an early peal of the death knell of major league baseball in Washington. Resurrection took more than 33 years.

After the collapse of 1970, Short blew up the team. By May 1971, the Senators' owner released or traded away Ken McMullen, Ed Stroud, Dave Baldwin, Hank Allen, Barry Moore, Brant Alyea, Lee Maye, Bob Humphreys, Dennis Higgins, Mike Epstein, Darold Knowles, Joe Coleman, Jim Hannan, and Ed Brinkman. The 1971 Senators, a dysfunctional team of strangers, made a sorry spectacle, losing 96 games – with sore-armed malcontent Denny McLain its perfect symbol. The wretched club wore out Williams. Del Unser said, "I think after awhile he wasn't as excited about [managing]. I think he just got tired of it.

We were a bad club. Some of the chemistry, the craziness, the fun was gone."

When the 1971 season ended, the Washington Senators died. As he had done before with the Minneapolis Lakers, Short moved his team, this time to Arlington, Texas. A hanging in effigy during the Senators' final game in Washington and a fan's beer poured over his head during an Orioles' game at Memorial Stadium in 1972 marked Washington's meager revenge.

182

No one thought Short could pry baseball from the nation's capital. Fans, the federal government and the D.C. Armory Board saw the national pastime as their private entitlement. Even Short's legitimate gripes – the lack of fences and brighter lights in stadium parking lots, cold hot dogs and warm beer, exhibition football games at RFK during torrential downpours, and a poor stadium lease agreement – fell on complacent, deaf ears.

Short did get parking lot fences and lights with higher wattage, but only after President Nixon intervened. Otherwise, few felt the slightest compunction to help a millionaire owner, even one wallowing in debt. People in the Washington area trusted Nixon, Bowie Kuhn and Congress to block any move to another city the nefarious Short threatened. "Let him grouse," they thought, "the Senators aren't going anywhere."

Everyone underestimated Short. In September 1971, the same silver tongue that coaxed Williams back into baseball convinced 10 American League owners to approve his club's move to Texas. With that, baseball in Washington disappeared. The joy of 1969 turned to dismal despair.

The loss of the Senators left Ron Menchine, a life-long Washington sports fan, dejected. One half of the Senators' radio broadcast team from 1969-71, he toiled in obscurity for 13 years. As a broadcast specialist for the Army, he taped a show of sports highlights sent to Fort Churchill in Manitoba, Canada called "Night Train to Churchill." Later, he broadcast Atlantic Coast Conference basketball at WDNC in Durham, North Carolina. He announced Navy football for WNAV in Annapolis and WBAL in Baltimore.

When Short purchased the Senators and put the team's radio and television contracts up for bid, Menchine was the sports' editor at WWDC radio in Washington, D.C. In a surprise outcome, Menchine's station outbid long-time incumbent WTOP for the club's broadcast rights.

Menchine said, "At the age of 35, I was doing major league baseball." He worked side-by-side with partner Shelby Whitfield, the team-employed Voice of the Senators. In 1971, he teamed with Tony Roberts.

Erudite, sophisticated, with a broad vocabulary and a rich baritone voice made smooth with Jack Daniel's, his favorite whiskey, Menchine soon won over Washington fans used to hearing John McLean and Dan Daniels. He brought a deep love for baseball to his work, even though he last broadcast the game as a college student at the University of Maryland from 1953-56.

There, he learned his craft from professionals working in the area at the time – Ernie Harwell, Bob Wolff and Jim Simpson. Harwell and Wolff later received the National Baseball Hall of Fame's Ford C. Frick award for excellence in broadcasting. These men arranged auxiliary booths in the press box for Menchine to sit in and record himself announcing major league baseball games. Afterward, Harwell, Wolff and Simpson critiqued his work.

Menchine said, "The most important thing that I learned from all of them was that preparation is the backbone of your work. I would go through the press guides and learn the nuances of the ballplayers, a little background information on the various players. Where they had gone to college; what their hobbies were. Things you could throw into a broadcast. It makes all the difference in the world. If you prepared for a game, you never felt at a loss for words."

Menchine enjoyed a productive career as a broadcaster, voice-over specialist for radio advertising, and author of books on baseball and World War II postcards. Washington baseball fans remember and respect him for the eloquent bravado he displayed during the Senators' final game in Washington, the saddest moment in Menchine's career.

He said, "I had lunch that afternoon with Ron Weber, who did Capitals' ice hockey for many years. It was a rainy day. I told Ron, 'I hope the game's rained out.' I didn't want to broadcast because of the emotions involved. As it turned out, under the circumstances, it may have been the best work I ever did."

Menchine described the game's melancholy, but memorable moments – Howard's home run, the Senators' late inning comeback, the fans storming the field, the game being forfeit to the Yankees with one out to go. During the game, he held inside his deep personal loss. Years later, he said, "This is my lifetime job, my dream job come true. I'd been waiting all my life to do major league baseball and after three years it was taken away from me."

The toxic combination of Bob Short's wanderlust and the local region's apathy left Menchine and Washington baseball fans with nothing – except for the memories. Short moved a baseball franchise, but could not pack away the pleasant reveries Washington Senators' fans from Chevy Chase, Maryland to Centreville, Virginia held deep inside their minds and hearts.

Many recalled the first game with Dad when they glimpsed the green field peeking through the narrow openings on the mezzanine level, offering just a glimpse of its beauty. Then, after the long trek up RFK's concrete switchback ramps, hustling through the narrow portals to see the diamond below, wide and clear in emerald splendor.

Others remembered the first time they arrived early to get an autograph from their favorite player, or watch batting practice, or celebrate a birthday. Maybe the Senators won in the bottom of the 9th inning or Frank Howard hit a long home run.

Short could never steal memories of the incomparable smells of Washington baseball. Odors that swirled into a sublime mix of summer heat and humidity, the hint of a breeze at sunset, cigar smoke, beer, hot dogs and pretzels. The pizza, sold in those square white boxes that made perfect bases for backyard baseball games the next afternoon (I'm Brinkman! I'm Cazzie! I'm Unser! No kid dared pretend to be Howard), had an indescribable odor all its own.

The sounds were extraordinary, too: the organ, the unprompted rhythmic clapping for a rally, the gentle conversation between friends, and the eerie percussion of thousands of wooden bats pounding against concrete on Bat Day. Most unique, the loud pop-pop-pop of beer and soda cups in the upper deck, a dirge mourning defeat most years, but in 1969 often a victory salute.

Told to other generations with a little dramatic embellishment, these memories kept the faint heartbeat of baseball in Washington alive.

The Senators' 1998 reunion made that pulse beat a little quicker. It reached its peak that sunny November morning when Ted Williams spoke to the adoring crowd. Sadly, the frail legend could not go on forever. Exhausted, he motioned to his son, John Henry, said good-bye to the fans and his players, and then gingerly lowered himself into his wheelchair. John Henry wheeled his father off the stage, out a side door, and back to his hotel room.

With that, as seasons end, fading into record books and memories, the 1969 Senators reunion drew to a close. The old Senators, one by one, left the Westfields Inn and Conference Center, passing through the revolving door that transformed them from heroes back into regular men, as obscure and wonderful as anyone might be. One, Howard, remains a local legend. Another, Williams, endures in death as an American legend. The others returned to simple, everyday lives. Yet, to those who watched them play in the boundless summer of 1969, the year impossible dreams came true, all remain heroic in the green field of our memories and abide forever young in our hearts.

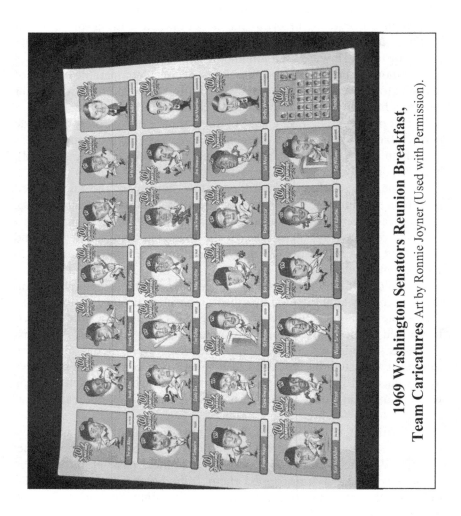

1969 Washington Senators Reunion Breakfast, Team Caricatures Art by Ronnie Joyner (Used with Permission).

RFK Stadium, Summer 1969
Private Collection of Mark Hornbaker (Used with Permission)

Epilogue for the 50th Anniversary Edition
A Relentless Hope

"When the LORD restored the captives of Zion, we thought we were dreaming.
Then our mouths were filled with laughter; our tongues sang for joy."

-Psalm 126:1-2

The 1969 Senators' season meant far more than Frank Howard's 48 home runs, Lee Maye's grand slam that guaranteed a winning season, Dick Bosman's ERA title, scores of heroic performances and several improbable comeback victories. After Bob Short moved the Senators to Texas after the 1971 season, the Senators gave Washington baseball fans the only thing they had besides memories -- hope.

1969 reminded fans that, for one great Summer, baseball mattered here, brought lasting joy, and united the entire region. Year after year, decade after decade, fans held onto the dream that a team like that might play ball in Washington again. They held that undying, relentless hope through years of unrequited expectations and last-minute broken promises.

Hope inspired thousands to attend "Bring Baseball Back" rallies and tens of thousands to pay exorbitant prices for exhibition games that featured creaky old timers or half-interested major leaguers playing in a stadium configured for football, complete with an absurd 250 foot left field wall.

Hope compelled people to pray that baseball would ultimately see the wisdom in granting an expansion team or moving a struggling franchise to the nation's fifth largest media market -- but then watched incredulous as cities like Tampa Bay and Miami got teams instead.

Hope sustained faith that baseball would return even after San Diego found an owner less than a day before a deal to sell the Padres to a D.C. owner was consummated and Houston voters, by one-tenth of one percent, voted to fund a new stadium, leaving D.C. in exile again.

On several occasions, Frank Howard made a compelling business case for baseball to return to the nation's capital. In 1999, he said, "Let's say you go from Washington, D.C. to Richmond, Virginia, which is 90 miles away. Let's say you go from Washington, D.C. out west to Front Royal, Virginia, which is Fairfax County, Fauquier County, Loudoun

County; let's say you go north up into Frederick, Maryland and Hagerstown, and – believe it or not – there's probably as much Washington sentiment up (there) as there is sentiment toward Baltimore. Between that Northern Virginia, Southern Virginia, Northwestern Maryland part of our area, you've got five million people living. And you've got a growth factor of about seven million in the next 25 years.

"You've got the highest per capita income of any area in the country. You've got radio and television and media coverage that rates in the top five. So, if you're looking at the big picture, there's no way that the greater Washington area does not merit or deserve major league baseball. I think it's going to come. I think it's going to happen. When, I don't know."

But it required more than cold, logical economics to convince owners to approve a team for Washington. Logic speaks to the head. It's the heart that drives action. Washington baseball fans needed an advocate who could describe their relentless hope in a charismatic, heartfelt way.

Who better to play that role than Ted Williams?

It happened on November 8, 1998, in the last minute of the 1969 Senators' reunion breakfast. Williams had already captivated the room, but had 25 more vital words to say. The 80-year old man, frail yet still electric when he spoke, gave the event its coda and the drive to bring baseball back to D.C. its heart. Media covering the event wrote and broadcast his words to the nation.

Williams said, "Keep the faith about Washington. Because I can't think of a better place, and probably the best place, to have major league baseball come back."

Ted Williams, the great man who convinced the Hall of Fame to open its doors to Negro League players, had smashed the final barrier keeping D.C. out of the big leagues. The Splendid Splinter spoke a truth that baseball could no longer ignore or deny. Just shy of seven years later, baseball returned.

Thus, the gift of the 1969 Senators became, at long, long last, hope fulfilled.

Statistics

1969 Washington Senators Roster and Statistics

WON-86 LOST-76
MGR: Ted Williams, 86-76
AWAY: 39-42 HOME: 47-34

VS. AL EAST: 51-39
VS. AL WEST: 35-37
ONE RUN GAMES: 27-29
DOUBLEHEADERS: 7-2-7

Pitchers	B	T	HT	WT	YR	W	L	ERA	G	GS	CG	IP	H	BB	SO	AB	H	BA
Dave Baldwin	R	R	6'2"	200	4	2	4	4.05	43	0	0	66.2	57	34	51	7	0	.000
Frank Bertaina	L	L	5'11"	180	6	1	3	6.56	14	5	0	35.2	43	23	25	11	4	.364
Dick Bosman	R	R	6'3"	205	4	14	5	2.19	31	26	5	193	156	39	99	64	6	.094
Cisco Carlos	R	R	6'3"	205	3	1	1	4.58	6	4	0	17.2	23	6	5	5	1	.200
Joe Coleman	R	R	6'3"	177	5	12	13	3.27	40	36	12	247.2	222	100	182	84	9	.107
Casey Cox	R	R	6'5"	200	4	12	7	2.78	52	13	4	171.2	161	64	73	47	5	.106
Jan Dukes	L	L	5'11"	175	1	0	2	2.45	8	0	0	11	8	4	3	1	0	.000
Jim Hannan	R	R	6'3"	200	8	7	6	3.64	35	28	1	158.1	138	91	72	52	6	.115
Dennis Higgins	R	R	6'4"	190	4	10	9	3.48	55	0	0	85.1	79	56	71	11	1	.091
Bob Humphreys	R	R	5'10"	170	8	3	3	3.05	47	0	0	79.2	69	38	43	13	1	.077
Darold Knowles	L	L	6'0"	185	5	9	2	2.24	53	0	0	84.1	73	31	59	13	1	.077
Frank Kreutzer	R	L	6'1"	190	6	0	0	4.50	4	0	0	2	3	2	2	0	0	---
Jim Miles	R	R	6'2"	205	2	0	1	6.20	10	1	0	20.1	19	15	15	3	1	.333
Barry Moore	L	L	6'1"	190	5	9	8	4.30	31	25	4	134	123	67	51	43	9	.209
Camilo Pascual	R	R	5'11"	185	16	2	5	6.83	14	13	0	55.1	49	38	34	17	4	.235
Jim Shellenback	L	L	6'2"	200	3	4	7	4.04	30	11	2	84.2	87	48	50	27	5	.185

190

	B	T	HT	WT	YR	G	AB	H	2B	3B	HR	R	RBI	BB	SO	SB	BA	SA
Catchers																		
Paul Casanova	R	R	6'4"	200	5	124	379	82	9	2	4	26	37	18	52	0	.216	.282
Jim French	R	R	5'7"	182	5	63	158	29	6	3	2	14	13	41	15	1	.184	.297
Doug Camilli	R	R	5'11"	195	9	1	3	1	0	0	0	0	0	0	2	0	.333	.333
Infielders																		
Bernie Allen	L	R	6'0"	185	8	122	365	90	17	4	9	33	45	50	35	5	.247	.389
Ed Brinkman	R	R	6'0"	170	9	151	576	153	18	5	2	71	43	50	42	2	.266	.325
Tim Cullen	R	R	6'1"	185	4	119	249	52	7	1	1	22	15	14	27	1	.209	.249
Mike Epstein	L	L	6'4"	230	4	131	403	112	18	1	30	73	85	85	99	2	.278	.551
Toby Harrah	R	R	5'11"	165	1	8	1	0	0	0	0	4	0	0	0	0	.000	.000
Gary Holman	L	L	6'1"	200	2	41	31	5	1	0	0	1	2	4	7	0	.161	.194
Ken McMullen	R	R	6'3"	195	8	158	562	153	25	2	19	83	87	70	103	4	.272	.425
Zoilo Versalles	R	R	5'10"	150	11	31	75	20	2	1	0	9	6	3	13	1	.267	.320
Outfielders																		
Hank Allen	R	R	6'0"	190	4	109	271	75	9	3	1	42	17	13	28	12	.277	.343
Brant Alyea	R	R	6'3"	215	3	104	237	59	4	0	11	29	40	34	67	1	.249	.405
Dick Billings	R	R	6'1"	190	2	27	37	5	0	0	0	3	0	6	8	0	.135	.135
Sam Bowens	R	R	6'2"	195	7	33	57	11	1	0	0	6	4	5	14	1	.193	.211
Frank Howard	R	R	6'7"	260	12	161	592	175	17	2	48	111	111	102	96	1	.296	.574
Lee Maye	L	R	6'2"	190	11	71	238	69	9	3	9	41	26	20	25	1	.290	.466
Dick Smith	R	R	6'5"	200	1	21	28	3	0	0	0	2	0	4	7	0	.107	.107
Ed Stroud	L	R	5'11"	175	4	123	206	52	5	6	4	35	29	30	33	12	.252	.393
Del Unser	L	L	5'11"	180	2	153	581	166	19	8	7	69	57	58	54	8	.286	.382

Sources: Baseball Encyclopedia, 2004 Edition; Washington Senators 1969 Press-Radio TV Guide; Retrosheet

Bibliography

Books

Aaron, Hank. *I Had a Hammer: The Hank Aaron Story*. New York: Harper Collins, 1991.

Andre, Sam E., ed. *Street and Smith's Official Yearbook: 1969 Baseball*. New York: Conde Nast Publications, 1969.

Baldwin, Dave. *Snake Jazz*. Philadelphia: Xlibris Corporation, 2007.

Boswell, Thomas (Dick Schaap, ed.). "All of Us Bear the Marks of the Lash." In *How Life Imitates the World Series*. New York: Doubleday & Company, Penguin Books, 1982: 97-112.

_____. "Sometimes I Think He's Too Good for the Game." In *How Life Imitates the World Series*. New York: Doubleday, 1982: 184-190.

Frommer, Frederic J. *The Washington Nationals 1859 to Today: The Story of Baseball in the Nation's Capital*. Lanham, MD: Taylor Trade Publishing, 2006.

Gagnon, Cappy. *Notre Dame Baseball Greats: From Anson to Yaz*. San Francisco: Arcadia Publishing, 2004.

Gough, David and Jim Bard. *Little Nel: The Nellie Fox Story; an Up-Close and Personal Look at Baseball's "Mighty Mite."* Alexandria, VA: D.L. Megbec Publishing, 2000.

Halberstam, David. *The Teammates: A Portrait of Friendship*. New York: Hyperion Books, 2003.

Hartley, James R. *Washington's Expansion Senators (1961-1971)*. Germantown, MD: Corduroy Press, 1998.

James, Bill and Jim Henzler. *Win Shares*. Morton Grove, IL: STATS Publishing, 2002.

Leavengood, Ted and Bosman, Dick. *Dick Bosman on Pitching: Lessons from the Life of a Major League Ballplayer and Pitching Coach*. Lanham, Maryland: Rowland & Littlefield, 2018.

Lingo, Will, ed. *Baseball America Directory 2008*, Durham, N.C., Baseball America, Inc., 2008.

Maraniss, David. *Clemente: The Passion and Grace of Baseball's Last Hero*. New York: Simon & Schuster, 2006.

Neft, David S., Richard M. Cohen, and Michael L. Neft. *The Sports Encyclopedia: Baseball 2000, 20th Edition*. New York: St. Martin's Press, 2000.

Okkonen, Marc. *Baseball Uniforms of the Twentieth Century: The Official Major League Baseball Guide*. New York: Sterling Publishing, 1993.

Palmer, Pete, and Gary Gillette, eds. *The Baseball Encyclopedia, 2004.* New York: Barnes and Noble Publishing, 2004.

Ritter, Lawrence S. *Lost Ballparks: A Celebration of Baseball's Legendary Fields.* New York: Penguin, Viking Studio Books, 1992.

Seidel, Michael. *Ted Williams: A Baseball Life.* Lincoln, NE: University of Nebraska Press, 2000.

Smith, Curt. *Voices of the Game.* South Bend, IN: Diamond Communications, 1987.

Smith, Don and Ed Croke, eds. *Professional Baseball the First 100 Years: Official Centennial Edition.* New York: Poretz-Ross Publishers, Inc., 1969.

Spatz, Lyle, ed. *The SABR Baseball List and Record Book.* New York: Simon & Schuster, Scribner, 2007.

Stang, Mark and Phil Wood. *Nationals on Parade: 70 Years of Washington Nationals Photos.* Wilmington, OH: Orange Frazer Press, 2005.

Thorn, John, Pete Palmer, and Michael Gershman, eds. *Total Baseball: The Official Encyclopedia of Major League Baseball, Fourth Edition.* New York: Penguin Books, Viking, 1995.

Washington Senators Baseball Club. *1969 Press-Radio Television Guide*, 1969.

_____. *American League Official Scorecard Program: Welcome Back to Baseball*, 1969.

West, Steve and Nowlin, Bill. *The Team That Couldn't Hit: The 1972 Texas Rangers.* Phoenix, Arizona: Society for American Baseball Research, 2019.

Whitfield, Shelby. *Kiss It Goodbye.* New York: Abelard-Schuman, 1973.

Wilkerson, Isabel. *The Warmth of Other Suns: The Epic Story of America's Great Migration.* New York: Vintage Books, a Division of Random House, Inc., 2011.

Williams Ted and John Underwood. *The Science of Hitting.* New York: Simon & Schuster, 1970.

_____. *My Turn at Bat: The Story of My Life (New Edition).* New York: Simon & Schuster, Fireside Books, 1988.

Interviews by Author

(Note: All interviews were conducted by telephone and recorded unless otherwise noted).

Allen, Bernie. Transcript. July 2, 2007.

Allen, Carol. Westfields Inn and Conference Center, Chantilly, VA, November 7, 1998.

Allen, Hank. November 14, 1998.

Alyea, Brant. May 24, 2007.

Baldwin, Dave. April 25, 2007.

Bosman, Dick. January 6, 1999.

Brinkman, Ed. February 12, 1999.

Byrd, Mark. Westfields Inn and Conference Center, Chantilly, VA, November 7, 1998.

Cassell, Rob. Westfields Inn and Conference Center, Chantilly, VA, November 7, 1998.

Cox, Casey. Westfields Inn and Conference Center, Chantilly, VA, November 7, 1998.

French, Jim. Transcript. May 23, 2007.

Gallagher, Keith. Westfields Inn and Conference Center, Chantilly, VA, November 7, 1998.

Hamlin, Kevin. Westfields Inn and Conference Center, Chantilly, VA, November 7, 1998.

Hartley, James. Silver Spring, MD, November 28, 2007.

Higgins, Dennis. Westfields Inn and Conference Center, Chantilly, VA, November 7, 1998.

Howard, Frank. February 9, 1999.

Hudson, Sid. May 29, 1998.

Humphreys, Bob. Transcript. June 6, 2007.

Knowles, Darold. January 15, 2007.

Maye, Arthur Lee. November 18, 1998.

McMullen, Ken. Transcript. January 4, 2007.

Menchine, Ron. Country Club of Maryland, Baltimore, MD, February, 2005.

Morgan, Charles. Westfields Inn and Conference Center, Chantilly, VA, November 7, 1998.

Oppermann, Paul. November 27, 2007.

Schlesinger, Richard. Westfields Inn and Conference Center, Chantilly, VA, November 7, 1998.

Stroud, Ed. Transcript. June 4, 1998.

Summers, Jack. Westfields Inn and Conference Center, Chantilly, VA, November 7, 1998.

Terwilliger, Wayne. January 7, 1999.

Unser, Del. March 18, 2008.

Newspapers, Magazines and Journal Articles

(Note: *Washington Post* and *Los Angeles Times* articles were obtained
from ProQuest Historical Newspapers).

Addie, Bob. "Addie's Atoms: A Tribute to Hondo." *Sporting News*, July
26, 1969: 14.
_____. "Back to Business." *Washington Post*, July 25, 1969: D1.
_____. "Happy Stottlemyre Calls Himself Lucky." *Washington Post*,
April 8, 1969: D5.
_____. "Homer, Sweet Homer." *Washington Post*, April 11, 1969: D3.
_____. "Musical Chair Time." *Washington Post*. July 5, 1969: C1.
_____. "Nats Ready to Pull Out of Buffalo." *Washington Post*. July 28,
1969: D1.
_____. "New Ball Game." *Washington Post*. April 2, 1969: D1.

_____. "Senators Present Williams 11-3 Gift: Howard Hits 41st Homer
Against A's." *Washington Post*, August 31, 1969: K1+.
_____. "Short Irate Over Field, May Sue." *Washington Post*, August 6,
1969: D1.
_____. "Short Often Long." *Washington Post*. February 8, 1969: D1.
_____. "Tickets Aplenty." *Washington Post*, July 24, 1969: C2.
_____. "Unaccustomed to Crowds." *Washington Post*. July 12, 1969: C1.
Asher, Mark. "It's a Steal, French Finds on Key Dash." *Washington
Post*, May 5, 1969: D1.
Attner, Paul. "Allen's Thwarted Dash for Home Just One of Nats' Many
Mistakes: Williams Refuses to Assign Goat's Role." *Washington
Post*, July 9, 1969: C4.
_____. "Just Ask French: Senators Terrific in All Departments."
Washington Post, July 8, 1969: B1.
Brady, Dave. "Not All Errors on Diamond." *Washington Post*, April 8,
1969: D1+.
Coons, Ron. "Nine Int. Pitchers Fail to Curb Nat Sluggers." *Sporting
News*, August 23, 1969: 34.
Denlinger, Kenneth. "Baseball's Great Men, Moments Are Honored:
Williams Skips Banquet." *Washington Post*, July 22, 1969: D1+.
Gildea, William. "Groundskeeper Mooney Faces Stupendous Task."
Washington Post, August 5, 1969: D1.
_____. "Nat Booster Aims for One Million Fans." *Washington Post*,
March 22, 1969: D1.

_____. "Nats Sign Williams to Five-Year Contract: Best-Ever Pact Inked at Midnight." *Washington Post*, February 22, 1969: E1+.

_____. "Nats Signing of Williams Draws Near." *Washington Post*, February 21, 1969: B1+.

_____. "Nixon Told to Keep Attending." *Washington Post*, July 16, 1969: D3.

_____ "On Today's Scene: Stadium Infected by Natsomania." *Washington Post*, July 16, 1969: D3.

_____. "Return to Baseball Surprises Williams, Too." *Washington Post*, February 16, 1969: D1+.

_____. "Ruth Voted Greatest Ever; Johnson on All-Time Team: Williams Named to All-Living Club." *Washington Post*, July 22, 1969: D1+.

_____. "We Can Take Off from Here, Williams Says of Senators." *Washington Post*, July 17, 1969: D4.

_____. "Williams Happy as a Rookie: Senators Hitting Like Old No. 9." *Washington Post*, April 10, 1969: H1+.

Guback, Steve. "Nixon's Baseball Pitch Hard to Handle." *Washington Star,* April 8, 1969: A1+.

Jock. "Would Mike Epstein Like to Be a Yankee? What Can I Tell You? Don't Ask." May-June 1970: 98-102.

Lamey, Mike. "Cover Boy? Alyea Can't Get Over It." *Sporting News*, May 9, 1970: 3.

Leavengood, Ted. "Do You Believe in Magic? Baseball Returns to D.C." *Elysian Fields Quarterly: The Baseball Review*, Summer 2005: 9-19.

Los Angeles Times, 1969. "Ted Williams' Rookie Year as Manager: 'Just Great.'" October 4: C1+.

MacPherson, Myra. "Some Innovations, But the Same Old Score." *Washington Post,* April 8, 1969: B1.

Marcks, Drew. "1,700 Crowd Airport to Greet Nats." *Washington Post*, July 7, 1969: C1.

Minot, George, Jr. "All-Stars to Try Again this Afternoon at 1:45: Rain Sets Game Back First Time." *Washington Post*, July 23, 1969: D1+.

_____. "Appearance of Knowles Cheers Nats." *Washington Post*, May 24, 1969: C1.

_____. "Bosman Blanks Bosox on Seven Hits: Senators Win, 5-0, Unser Has Three RBI." *Washington Post*, July 7, 1969: C1+.

_____. "Bosman Hurls One-Hitter at Indians: Streaking Senators Defeat Tiant, 5-0." *Washington Post*, May 3, 1969: C1+.

_____. "Brinkman's Single Beats Orioles: Senators Win, 3-2, with Run in Ninth." *Washington Post*, September 16, 1969: D1+.

_____. "Casanova Needed a Little Loving: Selkirk's Shock Treatment Leaves Catcher Badly Burned." *Washington Post*, June 30, 1968: D4.

_____. "Casanova's Five RBI Sink White Sox: Catcher's Homer, Single, Fly Help Senators Win, 7-5." *Washington Post*, June 1, 1969: D1.

_____. "Cullen Stars as Senators Romp, 7-3: Even Triple Play Can't Save Tigers." *Washington Post*, July 16, 1969: D1+.

_____. "Disputed Homer in Eleventh Beats Nats: F. Robinson Lands Orioles 6-3 Bulge." *Washington Post*, June 25, 1969: C1+.

_____. "Gutteridge Turns to Rule Book, Discovers Umps Were Right." *Washington Post*, June 1, 1969: D2.

_____. "Howard Blasts Number Seven, Senators Rip Tribe, 10-3." *Washington Post*, April 26, 1969: D1+.

_____. "Howard Doubtful of All-Star Start: But He Will Play." *Washington Post*, July 6, 1969: H1.

_____. "Howard Hits 33rd as Senators Sweep: 31,700 Revel in 502-Footer." *Washington Post*, July 14, 1969: D1+.

_____. "Howard Hits Two More, Nats Win, 9-6: Sixteen-Hit Attack Lifts Team Mark to .361." *Washington Post*, April 11, 1969: D1.

_____. "Howard Put on Trade Block as Demands Enrage Short: McMullen Holds Out for $40,000." *Washington Post*, March 2, 1969: 145+.

_____. "Howard Shatters Tribe with 31st, 32nd: Reliever Cox Hurls Twenty Straight Outs, Senators Win, 7-2." *Washington Post*, July 8, 1969: B1+.

_____. "Indians Cut Down Senators, 6-5: Hank Allen Nailed at Plate in Ninth." *Washington Post*, July 9, 1969: C1+.

_____. "Knowles Loses Nickname, But Lives Up to it: Happy Senators' Reliever Unhappy with Air Force." *Washington Post*, June 8, 1969: D1.

_____. "Late Outburst Lifts Nats to 10-6 Triumph." *Washington Post*, March 24, 1969: C1.

_____. "Learning Baseball Lessons Helps Alyea Improve Closet: Senators' Poet, Music Lover, Fashion-Plate." *Washington Post*, June 1, 1969: D4.

_____. "Maye's Grand Slam Trips Indians: Senators Certain of Winning Year." *Washington Post*, September 27, 1969: E1+.

_____. "McCovey Hits Two as NL Breezes, 9-3: 45,259 See Five Homers in Star Game." *Washington Post*, July 24, 1969: C1+.

_____. "Nats Ask Waivers on Phil Ortega." *Washington Post*, March 30, 1969: D3.

_____. "Nats Closer to Signing Williams: Short, Slugger Hint Readiness." *Washington Post*, February 14, 1969: C1.

_____. "Nats Lose Eighth -- Reluctantly: Dawdling Humphreys Irritates Williams." *Washington Post*, March 15, 1969: D1+.

_____. "Nats Lose Opener to Yanks, 8-4." *Washington Post*, April 8, 1969: A1+.

_____. "Nats Make It Big Day, 9-3: Boston Bows to Williams." *Washington Post,* April 24, 1969: C1.

_____. "Nats Shut Out Expos for Second Victory: Coleman Sharp in Five-Inning Stint." *Washington Post*, March 19, 1969: D1+.

_____. "Pascual, Baldwin Halt Tribe." *Washington Post*, May 4, 1969: C1.

_____. "Pascual Is Dazzling, But Nats Fizzle, 5-2." *Washington Post*, March 10, 1969: D1+.

_____. "Peterson Clouts Three as Nats Win, 18-5: Braves First Victims of Spring." *Washington Post*, March 16, 1969: C1.

_____. "Peterson Dealt to Indians for Rookie Pitcher." *Washington Post*, April 1, 1969: D3.

_____. "Senators Ambush Twins with Three in Eighth: Stroud's Triple Revives Nats." *Washington Post*, August 17, 1969: D1+.

_____. "Senators Envision Happy New Year: Fans Hated to See '69 End." *Washington Post*, October 5, 1969: H1.

_____. "Senators Face A's in Start of Western Swing." *Washington Post*, May 6, 1969: D1.

_____. "Senators Pay Forfeit as Fans Danced at Wake: Wild Ending Tops Howard's Home Run." *Washington Post*, October 1, 1971: D1+.

_____. "Senators Pay Visit to Twins." *Washington Post*, June 6, 1969: D1+.

_____. "Senators Swamp Tigers in Tenth: Alyea's Home Run Caps Five-Run Rally, Relieves Joe Coleman." *Washington Post*, June 21, 1969. E1+

_____. "Senators Take Twinbill by 3-2 Scores: Sweep Cools Off Greedy White Sox." *Washington Post*, May 19, 1969: D1+.

_____. "Senators Win, Hand Title to Orioles: McMullen's Bat Pounds Tigers, 11-6." *Washington Post*, September 14, 1969: D1+.

_____. "Senators Win Two; Howard Homers: Hannan, Carlos, Rain Stop Angels."*Washington Post*, September 3, 1969: D1+.

_____. "Short Now Optimist on Nats' Attendance." *Washington Post*, July 16, 1969: D1.

_____. "Short Quickly Signs Pascual for $45,000." *Washington Post*, February 27, 1969: C1+.

_____. "Short Re-Enters Sports World as Nats' Owner." *Washington Post*, December 4, 1968: D1.

_____. "Short Will Talk to Fox about Managing Nats." *Washington Post*, February 11, 1969: C1.

_____. "Three Homers Wrap Up Sweep by Senators." *Washington Post*, June 30, 1969: D1+

_____. "To Home Hero, Another Game: All-Stars Howard, Knowles." *Washington Post*, July 20, 1969: D1.

_____. "Unser's Homer Beats Orioles, 11-8: Senators Blow 6-1 Edge After Howard Hits Number Twenty-Two." *Washington Post*, June 26, 1969: D1+.

_____. "Unser's Shot in Twelfth Stuns Twins: Epstein, Howard, Killebrew Connect."*Washington Post*, June 9, 1969: D1+.

_____. "Williams Has Touch: Nats' Boss Can Handle Own Pitchers, Too." *Washington Post*, July 13, 1969: C1.

_____. "Williams, Nixon Stars of Opener." *Washington Post*, April 6, 1969: D1+.

_____. "Williams Thinks Senators Don't, But Their Attitude Pleases Him: Hitters Talented from Neck Down." *Washington Post*. March 4, 1969: D1+.

_____. "Winning Occupies His Mind as Williams Goes to Boston: 'What's Going to be Different?'" *Washington Post*, April 20, 1969: D1.

_____. "Yanks Edge Senators in Eleventh, 3-2: Thirteen Nats Stranded; Cox Dealt Third Loss." *Washington Post*, July 21, 1969: C1+.

_____. "Yanks Rap Skidding Senators, 8-2: Runaway Occurs After Hannan Hurt." *Washington Post*, April 16, 1969: E1+.

O'Donoghue, Don H. "Reconstruction for Medial Instability of the Knee: Technique and Results in Sixty Cases." *Journal of Bone and Joint Surgery* 55-A, no. 5 (July 1973): 941-55.

Povich, Shirley. "Grownup Kid Revisits the Old Neighborhood." *Washington Post,* April 24, 1969: C1.

_____. "Owners Catch a Live One in Bowie Kuhn." *Washington Post,* February 20, 1969: P1.

_____. "This Morning with Shirley Povich." *Washington Post,* April 8, 1969: D1.

_____. "This Morning with Shirley Povich." *Washington Post,* April 10, 1969: H1.

_____. "This Morning with Shirley Povich." *Washington Post,* April 16, 1969: E1.

_____. "This Morning with Shirley Povich." *Washington Post,* August 31, 1969: K1.

_____. "This Morning with Shirley Povich." *Washington Post,* February 9, 1969: C1+.

_____. "This Morning with Shirley Povich." *Washington Post,* February 13, 1969: C1.

_____. "This Morning with Shirley Povich." *Washington Post,* February 16, 1969: C1.

_____. "This Morning with Shirley Povich." *Washington Post,* February 17, 1969: C1.

_____. "This Morning with Shirley Povich." *Washington Post,* February 26, 1969: D1+.

_____. "This Morning with Shirley Povich." *Washington Post,* February 27, 1969: C1.

_____. "This Morning with Shirley Povich." *Washington Post*, January 26, 1969: E1.

_____. "This Morning with Shirley Povich." *Washington Post*, July 3, 1969: E1.

_____. "This Morning with Shirley Povich." *Washington Post*, July 17, 1969: D1.

_____. "This Morning with Shirley Povich." *Washington Post*, July 20, 1969: C1.

_____. "This Morning with Shirley Povich." *Washington Post*, July 24, 1969: C1.

_____. "This Morning with Shirley Povich." *Washington Post,* March 4, 1969: D1.

_____. "This Morning with Shirley Povich." *Washington Post,* March 16, 1969: D1+.

_____. "This Morning with Shirley Povich." *Washington Post,* May 27, 1969: C1.

_____. "Williams Faces Inner Struggle with Nats." *Washington Post,* April 7, 1969: D1.

_____. "Williams Reroutes Florida Traffic Pattern." *Washington Post,* March 2, 1969: 145+.

Siegel, Morris. "Coleman Hasn't Forgotten His Two Seasons with Ted." *Washington Times*, March 17, 1992.

_____. "Short Overplays Role as a Super-Salesman." *Washington Star,* April 2, 1969: D1.

Smith, Lester. "Senators Set Pace in Majors' Higher Ticket Prices." *Sporting News*, April 12, 1969: 36.

Sporting News, 1970. "Coleman Not Ted's Top Fan." October 24, 1970.

Stann, Francis. "Here's Quick Callover as Long Season Starts." *Washington Star*, April 6, 1969: F2.

_____. "Win, Lose, or Draw: Cazzie Says Senators Are Making Own Breaks." *Washington Star*, May 5, 1969: F1.

_____. "Win, Lose, or Draw: Ted Will Finish His Job Because That's His Way." *Washington Star,* April 6, 1969: F1.

Turan, Kenneth. "'Stupid' All-Star Ticket Sale Leaves Many Fans Furious." *Washington Post.* July 11, 1969: D1.

Underwood, John. "Teaching Them Ted's Way." *Sports Illustrated,* March 17, 1969: 18-23.

_____. "The Newest Senator in Town." *Sports Illustrated*, February 24, 1969: 20-21.

warren, Stephen J. "1969's Unsung Heroes: Casey Cox and Dennis Higgins." *Nats News*, Spring 2001: 12–13.

_____. "Dick Bosman: A Life in Baseball." *Nats News*, Summer 2000: 10-11.

_____. "Sid Hudson: A Baseball Life." *Nats News*, Summer 1998: 8-9.

_____. "Twig." *Nats News*, Fall 1998: 10–11.

Washington Post, 1969. "16-13 Saturday Nightmare Has Nats Mumbling About a House of Horrors: Manager Williams 'Could Scream.'" May 12: D2.

_____. "Howard Heats Up Dispute, Says $300,000 Tag Is Firm." March 5: E1.

_____. "Nats Sign Howard to $90,000 Pact: Trade Was Never Close." March 16: D1.

_____. "Senators' Spring Batting, Pitching." April 7, 1969: D6.

_____. "Senator Ticket Prices Raised to Tops of $5, Low of $2: $4 Boxes Quadrupled." February 23: H1+.

_____. "Whitfield Set as Nats' 'Voice.'" February 26: D3.

_____. "Williams Views Senators' Job as Challenge: Early Pennant Not Considered Likely." February 15: C1.

_____. "Williams Will Follow McCarthy's Formula: 'Ten Commandments of Baseball.'" February 22: E1.

Washington Post, 1972. "Coleman Injured by Line Drive." March 28: C1.

Whittlesey, Merrell. "Air Force Vet Knowles Flying High in Nats' Bullpen." *Sporting News*, June 21, 1969: 23.

_____. "Casey Cox Making Capital of Three Cs." *Sporting News*, June 28, 1969: 9, 16.

_____. "Don't Believe Idle Talk About Ted Quitting Senators." *Sporting News*, September 13, 1969: 5.

_____. "Gridders Rip Soft Turf; Senators Fighting Mad." *Sporting News*, August 23, 1969: 17.

_____. "HR-Hitting Hondo Likes to Bat Breeze on Walks." *Sporting News*, July 26, 1969: 21.

_____. "One Huge Plus for Nats -- It's Glamour." *Sporting News*, April 12, 1969: 37.

_____. "Platter or Plate, Lee Maye of Nats Cuts a Groovy Tune." *Sporting News*, August 23, 1969: 17.

_____. "Senator Alyea Earns Huzzahs for Assault on Left-Wingers." *Sporting News*, June 14, 1969: 22.

_____. "Ted and His Senators Are the Toast of the Town." *Sporting News*, April 26, 1969: 27.

_____. "Ted Finally Convinced Writers Nats Were For Real." *Sporting News*, October 18, 1969: 27.

_____. "Ted Made Camp Busy, Different." *Washington Star,* April 6, 1969: F2.

Wiebusch, John. "Nats Down Angels on McMullen's Fly in Tenth Inning, 8-7." *Los Angeles Times*, August 3, 1969: B1.

Electronic Sources

Admiral Merchants Motor Freight, Inc. http://www.ammf.com.

Apollo 11 Site. http://www.nasm.si.edu/collections/imagery/Apollo/AS11/a11facts.htm.

Baldwin, Dave. Linkedin Profile. https://www.linkedin.com/in/dave-baldwin-528b628.

Ballpark Digest. "Seattle's Sicks Stadium." http://www.ballparkwatch.com/stadiums/past/sicks_stadium.htm.

Baseball Page. "Frank Howard." http://www.thebaseballpage.com/players/howarfr01.php.

Baseball Reference. http://www.baseball-reference.com.

Berkow, Ira. "At 81, Coach Accessorizes a Title with an Earring." July 11, 2006 https://www.nytimes.com/2006/07/11/sports/baseball/11wayne.html

Buck, Ray. "At 88, Wayne Terwilliger forgets to act his age." February 19, 2014, Updated November 12, 2014. Special to the Dallas Star-Telegram. https://www.star-telegram.com/sports/article3846510.html

Charters, Kyle. "Old National presents: A long-awaited spring game return." April 5, 2018. https://purdue.rivals.com/news/old-national-presents-a-long-awaited-spring-game-return.

Cox, Timothy. "Home-grown major leaguer still enjoys

the game as Astros scout." July 11, 2017, New
Castle News.
http://www.ncnewsonline.com/news/home-grown-
major-leaguer-still-enjoys-the-game-as-
astros/article_229f12ec-65af-11e7-bf20-
1be22dedbec3.html.

Diunte, Nick. "Paul Casanova: Everyone's 'Hermano.'"
La Vida Baseball, August 2017.
https://www.lavidabaseball.com/paul-casanova-
everyones-brother/.

Electric Earl. "Arthur Lee Maye." Doo-Wop Society.
http://www.electricearl.com/dws/ALmaye.html.

Frisaro, Joe. "Marlins Name Minor League Coaching Staffs."
MLB.Com, January 8, 2016.
https://www.mlb.com/news/marlins-name-minor-league-coaching-
staffs/c-161355504.

Hagen, Paul. "Where are they now? Del Unser." MLB.com, November
1, 2017.
https://www.mlb.com/news/where-are-they-now-del-unser/c-
260355380.

Hampden-Sydney 2008 Baseball Media Guide.
http://www2.hsc.edu/athletics/baseball/2008/baseball_mediaguide08
.pdf.

Hoffman, Paul. "Jim French." SABR Bio Project, December 15, 2016.
https://sabr.org/bioproj/person/ea4fdff7.

Itazuke Air Force Base Alumni Association. http://www.itazuke.org/.

Johnson, Mike. "Bosman calls it a career." September 26, 2018,
Kenosha News.
https://www.kenoshanews.com/sports/local_sports/bosman-calls-it-a-
career/article_9abb7899-f790-53f4-99e6-414ac10550db.html.

Kuttler, Hillel. "Epstein: Proud of Being Known as 'Super Jew.'" March
12, 2016, Jewish Baseball Museum.
http://jewishbaseballmuseum.com/spotlight-story/the-mike-epstein-
file/.

Kyger, Ernie. "WWDC Press Conference Announcing Signing of Ted
Williams to Manage the Washington Senators,
https://youtu.be/lmVTQkaUT1M.

Leavengood, Ted. Green, Chip, ed. "Mike Epstein." SABR Bio Project,
2015.
https://sabr.org/bioproj/person/a92f9e38.

Long Beach Parks, Recreation, and Marine. "Baseball Hall of Fame.
2019.

http://www.longbeach.gov/park/recreation-programs/sports-and-athletics/baseball-hall-of-fame/#casey_cox.

Los Angeles Lakers History. http://www.nba.com/lakers/history/lakers_history_new.html.

Major League Baseball Players Alumni Association. "Who We Are," http://mlb.mlb.com/mlb/features/alumni/article.jsp?article=about_us.

Markusen, Bruce. "Moore Provides Law and Order for Alumni: Attorney Has Been Involved with Alumni Association for More Than 25 Years." *MLB.com*, January 15, 2008. http://mlb.mlb.com/mlb/features/alumni/article.jsp?article=moore.

National Baseball Hall of Fame, Ford C. Frick Award Nominees. http://web.baseballhalloffame.org/hofers/Frick.jsp

Niland, Marty. "McMullen draws birthday love from D.C. fans." MASN Sports, June 4, 2018. http://www.masnsports.com/nationals-buzz/2018/06/marty-niland-ken-mcmullen-draws-birthday-love-from-dc-fans.html.

Purdue Football Information Guide 2007, Supplemental Material. http://grfx.cstv.com/photos/schools/pur/sports/m-footbl/auto_pdf/07-fb-mg-supplemental.pdf.

Republican Club of Greater Largo. www.largorepublicans.com. 2017.

Retrosheet. http://www.retrosheet.org. (Note: The information used herein was obtained free of charge from and is copyrighted by Retrosheet. Interested parties may contact Retrosheet at www.retrosheet.org).

Richard Harding Poff Biographical Information. http://bioguide.congress.gov/scripts/guidedisplay.pl?index=P00401.

Riverside Sports Hall of Fame. "Induction Awards Dinner, 2019." https://www.riversidesporthalloffame.com/induction-awards-dinner/.

Stahl, John. "Bob Humphreys." SABR Bio Project, 2011. https://sabr.org/bioproj/person/b490a227.

Twins Trivia. "Bernie Allen Interview." 2014. https://twinstrivia.com/interview-archives/bernie-allen-interview/.

University of Notre Dame. "About Notre Dame: History of the University." http://nd.edu/aboutnd/history.

Venezuelan League. http://www.baseball-reference.com /bullpen/Liga_Venezolana_de_Beisbol_Profesional.

Virginia Tech 2007 Baseball Media Guide. http://www.hokiesports.com/baseball/bb07mg.pdf.

Warren Sports Hall of Fame. "Honored Inductees, Ed Stroud, 1989, Charter Member." 2018. https://warrensportshof.com/inductees.php.

Wayne Terwilliger. "Making History."
  http://www.wayneterwilliger.com.
Western High School, Cincinnati, OH, Baseball Players.
  http://www.thebaseballcube.com/high-schools/western-hills-
  1344.shtml.
Wolf, Gregory, H. "Joe Coleman." SABR Bio Project, August 1, 2016.
  https://sabr.org/bioproj/person/fa3ea9bf.
Zink, David. "ZINK: Shellenback joins Ramona's sports hall of fame."
  The Press-Enterprise, April 21, 2015.
  https://www.pe.com/2015/04/21/zink-shellenback-joins-ramonas-
  sports-hall-of-fame/.

Other Sources

Hartley, Jim. Photos of Washington Nationals vs. Philadelphia Phillies, April 4, 2005.

Nats News, May 2005: 11.

Menchine, Ron and Tony Roberts (broadcasters). "New York 9 Washington 0 (Forfeit)." *Miley Collection*, September 30, 1971. (cassette).

Washington Post, 1969. Photograph of helicopter hovering over RFK Stadium outfield. (No photo credit). August 8: D1.

Williams, Ted. Remarks at 1969 Senators' Reunion Breakfast. November 8, 1998.

Wood, Phil. Remarks at 1969 Senators' Reunion Breakfast. November 8, 1998.

Index

209

candor, 118, 119;
winning streak, 116;
work habits, 63, 113, 116,
117, 118
Bosman, Pam, 115,
118, 119
Boston, Mass, 38, 44, 45, 46,
48, 49, 51, 63, 114, 115,
120, 125, 153
Boston Red Sox, 21, 25, 45, 46,
48, 49, 56, 66, 93, 100, 110,
114, 117, 121, 125, 146,
167, 174, 176, *180*,
Williams named
greatest, 17, 125;
Williams returns,
46, 48-49
Bowens, Sam, 2, 44, 106
Bradford, Buddy, 73
Brett, Ken, 174
Brinkman, Ed, 2, 4, 13, 22, 24,
48, 49, 57,58, 67, 70, 73,
100, 107, 110, 114, 120,
125, 128, 129, 139, 142,
144, 146, 155, 157, 159,
161, 163, 164, 166, 167,
168, 169, 172, 175, 176,
182, 185, aches to win, 159,
163, 164, 166, 167; at
Western Hills, 164;
batting cage behavior,
22,165; bonus baby, 164;
coach, 169; fielding
records, 168; friends; leads
"Nasty Nats", 48, 49, 52,
114, 142, left off All-Stars,
125; makes All-Stars, 168;
mod fashions, 163, 164,
167, 168; Nellie's bottle
bats, 165, 166; sense of
humor, 49, 100, 107, 139,
142, 157, 163; teases

Hondo, 107, 139, 142, 157,
163; traded to Tigers, 4, 70,
168, 175, 182; Williams
teaches, 24, 165; with
Martin, 168; wins job, 164
Brooklyn Dodgers, 29, 143,
144, 153, 155, 156, 158
(*see also LA Dodgers*)
Brown, Ike, 154
Brown, Kevin, 64
Brown, Larry, 52
Brunswick, MO, 79
Buffalo, NY, 21, 29, 59, 116,
AAA Bisons, 29, 115, 116;
War Memorial Stadium
(aka Rock Pile), 29, 115
Buford, Don, 116
Burke, Joe, 50
Burlington, NC, 53
Burn Brae Theater, 1, 115
C-130 Transport, 78
Cabrera, Miguel, 31
California, 66, 94, 106, 109,
121, 127, 153, 170
California Angels, 60, 71, 94,
100, 127, 128, 132, 148,
151, 155, 157, 158, 176
(*see also LA Angels*)
Camacho, Joe, 2, 6, 17, 21, 37,
99, 172, bench coach,
6, 21; catches Nixon
toss, *33*, 37; runs camp
with Williams, 17
Camilli, Doug, 2, 21
Campaneris, Bert, 83
Canada, 183
Caracas, VZ, 87
Cardenas, Leo, 134
Carew, Rod, 43, 92
Carlos, Cisco, 2
Carlton, Steve, 126
Carolina League, 40, 53

211

213

215

219

About the Author

A Whole New Ballgame is Stephen J. Walker's first book. His articles on Washington Senators' baseball have appeared in the Society for American Baseball Research (SABR) national and regional publications as well as the Washington Baseball Historical Society's quarterly newsletter, *Nats News*. Stephen, his wife Debbie, and their youngest son live in Ellicott City, Maryland. Steve's two older sons have "launched." One works as an attorney in New York City, the other works in Maryland as a software developer for a Fortune 100 technology company.

Made in the USA
Las Vegas, NV
21 November 2023

81261150R00134